OXFORD WORLD'S CLASSICS

THE CONFIDENCE-MAN

HERMAN MELVILLE was born in New York City in 1819, a de-
scendant of English and Dutch colonial families. His father died
bankrupt in 1832, leaving his widow and eight children in penury.
Three years later, at the age of 15, Melville left school and worked as
a clerk, first in a bank and then for his brother's fur business. After
spells working on his uncle's farm in Massachusetts, and teaching,
he sailed on a trading ship to Liverpool in the summer of 1839, a
trip that was to form the basis for *Redburn* (1849). In 1841 he joined
the whaling ship *Acushnet*, bound for the South Seas, abandoning it
with a companion in the Marquesas Islands. This and other voyages
on whaling boats were to provide the material for *Moby-Dick* (1851).
The South Seas became the setting and subject for his novels *Typee*
(1846) and *Omoo* (1847). In 1850 Melville moved with his wife and
son to a farm near Pittsfield, Massachusetts, and became a close
friend of his neighbour, Nathaniel Hawthorne, to whom *Moby-Dick*
is dedicated. His *Piazza Tales* appeared in 1856, and a year later *The
Confidence-Man* was published. The increasingly metaphysical and
exploratory cast of his writing meant that his popularity had begun
to wane long before, however, and by 1866 he was forced to make a
living as an inspector of customs at the port of New York. He died
in obscurity in 1891, leaving a number of poems and *Billy Budd,
Sailor* in manuscript.

TONY TANNER was Professor of English and American Literature
at King's College, Cambridge. His books on American literature
include *The Reign of Wonder*, *City of Words*, and *Scenes of Nature,
Signs of Men*. He also edited Melville's *Moby-Dick* for the Oxford
World's Classics.

JOHN DUGDALE wrote his Cambridge Ph.D. dissertation on the
novelist Thomas Pynchon. He has books forthcoming on Thomas
Pynchon and Sam Shepard.

OXFORD WORLD'S CLASSICS

*For over 100 years Oxford World's Classics have brought
readers closer to the world's great literature. Now with over 700
titles—from the 4,000-year-old myths of Mesopotamia to the
twentieth century's greatest novels—the series makes available
lesser-known as well as celebrated writing.*

*The pocket-sized hardbacks of the early years contained
introductions by Virginia Woolf, T. S. Eliot, Graham Greene,
and other literary figures which enriched the experience of reading.
Today the series is recognized for its fine scholarship and
reliability in texts that span world literature, drama and poetry,
religion, philosophy and politics. Each edition includes perceptive
commentary and essential background information to meet the
changing needs of readers.*

OXFORD WORLD'S CLASSICS

HERMAN MELVILLE

The Confidence-Man
His Masquerade

With an Introduction by
TONY TANNER
and
Explanatory Notes by
JOHN DUGDALE

OXFORD
UNIVERSITY PRESS

OXFORD
UNIVERSITY PRESS

Great Clarendon Street, Oxford OX2 6DP

Oxford University Press is a department of the University of Oxford.
It furthers the University's objective of excellence in research, scholarship,
and education by publishing worldwide in

Oxford New York

Athens Auckland Bangkok Bogotá Buenos Aires Calcutta
Cape Town Chennai Dar es Salaam Delhi Florence Hong Kong Istanbul
Karachi Kuala Lumpur Madrid Melbourne Mexico City Mumbai
Nairobi Paris São Paulo Singapore Taipei Tokyo Toronto Warsaw

with associated companies in Berlin Ibadan

Oxford is a registered trade mark of Oxford University Press
in the UK and in certain other countries

Published in the United States
by Oxford University Press Inc., New York

Introduction and Chronology © Tony Tanner 1989
Other editorial material © John Dugdale 1989

First published as a World's Classics paperback 1989
Reissued as an Oxford World's Classics paperback 1999
Reissued 2008

British Library Cataloguing in Publication Data

Data available

Library of Congress Cataloging in Publication Data

Melville, Herman, 1819–1891.
The confidence-man: his masquerade / Herman Melville; with an
introduction by Tony Tanner and explanatory notes by John Dugdale.
(Oxford world's classics)
Bibliography: p.
I. Tanner, Tony. II. Dugdale, John. III. Title.
PS2384.C6 1989 813'.4—dc19 88–16958

ISBN 978–0–19–955485–0

12

Printed and bound in Great Britain by Clays Ltd, Elcograf S.p.A.

CONTENTS

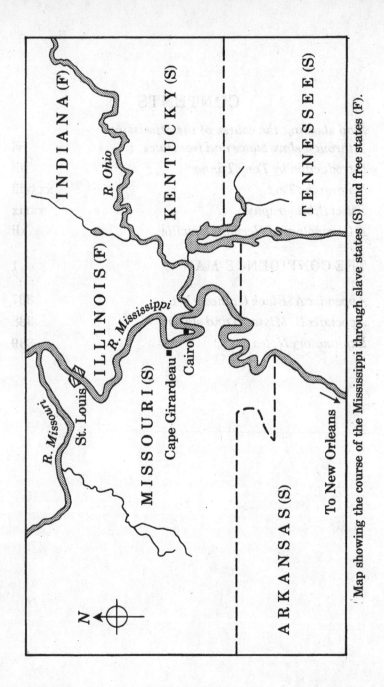

Map showing the course of the Mississippi through slave states (S) and free states (F).

INTRODUCTION

IN 1855 P. T. Barnum published his autobiography, *Life*. He started his career as a showman by exhibiting an aged negress, fraudulently claimed to have been George Washington's childhood nurse. His successful career as showman and entrepreneur was based on pioneering work in developing modes of extravagant publicity and advertising. Later he was to organize his famous circus which he advertised quite simply as 'the greatest show on earth'. He quite shamelessly admits, indeed brazenly boasts, that from the start, when he worked in a store, deception was the spirit, if not the name, of the game. 'The customers cheated us in their fabrics: we cheated the customers with our goods. Each party expected to be cheated, if it was possible.' He describes a life devoted to hoaxing (and entertaining) a public, perhaps excessively gullible or perhaps content enough to be deceived if it also meant being amused.

Also in 1855 Herman Melville published *Israel Potter: His Fifty Years of Exile*. Israel is an American loser—a failure and a victim. After fighting for his country he spends years of exile in England and Europe. When he finally manages to return to America he finds his family homestead burnt down and being ploughed over, while he himself is spurned by his ungrateful country and left to die in poverty and obscurity. 'He was repulsed in efforts, after a pension, by certain caprices of law. His scars proved his only medals. He dictated a little book, the record of his fortunes. But long ago it faded out of print— himself out of being—his name out of memory.' His is a case of total obliteration and erasure—he is one of those many Americans whom Thomas Pynchon was to designate as 'the praeterite', all those discarded, passed over, negated, or otherwise junked by the dominant power systems. But Melville also includes in this novel a portrait of the man who was the most successful American of them all—Benjamin Franklin. He perfectly catches that mixture of cunning and innocence which seems to have been the essence of the man. 'The diplomatist and the shepherd are blended; a union not without warrant; the apostolic serpent and dove. A tanned Machiavelli in tents.' And Melville goes on to describe him as, effectively, *the* archetypal American:

Having carefully weighed the world, *Franklin could act any part in it*. By nature turned to knowledge, his mind was often grave, but never serious. At time he had seriousness—extreme seriousness—for others, but never for himself. Tranquillity was to him instead of it. This philosophical levity of tranquillity, so to speak, is shown in his easy variety of pursuits. Printer, postmaster, almanac maker, essayist, chemist, orator, tinker, statesman, humorist, philosopher, parlor-man, political economist, professor of housewifery, ambassador, projector, maxim-monger, herb-doctor, wit:—Jack of all trades, master of each and mastered by none—*the type and genius of his land*. (My italics.)

In his *Autobiography*, itself a calculated product, a piece of publicity, an advertisement, Frankin displays a curiously instrumental attitude towards himself—as if the image of himself can be made, constructed, always with an eye on the public. It is as though he is always detached from the self that acts and performs in the world, manipulating it with a cool and calculating amiability which is not quite cynicism, not quite hypocrisy, but which does suggest a degree of smooth and protean adaptability. This can make one wonder about the core morality, the determining values and the commitments, the emotional capacities, of the internal manager, promoter, producer of all his fluent, sometimes devious, adjustments, his opportunistic, often brilliant, improvisations. Who, or what, is in charge of the show? One might have asked the same thing of P. T. Barnum. Both men, certainly, showed an uncanny promotional flair.

In his essay in 'The Poet', published in 1844, Emerson repeatedly deploys a word which is at the centre of his thinking—'metamorphosis'. The poet 'sees the flowing or metamorphosis'; his speech 'flows with the flowing of nature'; his mind 'flows into and through things . . . and the metamorphosis is possible'; 'the metamorphosis once seen, we divine that it does not stop.' This emphasis on 'incessant metamorphosis', on the 'fluxional', the 'flexible', the 'plastic', the 'ductile', the 'fluid and volatile' is everywhere in Emerson. It stems from his root conviction that the real evil in the world is everything that can be subsumed under the notion of 'fixity': 'There are no fixtures in nature'; 'The quality of the imagination is to flow, and not to freeze'; 'The only sin is limitation.' A lot of this reiterated stress on the supreme value of endless metamorphosis stems from his antipathy to the past, to all institutions, to previous authorities, to social structures, indeed to the 'jail-yard of individual relations'—to anything that binds, limits, constrains, commits. Indeed, in his seminal essay 'Self-Reliance'—seminal for America—he rather alarmingly announced 'I will have no covenants but proximities'. From one point of view this could seem like a willingness, indeed a determination, to dissolve identity in present contingency and certainly Emerson seems willing to embrace an extreme discontinuity of self: 'A foolish consistency is the hobgoblin of little minds . . . live ever in a new day'; 'Our moods do not believe in each other.' We should take our cue from nature, and nature, as Emerson sees it, is perpetual change: 'this surface on which we now stand is not fixed, but sliding.' So slide with it: 'we live amid surfaces, and the true art of life is to skate well on them.' Everything is 'flowing' so—'go with the flow'. That Californian injunction of the 1960s is pure Emerson. For Emerson metamorphosis was evolutionary, ascensional, a constant move towards higher and ever higher forms. Clearly this overlooks or minimizes the possibility of regressive or degenerative metamorphosis, a devolution or degradation to lower forms—the Kafka vision. And whatever else, the emphasis on sliding, skating, flowing could suggest an enthusiastic endorsement of a self a good deal more adaptive and protean than Franklin's deft self-technologist. And was there any enduring depth of self under this eager notional capitulation to shifting surface and incessant transience? Emerson had his own answer to this problem of the ultimate identity of the fluid, mutating self:

Man is not a farmer, or a professor, or an engineer, but he is all. Man is priest, and scholar, and statesman, and producer, and soldier. In the *divided* or social state these functions are parcelled out to individuals, each of whom aims to do his stint of the point work, whilst each other performs his . . . The state of society is one in which the members have suffered amputation from the trunk, and strut about like so many walking monsters—a good finger, a neck, a stomach, an elbow, but never a man. Man is thus metamorphosed into a thing, into many things.

Individuation is amputation; socialization is fragmentation. There is, after all, bad metamorphosis—from a mystical unitary totality into partiality and reification. Emerson can solve his problem—or conjure it away—by positing a transcendental identification of the real self with the All. Meanwhile, in the 'divided' state which is society, all those fingers and elbows can go on sliding and skating around on the shifting surface of things, abjuring consistency, refusing covenants, eluding relations. It can be seen that there is a high potential for anarchy in Emerson's descriptions and prescriptions. Certainly, there is not the slightest interest in what might make for and sustain any kind of community or communality. The self-reliant Emersonian self is determinedly anti-social.

So, in his own very different way, is Edgar Alan Poe's 'diddler'. In 1843 Poe wrote an essay entitled 'Diddling Considered as One of the Exact Sciences'. Jeremy Diddler was in fact a character in an English play ('Raising the Wind', 1803, by James Kenney) who borrowed small amounts of money with no intention of repaying them, but Poe sees something more profound in the art to which he gave his name: 'A crow thieves; a fox cheats; a weasel outwits; a man diddles.' He is indeed a self-reliant self—against the world: 'He regards always the main chance. He looks to Number One. You are Number Two, and must look to yourself.' But Poe's diddler is not just a generic cheat, though cheating is all he does. He has very distinctive characteristics. 'Diddling rightly considered, is a compound, of which the ingredients are minuteness, interest, perseverance, ingenuity, audacity, *nonchalance*, originality, impertinence, and *grin*.' Poe was himself a unique sort of literary diddler, playing every kind of trick and hoax on his readers and indeed manifesting in his art just those qualities he ascribed to the more overtly financial diddler. And his portrait seems almost prophetic. In July 1849 the *New York Herald* carried an item headed 'Arrest of the Confidence Man' which began:

For the last few months a man has been travelling about the city, known as the 'Confidence Man;' that is, he would go up to a perfect stranger in the street, and being a man of genteel appearance, would easily command an interview. Upon this interview he would say, after some little conversation, 'have you confidence in me to trust me with your watch until to-morrow;'

the stranger, at this novel request, supposing him to be some old acquaintance, not at the moment recollected, allows him to take the watch, thus placing 'confidence' in the honesty of the stranger, who walks off laughing, and the other, supposing it to be a joke, allows him so to do. In this way many have been duped . . .

This reads exactly like one of the examples Poe gives of successful diddles. And, of course, it gave Melville the title—even perhaps the idea—for his last novel.

Later in the same year, Melville's friend Evert Duyckinck, writing in the *Literary World*, commented on an editorial in another paper concerning the 'Confidence Man':

The Confidence Man, the new species of the Jeremy Diddler recently a subject of police fingering, and still later impressed into the service of Burton's comicalities in Chambers Street, is excellently handled by a clever pen in the *Merchants' Ledger*, which we are glad to see has a column for the credit as well as for the debit side of humanity. It is not the worst thing that can be said for a country that it gives birth to a confidence man:—
' . . . It is a good thing, and speaks well for human nature, that, at this late day, in spite of all the hardening of civilization and all the warning of newspapers, men *can be swindled*. The man who is *always* on his guard, *always* proof against appeal, who cannot be beguiled into the weakness of pity by *any* story—is far gone, in our opinion, towards being a hardened villain. He may steer clear of petty larceny and open swindling—but mark that man well in his intercourse with his fellows—they have no confidence in him, and he has none in them. He lives coldly among his people, he walks an iceberg in the marts of trade and social life—and when he dies, may Heaven have that confidence in him which he had not in his fellow mortals!'

These cogent and eloquent—and perceptive—comments raise profound issues which are at the heart of Melville's novel, issues concerning the crucial role of 'trust' in society—not to say in humanity. I note in passing that the two men who most notably *cannot be swindled* in the novel (Mark Winsome and Egbert) are based on Emerson and Thoreau and in their casuistical impermeability to pity they are just as ice-cold as the writer in the *Merchant's Ledger* predicted such a type would be.

Clearly by running together descriptions of Poe's diddler, Emerson's sliding self-reliant metamorphoser, Franklin's craftily adaptable self, P. T. Barnum the hoaxer–showman, and the historically actual American confidence man of 1849, I am suggesting that they have something in common, and something which is peculiarly American. I stress this because, while there seem to be trickster figures in every culture's mythology or folk-lore, so that Hermes has innumerable relations and descendants, and while Proteus, too, is only one of many 'shape-shifters' in world narrative, and while some people have no doubt abused other people's trust since at least the time when there were signs and signals with which to deceive them, the 'confidence man' is a figure of quite special—and central—importance in American culture and history. To appreciate better what Melville is doing in his extraordinary novel, it is really essential to try to see it in its historical context—that is, as being very specifically concerned with matters and phenomena generated in and by the conditions of American society, or lack of it, in the first half of the nineteenth century when the euphoria of Independence had not yet been sobered by the Civil War. Of course the novel touches on matters of universal importance and concern, but some of these universal problems first began to emerge in their modern form in the America of this time.

In the chapter entitled 'American Ideals 1800', in his magisterial *History of the United States of America during the Administrations of Thomas Jefferson and James Madison*, Henry Adams contrasts the animating spirit of these times with the aims and aspirations of the first colonists:

In the early days of colonization, a very new settlement represented an idea and proclaimed a mission. . . . No such character belonged to the colonization of 1800. From Lake Erie to Florida, in long, unbroken line, pioneers were at work, cutting into the forests with the energy of so many beavers, and with no more express moral purpose than the beavers they drove away. The civilization they carried with them was rarely illumined by an idea; they sought room for no new truth, and aimed neither at creating, like the Puritans, a government of saints, nor, like the Quakers, one of love and peace . . . To a new society, ignorant and semi-barbarous, a mass of demagogues insisted on applying every stimulant that could inflame its worst appetites, while at the same instant taking away every influence that had hitherto helped to restrain its passions. Greed for wealth, lust for power, yearning for the blank void of savage freedom such as Indians and wolves delighted in,—these were the fires that flamed under the cauldron of American society, in which, as conservatives believed, the old, well-proven, conservative crust of religion, government, family, and even common respect for age, education, and experience was rapidly melting away, and was indeed already broken into fragments, swept about by the seething mass of scum ever rising in greater quantities to the surface.

Adams was a conservative, and a pessimist, and doubtless there is some personal feeling behind these patrician words, but it clearly did seem to many observers that, having as it were slipped the leash of England—broken free of old ties—America in the nineteenth century was becoming a place of both vertiginous activity and radical uncertainty of direction. And the Americans themselves: what kind of people were these citizens of this new republic turning out to be like? Alexis de Tocqueville saw them as dissolvers of the past, endlessly transforming their heritage, their environment, themselves:

Under their hand, political principles, laws, and human institutions seem malleable, capable of being shaped and combined at will. As they go forward, the barriers which imprisoned society and behind which they were born are lowered; old opinions, which for centuries had been controlling the world, vanish; a course almost without limits, a field without horizon, is revealed: the human spirit rushes forward and traverses them in every direction.

This of course is exactly what Emerson would praise and prescribe for the new American individual, but de Tocqueville draws out some of the possible pains and problems in this new, seemingly almost anarchic, state of society: 'Thus not only does democracy make every man forget his ancestors, but it hides his descendants and separates his contemporaries from him; it throws him back forever upon himself alone and threatens in the end to confine him entirely within the solitude of his own heart.' It is one thing to break up old, repressive hierarchies and jettison a tyrannous and burdensome past. But if the process goes on to sever all generational and social ties—call them chains, call them bonds, or covenants—then self-reliance might turn into a self-sealing solitude. It is no doubt good to get rid of imperious marks of rank and cruel badges of class division, but again new problems may arise: 'As each class gradually approaches others and mingles with them, its members become undifferentiated and lose their class identity for each other.' We know very well how insidious class distinctions, in every sense, can be—and de Tocqueville is another conservative. But when all signs of 'class identity' are erased, social identity itself can become endlessly problematical. This may be an exhilarating freedom from restrictive and coercive classifications, but it might make it harder and harder to know just whom you are talking to, as Melville—a very emphatic and passionate democrat—

shows in his novel. And one may drown in undifferentia-
tion, as one may indeed suffocate in hierarchy. What de
Tocqueville could see was that in this America there
was bound to be something like a permanent crisis
of authority. There was so much fluidity, so much
movement, that it might be impossible, and would
certainly be very difficult, to locate or establish or
recognize any stable guide-posts. 'Paternal authority' was
notably weakened and this could be taken as a paradigm
of the waning and dimming of all previous sources of
directional influence. Movement and expansion can mean
progress and development, but when 'the whole of society
is in motion' it can become increasingly difficult to orient,
or focus, or even locate, yourself. It is important to
remember that what was happening in America was not
the sudden upheaval and dislocation of a previously
stable and relatively settled society. Immigration and a
moving frontier meant an endless inpouring of strangers,
who in the general movement became endlessly re-
estranged. Melville's description of the embarking and
disembarking passengers on his Mississippi steamer
Fidèle makes it exactly a microcosm of America, the
frontier of America in particular, at this time: 'though
always full of strangers, she continually, in some degree,
adds to, or replaces them with strangers still more
strange.' In a society made up completely of strangers and
perpetually stirring itself, problems of communication,
recognition, identification, and, above all, trust and
confidence become *particularly* acute. And the problem
may have a further, and more worrying, twist: 'for in
democratic times what is most unstable, in the midst of
the instability of everything, is the heart of man.' It may
be difficult and confusing trying to work out who, or what,
your neighbour, or contiguous stranger, is. But what if
you should find that you have become a stranger to

yourself? Such a society was, of course, peculiarly liable to produce 'confidence men'. To someone with an eye as searching as Melville's it might become a matter of more moment whether it would—or could—produce anything else.

There was another characteristic of these early nine-teenth-century Americans identified by Adams which gives an added meaning or dimension to the notion of 'confidence':

'The hard, practical, money-getting American democrat . . . was in truth living in a world of dream, and acting a drama more instinct with poetry than all the avatars of the East, walking in gardens of emerald and rubies, in ambition already ruling the world and guiding Nature with a kinder and wiser hand than had ever yet been felt in human history. . . . Even on his practical and sordid side, the American might easily have been represented as a victim to illusion. If the Englishman had lived as the American speculator did,—in the future,—the hyperbole of enthusiasm would have seemed less monstrous.'

And Adams then describes the sort of visionary enthusiasm which could already see—or imagine—'magnificent cities' where there were actually only 'tremendous wastes, swamps and forests'—exactly the kind of wild 'confidence' in the future which Charles Dickens satirizes in *Martin Chuzzlewit* when a land agent describes the 'flourishing' city of Eden to an impressed Martin, who gradually discovers that it is 'not quite' built yet; Melville glances at this when his Confidence Man tries to arouse interest (and contributions) with his evocation of the 'thriving city' of New Jerusalem. Clearly this kind of visionary enthusiasm could make it difficult to distinguish between the imaginative prophet—say, Whitman—and the fraudu-lent speculator. Of both it might be said that 'his dream was his whole existence', as Adams said of the generic American of 1800, adding of this 'class of men' that 'whether imagination or greed led them to describe more than actually existed, they still saw no more than any inventor or discoverer must have seen in order to give him the energy of success'.

The result of all this living in, and on, and indeed off, the future was the emergence of America as a 'confidence culture'. The phrase is Gary Lindberg's, who describes how 'the visionary tradition has been one of the major continuities in American culture, linking land boomers and poets, prophets and profiteers'. Indeed, 'in the general atmosphere of boosterism and mutual congratulation, "America" itself came to exist primarily in the imagination' (*The Confidence Man in American Literature*, Oxford University Press, 1982.) Lindberg demonstrates that 'the confidence man sees more opportunities in New World fluidity, not merely to improve his lot by cleverness and technical proficiency but actually to recast the self through cunning imitation. He becomes the specialist in secondary, reproducible identities'. The very idea of 'the self-made man' (the phrase dates apparently from 1832) is peculiarly American since, aptly ambiguous, it suggests both the independent achievement of success and a more radical act of self-parenting. Jay Gatsby, who 'sprang from his own conception of himself', is only one of the more memorable of the many figures in American literature—and indeed history—who dismiss and erase or ignore their actual biological point of origin in favour of some more desirable, or profitable, or marketable, fabricated identity. Following other critics (R. W. B. Lewis, Kenneth Lynn, Daniel Hoffman), Lindberg puts together such figures as Franklin, Jefferson, William James, and more generic American folk types like the Yankee Peddler, the booster, the gamesman, the healer, along with writers such as Emerson and Whitman, as figures who all, in their very different ways, traffic in 'belief', or peddle in 'confidence'. And in his survey he shows how prevalent the figure of the confidence man is in American literature, from the earliest years of the republic, before he had been named, up to the present day. Carwin and Arthur Mervyn in Charles Brockden Brown's *Wieland* and *Arthur Mervyn*, Richard Jones in James Fenimore Cooper's *The Pioneeers*, Holgrave in Hawthorne's *The House of the Seven Gables* ('putting off one exterior, and snatching up another, to be soon shifted for a third'), Johnson J. Hooper's Simon Suggs ('It is good to be shifty in a new country'), the Duke and the Dauphin on Huckleberry Finn's raft, and Huckleberry Finn himself (not to mention Tom Sawyer), William Faulkner's Flem Snopes, Ralph Ellison's Invisible Man, Saul Bellow's Augie March—the list is indefinitely extendable: all these figures, in various ways, trade in and on trust and belief—in different ways and, of course, for widely different ends. It may be for the most ruthless exploitation and self-aggrandizement, as in the case of Flem Snopes; or it might be for sheer survival, as with Huck Finn. But in one way or another 'confidence' is the name of the game, and it is a peculiarly (not exclusively, but peculiarly) American game. And no book both demonstrates and explores this fact more profoundly, memorably, disturbingly than Melville's novel, which indeed confronts the Confidence Man in all his singularity and multiplicity.

I use the words advisedly since a reader coming to the novel for the first time would almost certainly think that there was no one confidence man, as the title suggests, but a whole series of them. Critics, most notably Bruce Franklin, have shown that a number of the figures who appear in very different dress are probably avatars of one 'original' confidence man—though even here there has been disagreement as to whether, for instance, the deaf mute of the first chapter is one of these avatars or not.

And there is certainly more than one confidence man on board the *Fidèle*, indeed often two are present at the same time trying to 'con' each other, as in the long central exchange between Francis Goodman and Charlie Noble, so that it must be uncertain how many of the characters are in fact one man in several disguises and how many are simply other confidence men at large. It is important to recognize that this uncertainty—are they all one, or all different people?—cannot be resolved, since this is central to the novel's deep intention: namely, to question whether man has a core self, whether there is any consistency or continuity-through-change of character; or whether man is indeed serial and partial, a plurality of fragmentary and momentary roles? Spreading outward through the book is growing doubt about the ontological status of individual identity, which means that it does not read like other novels of its time, precisely because it calls into question the conception of character and the conventions of representation which were current then and which, indeed, for many readers and writers, still prevail today.

Contemporaries certainly had trouble with it. 'A novel it is not, unless a novel means forty-five conversations held on board a steamer, conducted by passengers who might pass for the errata of creation, and so far resembling the Dialogues of Plato as to be undoubted Greek to ordinary men' (*The Literary Gazette*, 11 April 1857). Actually, that is no bad description. The forty-odd characters are so pastless, so unfamilied, so devoid of interiority, such strangers strange and estranged, that, to a conventional eye, they might well seem like some of nature's mistakes—fragmentary, unfinished, incomplete. For this is the kaleidoscope of the new world where 'varieties of mortals blended their varieties of visage and garb. A Tartar-like picturesqueness; a sort of pagan abandonment and assurance. Here reigned the dashing and all-fusing spirit of the West, whose type is the Mississippi itself, which, uniting the streams of the most distant and opposite zones, pours them along, helter-skelter, in one cosmopolitan and confident tide (Ch. 2).' At first that reads like a topographic and sociological description—and indeed the Mississippi setting is as important here as it is in, say, *Huckleberry Finn*. But in fact there is effectively no natural description in the novel, and it is more philosophical matters concerning 'fusion' and the 'uniting' of 'opposite zones' which gradually emerge, until the 'cosmopolitan and confident tide' finally takes on the form of the Cosmopolitan who, exactly half-way through the book, appears in his fantastic 'plumagy', many-hued and 'grotesque' dress, and announces himself as indeed the very spirit—if that is the right word—of 'fusion'. 'A cosmopolitan, a catholic man; who, being such, ties himself to no narrow tailor or teacher, but federates, in heart as in costume, something of the various gallantries of men under various suns. Oh, one roams not over the gallant globe in vain. Bred by it, is a fraternal and fusing feeling. No man is a stranger.' In an America which was showing itself to be inherently fissile and in which everyone was more or less a stranger, a figure emanating or preaching—or is it peddling?—'federation' and the 'fusing feeling' should surely be welcome. But fusion can become confusion and have deeply ambivalent results. Like the 'tide' described at the start, the cosmopolitan is also supremely 'confident', or at least a sweet-voiced spokesman for confidence, and most certainly the ultimate confidence man. There are far-reaching problems here and none more so than those raised by the word 'confidence', which has connotations ranging from the most sacred trust, generous optimism, enabling hope, compassion and friendship, privacy and discretion; on to the darker side of the word, involving deceit, subterfuge, and trickery, leading to distrust, suspicion, and estrangement. The word and its implications are debated on almost every page of the book, and here again the reviewer was quite accurate. The book is made up almost exclusively of conversations. People talk, argue, debate, heckle, tell and re-tell stories, and then discuss them. There is no action (only one blow is struck); there are no emotional or sexual relations (indeed no women, except for two widows—perhaps one?); the boat never gets to New Orleans (and there is no discernible captain); the last named port of call is Cairo, or, more specifically and appropriately, 'a grotesque-shaped bluff' called 'the Devil's joke', terms which describe what is going on on board, and perhaps the novel itself. The last landscape to be described, even referred to, is the 'swampy and squalid domain' which Pitch sees as he leans over the rail, looking after the departed PIO man (who has of course conned him) and pondering 'the mystery of human subjectivity in general'. That—and whether there finally is any—is what the book is pondering as well. It has no time for the mute externals of the given world, for it is above all interested in the words men say—and write—as they attempt to relate or exploit, to communicate or manipulate, to enlighten or outwit, to tell the truth or insert a lie.

The negro cripple who claims to be 'werry well wordy of all you kind ge'mmen's kind confidence' provides a felicitous pun with his dialect pronunciation, for the actors in this book, on this boat, are indeed 'wordy' and the connection between words and 'worth' or trustworthiness, indeed between language and value or integrity, is just what—in suitably various guises and disguises—this masquerade of a book is all about. And the most 'wordy' figure is the Confidence Man/Men, who does indeed initiate a series of latter-day Platonic dialogues with himself as an appropriately altered Socrates, metamorphosed by the new conditions of America into a slippery (sliding and skating), Franklinesque, shape-shifter and jack of many trades or poses—merchant, philanthropist, speculator, healer, even philosopher (or is it slave-trader?). Whatever else—and he receives precious little cash, and one free haircut, for all his pains and ploys (he is not a very successful confidence man)—he does perform a Socratic role. His various interlocutors are forced (or persuaded), in one way or another, to reveal themselves, or, better, they are variously unmasked, though whether simply to expose another mask cannot be ascertained. If much of his talk is as bewildering as 'Greek' to the 'ordinary man' this is precisely because his aim is mystification—but his end is hardly financial. 'Was the man a trickster, it must be more for the love than the lucre. Two or three dirty dollars the motive to so many wiles?' The motives of the Confidence Man are unknown and undiscoverable; we have no access to his interiority, if he has any. He has been called a satirist and a moralist, as he has been identified as Christ and Satan. But fixed identifications and classifications are just what this novel renders impossible. What we can say is that he is an agent of exposure, and many concealed qualities and aspects of people's natures are teased or provoked into the open. Once or twice positive qualities emerge: Mr Roberts, the merchant, is a kind man; the widow reads Corinthians 13 and is indeed somewhat bemusedly charitable. But usually some meanness, or greed, or downright inhumanity comes to light and manifests or declares itself. It may be a 'ship of fools' as one cynic shouts: it is certainly a ship of knaves. As Bruce Franklin showed, every kind of fraud and swindling is represented on board: quack-healers, herb-doctors, land agents, counterfeiters, card sharps, pseudo charity agents, transcendentalist philos-

ophers, false clergymen (he demonstrated conclusively
that the Episcopal minister is another confidence man),
every variety of contemporary American operator. And a
vast range of reference brings in and variously implicates
many historical figures, philosophers, writers, and also
mythical figures and 'gods'. The fusion/confusion starts to
spread through time as well as space, and there is hardly
any seeing where it will stop. For by the end all the lights
are out.

Let us consider how this unusual novel begins and
concludes. It starts on April the first at sunrise—hardly a
subtle clue. A man in 'cream-colors' appears 'as suddenly
as Manco Capac'—a founding divinity of the Inca Empire.
It is stressed that he has no luggage and no friends and is
'in the extremest sense of the word, a stranger'. He wears
a white 'fleecy' cap. Deaf and dumb, he writes out the
Corinthian definitions of Charity on a slate. The crowd
resent his 'intrusion' and regard both him and his writing
as 'somehow inappropriate to the time and place'. The
crowd are sceptical about him since they perceive 'no
badge of authority about him'. They then revile, mock,
and reject him and at the end of the chapter, looking
'gentle and jaded', he retreats or withdraws into sleep:
'his flaxen head drooped, his whole lamb-like figure
relaxed'. We are almost too pointedly asked to interpret
him as a Christ figure. But remember, it is April the first
for the reader as well! There are two other written signs
posted up on the ship. The barber's notice, 'NO TRUST',
initiates a series of postures and reactions of obdurate
and even violent cynicism and scepticism, distrust or
disbelief which the confidence man/men meets on every
appearance. And there is a placard 'offering a reward for
the capture of a mysterious impostor, supposed to have
arrived recently from the East; quite an original genius

in his vocation, as would appear, though wherein his originality consisted was not clearly given; but what purported to be a careful description of his person followed.' The crowd has gathered round this 'announcement' as if it is 'a theatre-bill'. They are eager for amusement, for illusion; they want a performance. Now, the East may be Bethlehem, or it may be New York. We are not given the 'careful description', an occlusion which leaves it open as to whether the man in 'cream-colors', who has certainly come 'from some far country beyond the prairies', fits it or not. Or perhaps the book which follows is the 'careful description'. The Cosmopolitan will be talked about as 'QUITE AN ORIGINAL' after his performance on the ship, and it is an open question whether the man in cream-colours is the original, originary, originating impostor in the book, or whether impostors have any 'origin'. Open, because he *might* be a reincarnation of Christ, or some other God who came down to earth to help mankind. Though in retrospect we may remember the white 'fleecy' cap when we are told of the 'knotted black fleece' of the negro cripple who appears immediately after he has, perhaps, 'waked up and landed', in any case faded into 'oblivion', an indeterminable mode of departing which marks the disappearance of all the subsequent avatars or con men. White fleece and black fleece might suggest opposites, even Manichaean ones, or they might turn out to be variations on a theme—the theme of generally 'fleecing' people, whether the victims lose their money or their masks, which runs through the book. There *may* be gods around. But it *is* April the first! And the barber whose message and stance seem so antithetical to those of the man in cream-colours, turns out to be named William Cream when the Cosmopolitan persuades him, briefly, to abandon his policy of 'NO TRUST'—and cons him. This is, perhaps, a 'creamy' hint that radical opposites might turn out to share more latent similarities than we think.

A premonitory listing of some of the confidence man's subsequent roles or masks is given when the crowd, aroused to suspicion and scrutiny by the first of the crippled cynics who calls him a 'sham' and a 'white impostor', asks the negro for 'documentary proof' that he is not 'spurious'. Of course he has no such 'waloable papers'. Then the tender and innocent-looking young Episcopal clergyman ('newly arrived from another part of the boat'—*he* might be the deaf mute of Chapter One) asks whether there is not someone who can 'speak a good word for you?'. There are plenty of speakers of good words on this boat and the negro answers:

Oh yes, oh yes, dar is aboard here a werry nice, good ge'mann wid a weed, and a ge'mann in a gray coat and white tie, what knows all about me; and a ge'mann wid a big book, too; and a yarb-doctor; and a ge'mann in a yaller west; and a ge'mann in a wiolet robe; and a ge'mann as is a sodjer; and ever so many good, kind honest ge'mann aboard what knows me as well as dis old darkie knows hisself, God bress him!

This list has aroused much comment. Some of the descriptions certainly fit some of the figures who subsequently appear, but others seem not to. This has been seen by some critics as a sign of absent-mindedness (age and ill health are adduced) as though Melville had carelessly strayed from a fixed programme or menu of characters he started with. This is, of course, entirely to miss the point. It is both impossible and irrelevant to work out how many of the figures who subsequently appear are adumbrated here, just as it is impossible to work out how many may or may not be avatars of a single confidence man. For one thing, these are far from 'careful descriptions', more like single attributes—clothes, appurtenances, accessories—which might apply to many figures both on and off the ship (at least three figures are carrying books prominently; four are soldiers of one kind or another, and so on); secondly, Melville's own descriptions of the characters are indeterminate in the extreme. Who would care to say whether he had or had not met this figure: 'A man neither tall nor stout, neither short nor gaunt; but with a body fitted, as by measure, to the service of his mind. For the rest, one less favoured perhaps in his features than his clothes . . . ' Hesitation, qualification, dubiety, modification, negative ascriptions along with a lot of wildly gaudy clothes—these are the mark of Melville's descriptions. And for a reason. He is demonstrating that you cannot really describe an individual, write him whole and all the way round, definitively and adequately. The signs are too elusive, approximative, partial, multivalent, promiscuously implicative. But as in his novel—which may annoy some readers—so it is in life, or at least life on board the *Fidèle*. How on earth can anyone be sure of identifying anyone—definitively, thoroughly, stably—in this 'cosmopolitan and confident tide' of 'strangers'? There are clothes, and bits and pieces—a weed, a tie, a book—and talk. It is not enough to 'identify' people in any but the most transient and superficial sense. But that is all these people have (it is all most people have in the modern urban crowd). And the negro's list concludes by invoking and thus implicating potentially everyone on board. On this ship it is simply impossible to tell who is or is not a confidence man (perhaps person, but as we noted, the passengers are overwhelmingly male) to some degree, in some way or another. And, by extension and implication, off this ship as well.

When the highly dubious Episcopal clergyman obligingly

dashes off to find one of the figures (or transform himself
into one of them) who will 'speak a good word' for the
negro, the adversarial, crippled cynic cries out 'Wild
goose chase! . . . Don't believe there's a soul of them
aboard.' It is certainly a moot point whether there are any
'souls' aboard this ship or in this masquerade. But it is a
'wild goose chase' in a profounder sense. The chase is a
quest for authentication, 'documentary proof', unassail-
ably reliable testimony, infallible evidence. But in this
world, where is that to be found? What would it look or
sound like? There are *no* 'badges of authority' on board
(the captain is an absence). Which man can speak for
another? Where are guarantees to be found? The confidence men, or the avatars, at times vouch for each other
(or themselves)—which is just to underline Melville's
point. In a society where self-authoring is as common as
self-parenting—people choose their parts then write their
lines—there is no longer any source of reliable author-
ization or legitimation, no captain to give guarantees,
and reference, and orders. All evidence about, emanating
from, other people is *potentially* suspect, synthetic, im-
provised. Of course from one point of view this is a
problem as old as human community—the problem of
trust. 'Confidence is the indispensable basis of all sorts of
business transactions. Without it, commerce between
man and man, as between country and country, would,
like a watch, run down and stop.' This is absolutely true
and of crucial importance for the State, both economic
and moral, of any society. You simply cannot have a
society—or indeed a life—founded on mistrust. 'But to
doubt, to suspect, to prove—to have all this wearing work
to be doing continually—how opposed to confidence. It is
evil!' The herb-doctor this time, and whether or not it is a
metaphysical evil, the habit of permanent doubt and
suspicion would be terminally corrosive of community

and relationship. Blind confidence, of course, has its vulnerabilities as it has its generosities. But some degree of trust is essential for any possibility of fruitful human relationship. And the request or demand for evidence and 'proof' of such impalpable qualities as honesty and authenticity is self-defeatingly dangerous. When Othello asks for 'ocular proof' that Desdemona is a whore, he is making that profoundly tragic mistake of asking for the wrong kind of evidence. As Iago says of Desdemona, with diabolical accuracy, her 'honour' is an 'essence that is not seen'. You can't see, or prove, honour, or fidelity, or trustworthiness. Iago can manufacture spurious evidence of seeming non-fidelity—nothing easier. He justs needs a few props—like a handkerchief (cf. weed or brass plate or book)—and a flow of insidiously insinuating and suggestive words, and he can do the trick. For Othello to trust that kind of 'evidence' against the admittedly ineffable and non-demonstrable 'honour' of Desdemona is, of course, his tragedy, a 'wild goose chase' of the most hideously mistaken kind. *The Confidence-Man* is not a tragedy, but Melville shows that absolutely fundamental problems, concerning trust and confidence, occur with special urgency and, perhaps, insolubility in the new world of America. Or, more largely, in the modern de-sacralized world which has to such a large extent lost not only its gods, but its guarantees: its sanctions and tacit assumptions, its bindings and bondings—in a word, its 'authority'. Just who and how much is to be trusted? There are no self-authenticating signs; but signs are all we have. The passengers on the *Fidèle* are perhaps only an extreme case of the now-common condition. And to *some* degree we have to trust trust, and have confidence in confidence.[1]

[1] See the volume *Trust* edited by Diego Gambetta (Basil Blackwell, 1988) in which the necessity and difficulty of establishing some form of

The 'wild goose chase' in this novel is picked up in the last chapter, in the concluding incident of the old man and the Counterfeit Detector. It is worth tracing out the final steps of the book. The Cosmopolitan goes down to the cabin to inspect a Bible, to see whether it does indeed include the cynical words of Sirach, quoted by Cream the barber: 'An enemy speaketh sweetly with his lips . . . I believed not his many words.' Professing not to believe such sceptical words can be found in the 'True Book', the Cosmopolitan approaches the old man reading the bible, asking him whether these words are there. The old man has no knowledge of them, but the Cosmopolitan finds them in Ecclesiasticus. The ensuing exchange is in some ways the most important in the book:

'Ah!' cried the old man, brightening up, 'now I know. Look,' turning the leaves forward and back, till all the Old Testament lay flat on one side, and all the New Testament flat on the other, while in his fingers he supported vertically the portion between, 'look, sir, all this to the right is certain truth, and all this to the left is certain truth, but all I hold in my hand here is apocrypha.'

'Apocrypha?'

'Yes, and there's the word in black and white,' pointing to it. 'And what says the word? It says as much as "not warranted;" for what do college men say of anything of that sort? They say it is apocryphal. The word itself, I've heard from the pulpit implies something of uncertain credit. So if your disturbance be raised from aught in this apocrypha,' again taking up the pages, 'in that case think no more of it, for it's apocryphal.'

'What's that about the Apocalypse?' here, a third time, came from the berth.

Here is the articulation of the orthodox certainty that

trust in all walks of life is discussed by writers from various disciplines. In particular see Gambetta's own concluding essay, 'Can we Trust Trust?'

revealed and established truth can be cleanly separated
out from all which is 'of uncertain credit' and the two
categories be rigidly delineated. The Cosmopolitan pur-
ports to be relieved but adds that it is potentially
misleading to have the Apocrypha inserted in the middle
between the True parts of the book. 'Fact is, when all is
bound up together, it's sometimes confusing. The uncanonical part should be bound distinct.' Melville's point—
one which his whole work is engaged in making—is that
it is not only impossible but potentially very dangerous
for any man, or society, to seek to reach, ascertain, and
proclaim absolute, unconditional certainty, rigid classifications of true and false, and good and bad. (It is the Ahab
drive, redisplayed in this book in its purity by the Indian-
hater John Moredock who sees all Indians as evil while he
is a kind and good Christian with his white family and
friends. It is a mark of the possible perversity to which
criticism can go that this schizophrenic, psychopathic
racist has been put forward as the hero of the novel. At
least he has clear ideas and the courage of his convictions
and is no con man! Such criticism simply re-enacts the
real dangers of the need and quest for fixed and stable
readings.) The quest for certainties leads to falsifications
and finally the Manichaean oppugnancy of oppositional
thinking. Black and white indeed. But for Melville, life
partakes of 'the *unravellable* inscrutableness of God'
(*Pierre*, my italics). Man lives precisely in the universe
where the Apocrypha is placed in the Book—in the
middle, the zone of uncertainty, the realm of the uncanonical. That the confidence man/men can best operate in
that realm, while pretending to wish to have a clear and
settled distinction between the canonical, the reliable, the
authoritative, and the 'not warranted', the ungrounded,
the provisional, and to have the latter 'bound' and seques-
tered (thus travestying the 'unravelling' aspirations of

traditional thought, and politics), is part of the dark irony
of Melville's vision.

A voice complains at the noise of these 'two geese'
gabbling and then the mysterious boy peddler enters and
proceeds to sell the old man a 'traveler's patent lock' and a
money-belt, thus making something of a mockery of his
previous claims not to distrust his fellow creatures. As a
bonus, the boy—all 'roguish parody'—gives the old man a
Counterfeit Detector which will lead to his final confusion.
To pass the time he tries out the Detector on some bills he
has recently been given. Once he starts to check the bills
against the list of what the Detector says should be
authenticating signs, he is reduced to a bemused bewil-
derment: 'I don't know, I don't know . . . there's so many
marks of all sorts to go by, it makes it a kind of uncertain.'
This effectively summarizes the perplexed cry which
comes from the heart of the book. In particular the old
man cannot find the 'microscopic', indeed effectively
'unobservable', 'figure of a goose' which, says the Detector,
should be there if the bill is 'good'. The Cosmopolitan
maintains that he can see the goose, with a fair intimation that the only goose on view is the old man himself.
Finally, he advises the old man: 'Then throw the Detector
away . . . it only makes you purblind; don't you see what a
wild goose chase it has led you?' The Detector and the
dollar bill are both printed items and the Detector may
be as 'counterfeit' as the bills it presumes to check (as
the ambiguity of the two words 'Counterfeit Detector'
suggests). Neither of these groups of 'marks' can verify, or
falsify, the other, and 'there are so many marks of all sort
to go by'. To look for absolute guarantees of authenticity
—this is indeed a wild-goose chase.

The implications of the conclusion are dark and
pessimistic. Retiring for the night, the old man asks for
his 'Life-preserver', which turns out to be a chair also

containing a chamberpot, and there is an almost crude faecal pun in the Cosmopolitan's ironic advice to 'have confidence in that stool for a special providence', for it seems the pot has been used: 'But bless me, we are being left in the dark here. Pah! what a smell, too.' How different from the coffin-turned-life-preserver which saves Ishmael at the end of *Moby-Dick*! Here there is only the odour of excrement in the air as the Cosmopolitan extinguishes the final light and leads the old man away into the ensuing darkness. It does seem to portend some kind of terminal exhaustion, obliteration, annihilation. Hints of apocalypse, using both biblical and pagan sources, are thick in the air of the last chapter, and are too obtrusive to be missed. It is a question of what we make of them. Is this an image or adumbration of the 'promised end', or is it the final, darkly humorous, flourish of the 'roguish parody' of our brilliant, mesmerizing, allusion-peddling author? The whole action of the book has taken place on April Fools' Day, related to ancient vernal celebrations of All Fool's Day; but Melville leaves it uncertain whether the last chapter takes place just before or just after midnight (the Cosmopolitan signs his Agreement with the barber at 'quarter to twelve o'clock, P.M.' and in his last conversation with the old man he alludes to this incident as being 'not a half-hour since'). Melville leaves us in teasing, and troubling, uncertainty to the last. Are we at the very end of the day of folly masquerade, in which confidence has, as it were, been carnivalized? Or is it now just over? The last chapter is indeed entitled 'The Cosmopolitan Increases in Seriousness' and so, we may feel, does the book. Certainly, by the last page, it does seem to be 'very late' and the possibility raised by the last words, that 'Something further may follow of this masquerade', might on the one hand imply that there might be a sequel, or on the other may be suggesting something more ominous. Certainly the end leaves us nothing to stand on and nothing to see by. And we still cannot be certain about the identity or significance of the Confidence Man, nor be sure of the implications and ramifications of 'His Masquerade'.

Bruce Franklin asserts, with a good deal of persuasive evidence, that 'in this universe man's Savior—Manco Capac, Vishnu, Christ, Apollo, the Buddhist's Buddha—is embodied by the Confidence Man, who is also man's Destroyer—Satan, Siva, the Hindu's Buddha. Melville's mythology converts all gods into the Confidence Man.' Such a reading is certainly allowed by Melville's super-abundantly allusive masquerade. We can also see more mundane and secular implications. Thomas Mann's suave confidence man, Felix Krull, while he is acting as a waiter in a luxurious hotel in Paris, often ponders a favourite idea: 'It was the idea of *interchangeability*. With a change of clothes and make-up, the servitors might often just as well have been the masters, and many of those who lounged in deep wicker chairs, smoking their cigarettes, might have played the waiter. It was pure accident that the reverse was the fact, an accident of wealth; for an aristocracy of money is an accidental and interchangeable aristocracy.' This idea is peculiarly relevant to the world of *The Confidence-Man* and Melville's own vision of reversibility and 'interchangeability'—of objects, words, concepts, roles, persons, gods. And Felix Krull puts his idea into action, occasionally leaving the hotel where he is a waiter, dressing up in fine clothes, and going to another fine hotel as a patron. 'This amounted, as one can see, to a kind of dual existence, whose charm lay in the ambiguity as to which figure was the real I and which the masquerade . . . I masqueraded in both capacities and the undisguised reality behind the two appearances, the real I, could not be identified because it actually did not exist.' Interchangeability is everywhere adumbrated on board the *Fidèle*, and by the same token there is a prevailing sense that it is becoming impossible to identify any 'real I', anywhere. This loss of confidence in the existence of some stable core identity increases throughout the century—thus Ibsen's Peer Gynt, *the* European confidence man of the nineteenth century, after playing so many roles and remaining so fluid, uncommitted, and opportunistic, finds that he is a series of surfaces but empty at the centre, like the onion he peels. A comparable sense of both the multiplicity and the sheer, ontological dubiety of the self is to be found in Pirandello; and an Italian critic, Guido Botta, rightly invoked his vision of man as '*un complesso di personaggi*' in connection with Melville's Confidence Man. (Anyone interested in the troubling relationship between roles and 'identity' in Pirandello should read, in particular, his novel *The Late Mattia Pascal*, and his play *Henry IV*.) The self as role-player has become something of a commonplace of sociology and psychology as, for example, in Erving Goffman's *The Presentation of Self in Everyday Life*, and, arguably, we are a good deal too complacent with the notion, too mindlessly comfortable in the 'endlessly-changeable accommodations' of the Confidence Man's 'Protean easy-chair'. But Melville was a pioneer and his novel has all the powerful and unsettling originality and strangeness, and at times awkwardness, and all the ambiguous and double-edged comedy and indeterminably, interminably worrying suggestiveness, of a work exploring new and dangerous ground.

It certainly breaks with existing conventions of novel-writing. It is set on no ordinary boat. 'The entire ship is a riddle'. It is also a writing desk, its rooms and promenades, saloons and balconies, passages and 'out-of-the-way retreats' being described in terms of the various spaces

and drawers in 'an escritoire'—and Melville keeps riddling
and writing, and the riddling of writing, well to the fore.
His ship is Fidèle; his theme is confidence; his complaint
is against those who demand 'severe fidelity to real life' in
a 'work of amusement'. How does, how can, how should
man keep faith with man, or an author with his readers?
Melville intrudes his own voice, or holds up his own slate,
in three short chapters (14, 33, and 44). He defends
himself against the charge of 'inconsistency' of characterization. It is a double defence. Surely 'to all fiction is
allowed some play of invention'; but, anyway, the fact is
that 'in real life, a consistent character is a *rara avis*'.
What he is maintaining is that it is conventional modes of
characterization which are false. It is a crucial passage:

That fiction, where every character can, by reason of its
consistency, be comprehended at a glance, either exhibits but
sections of a character, making them appear for wholes, or else
is very untrue to reality; while, on the other hand, that author
who draws a character, even though to common view incongruous in its parts, as the flying squirrel, and, at different
periods, as much at variance with itself as the caterpillar is with
the butterfly into which it changes, may yet, in so doing, be not
false but faithful to facts.

Melville is claiming a new kind of 'fidelity' for himself as
a writer, a fidelity to the actual radical discontinuity and
plurality of the self. What may follow from this perception
may hardly, perhaps, be decided. Some have seen the
figure of the Confidence Man as a nihilist, cynically
exploiting others; yet there is an undeniable resilience, a
participatory zest in his fluent exhortations. 'Life is a picnic *en costume*; one must take a part, assume a character,
stand ready in a sensible way to play the fool.' He is,
of course, diabolically plausible, an abuser of trust, but
the sour self-sequestration which results from habitual
suspicion—'I have confidence in distrust' says Pitch, but

note that he is a bachelor—can hardly be regarded as a preferred stance, for all that its robust scepticism can find ample justification. Melville, characteristically, makes all possible positions reciprocally subversive.

In his last intervention into his own text, he discusses the possibilities of creating 'original' characters in fiction, since in modern urban conditions figures are 'novel, or singular, or striking, or captivating, or all four at once', but not 'in a thorough sense, original'. Among all the dis-originated figures in contemporary America, origin-ality is going to be a rare phenomenon, in life and in fiction. 'The original character, essentially such, is like a revolving Drummond light, raying away from itself all round it—everything is lit up by it, everything starts up to it (mark how it is with Hamlet).' We may detect a final Melvillean irony here. He specifically asserts the 'impropriety' of calling the Cosmopolitan 'quite an original', yet in many ways, as critics have decided, the Cosmopolitan's effect on those he (and his, possibly, previous avatars) meets is exactly that of the Drummond light as described by Melville. One way and another, all 'start up' and are 'lit' by him. Does this make him a sort of modern Hamlet, that figure who, more perhaps than any other, served to lay bare the problems and ambiguities in the relations between doing, acting, performing, and 'playing'? It certainly makes him a kind of Drummond light. Now, the Drummond light was used most notably by P. T. Barnum to advertise and draw people into his Museum—his Masquerade, we might say. So where does that leave the Confidence Man and Melville? Hamlets and Shakespeares? Or counterfeiters and impresarios? Perhaps—and this would be the Melville touch—there is not, finally, very much difference.

TONY TANNER

NOTE ON THE TEXT

The Confidence-Man was first published on 1 April 1857
by Dix & Edwards in New York, and by Longman, Brown,
Green, Longmans & Roberts in London later that month.
This World's Classics edition follows the text of the
Constable Collected Edition (London, 1922–4).

SELECT BIBLIOGRAPHY

Biography, Letters

Howard, Leon, *Herman Melville; a biography* (Berkeley, 1951).

Leyda, Jan, *The Melville Log: A Documentary Life of Herman Melville, 1819–91* (New York, 1951).

Davis, Merrell R., and Gilman, William H., eds., *The Letters of Herman Melville* (New Haven, 1960).

Metcalf, Eleanor Melville, *Herman Melville: Cycle and Epicycle* (Cambridge, Mass., 1953).

General Criticism

Bloom, Harold, ed., *Herman Melville* (New York, 1986).

Branch, Watson, *Melville; the critical heritage* (London, 1974).

Chase, Richard, *Melville; a collection of critical essays* (Englewood Cliffs, 1962).

Feidelson, Charles, Jr., *Symbolism and American Literature* (Chicago, 1953).

Franklin, H. Bruce, *The Wake of the Gods: Melville's Mythology* (Stanford, 1963).

Fussell, Edwin, *Frontier: American Literature and the American West* (Princeton, 1965).

Lee, A. Robert, ed., *Herman Melville: reassessments* (London, 1984).

Mathiessen, F. O., *American Renaissance* (New York, 1941).

Parker, Hershel, *The Recognition of Herman Melville* (Ann Arbor, 1967).

Rogin, Michael Paul, *Subversive genealogy: the politics and art of Herman Melville* (New York, 1983).

Rosenberry, Edward H., *Melville* (London, 1979).

Seelye, John, *Melville: The Ironic Diagram* (Evanston, 1970).

Criticism of *The Confidence-Man: His Masquerade*

Blair, John G., *The confidence man in modern fiction: a rogue's gallery with six portraits* (London, 1979).

Foster, Elizabeth S., Introduction and Notes to Hendricks House edition (New York, 1954).

Franklin, H. Bruce, Introduction to Bobbs-Merrill edition (Indianapolis, 1967).

Lewis, R. W. B., Afterword to Signet edition (New York, 1964).

Lindberg, Gary, *The confidence man in American literature* (New York, 1982).

Quirk, Tom, *Melville's Confidence Man: from knave to knight* (Columbia, Missouri, 1982).

Sussman, Henry, 'The Deconstructor as Politician: Melville's *Confidence-Man*', *Glyph*, 4 (1978), 32–56.

Bibliographies

Important nineteenth-century criticism is collected in Hershel Parker, ed., *The Recognition of Herman Melville* (Ann Arbor, 1967), and in Watson G. Branch, ed., *Melville: The Critical Heritage* (London, 1974). Jeanetta Boswell's *Herman Melville and the Critics: A Checklist of Criticism 1900–78* (Metuchen, NJ, 1981) covers twentieth-century books and articles on Melville; those which deal with *The Confidence-Man* are also listed in the Annotated Bibliography (1919–70), compiled by Watson G. Branch, which is included in the Norton Critical Edition of the novel (New York, 1971), edited by Hershel Parker. For more recent criticism, see the annual MLA Bibliographies.

A CHRONOLOGY OF
HERMAN MELVILLE

1819   Born in New York City (1 August), son of Allan Melvill, a merchant, and Maria Gansevoort.

1830   Father declared bankrupt.

1832   Father dies, leaving mother with family of eight children and large debts.

1832–8   Employed in various short-lived jobs: in a bank, on a farm, in a store, teaching in an elementary school. Later takes engineering and surveying course.

1839   Signs on as merchant seaman on the *St. Lawrence*; makes the round trip to Liverpool described in *Redburn*. Teaches in school in New York State on return.

1840   Visits uncle in Galena, Illinois, then travels down Mississippi to Cairo, returning via Ohio River.

1841   Ships aboard the whaler *Acushnet*, bound for Cape Horn and the Pacific.

1842   Jumps ship with shipmate in the Marquesas Islands, and lives with cannibal tribe as recounted in *Typee*. Rescued by Australian whaler, but leaves the ship after a mutiny, and spends time in Tahiti, as described in *Omoo*.

1843–4   After period in Honolulu, returns to the USA as ordinary seaman in the frigate *United States*, the model for the *Neversink* in *White-Jacket*.

1846   *Typee*.

1847   *Omoo*. Marries Elizabeth Shaw, daughter of Chief Justice of Massachusetts, and settles in New York.

1849   *Mardi* and *Redburn*. Birth of first son, and second voyage to Europe.

1850   *White-Jacket*. Buys estate near Pittsfield, Massachusetts, close to home of Nathaniel Hawthorne.

1851   *Moby-Dick, or, The Whale*. Second son born.

1852   *Pierre, or, The Ambiguities*.

1853   Fire at publishers destroys remaining copies of his works. Fails to obtain post as US Consul. First daughter born.

1855   *Israel Potter*. Second daughter born.

1856   *The Piazza Tales*, a collection of his magazine stories. Travels to Europe and Holy Land for his health after completion of *The Confidence-Man: His Masquerade* in summer.

1857   *The Confidence-Man: His Masquerade*.

1858–65 Turns to verse, and makes fitful attempts to earn a living by means other than writing.

1866   *Battle-Pieces*, poems. Becomes Customs Inspector, for the next twenty years, in the port of New York.

1876   *Clarel: A Poem and Pilgrimage in the Holy Land*.

1888   *John Marr and Other Sailors*, poems.

1891   *Timoleon*, poems. Dies, 28 September.

1924   *Billy Budd, Sailor* published.

CONTENTS

CONTENTS

THE CONFIDENCE-MAN

HIS MASQUERADE

CHAPTER I

A MUTE GOES ABOARD A BOAT ON THE MISSISSIPPI

At sunrise on a first of April,* there appeared, suddenly
as Manco Capac at the lake Titicaca,* a man in cream-
colours, at the water-side in the city of St. Louis.*

His cheek was fair, his chin downy, his hair flaxen,
his hat a white fur one, with a long fleecy nap. He
had neither trunk, valise, carpet-bag, nor parcel. No
porter followed him. He was unaccompanied by
friends. From the shrugged shoulders, titters, whispers,
wonderings of the crowd, it was plain that he was, in
the extremest sense of the word, a stranger.

In the same moment with his advent, he stepped
aboard the favourite steamer *Fidèle,* on the point of
starting for New Orleans. Stared at, but unsaluted,
with the air of one neither courting nor shunning regard,
but evenly pursuing the path of duty, lead it through
solitudes or cities, he held on his way along the lower
deck until he chanced to come to a placard nigh the
captain's office, offering a reward for the capture of a
mysterious impostor, supposed to have recently arrived
from the East; quite an original genius in his vocation,
as would appear, though wherein his originality consisted was not clearly given; but what purported to
be a careful description of his person followed.

As if it had been a theatre-bill, crowds were gathered about the announcement, and among them certain chevaliers, whose eyes, it was plain, were on the capitals, or, at least, earnestly seeking sight of them from behind intervening coats ; but as for their fingers, they were enveloped in some myth ; though, during a chance interval, one of these chevaliers*somewhat showed his hand in purchasing from another chevalier, *ex-officio* a peddler of money-belts, one of his popular safe-guards, while another peddler, who was still another versatile chevalier, hawked, in the thick of the throng, the lives of Measan, the bandit of Ohio, Murrel, the pirate of the Mississippi, and the brothers Harpe,* the Thugs* of the Green River country, in Kentucky—creatures, with others of the sort, one and all exterminated at the time, and for the most part, like the hunted generations of wolves in the same regions, leaving comparatively few successors ; which would seem cause for unalloyed gratulation, and is such to all except those who think that in new countries, where the wolves are killed off, the foxes increase.

Pausing at this spot, the stranger so far succeeded in threading his way, as at last to plant himself just beside the placard, when, producing a small slate and tracing some words upon it, he held it up before him on a level with the placard, so that they who read the one might read the other. The words were these :—

'Charity thinketh no evil.'*

As, in gaining his place, some little perseverance, not to say persistence of a mildly inoffensive sort, had been unavoidable, it was not with the best relish that the crowd regarded his apparent intrusion ; and upon a more attentive survey, perceiving no badge of authority about him, but rather something quite the contrary— he being of an aspect so singularly innocent ; an aspect,

too, which they took to be somehow inappropriate to
the time and place, and inclining to the notion that his
writing was of much the same sort : in short, taking
him for some strange kind of simpleton, harmless enough,
would he keep to himself, but not wholly unobnoxious
as an intruder—they made no scruple to jostle him aside ;
while one, less kind than the rest, or more of a wag,
by an unobserved stroke, dexterously flattened down his
fleecy hat upon his head. Without readjusting it, the
stranger quietly turned, and writing anew upon the
slate, again held it up :—

'Charity suffereth long, and is kind.'

Illy pleased with his pertinacity, as they thought it,
the crowd a second time thrust him aside, and not
without epithets and some buffets, all of which were
unresented. But, as if at last despairing of so difficult
an adventure, wherein one, apparently a non-resistant,
sought to impose his presence upon fighting characters,
the stranger now moved slowly away, yet not before
altering his writing to this :—

'Charity endureth all things.'

Shield-like bearing his slate before him, amid stares
and jeers he moved slowly up and down, at his turning-
points again changing his inscription to—

'Charity believeth all things.'
and then—

'Charity never faileth.'

The word charity, as originally traced, remained
throughout uneffaced, not unlike the left-hand numeral
of a printed date, otherwise left for convenience in blank.

To some observers, the singularity, if not lunacy, of
the stranger was heightened by his muteness, and,
perhaps also, by the contrast to his proceedings afforded

in the actions—quite in the wonted and sensible order
of things—of the barber of the boat, whose quarters,
under a smoking-saloon, and over against a bar-room,
was next door but two to the captain's office. As if
the long, wide, covered deck, hereabouts built up on
both sides with shop-like windowed spaces, were some
Constantinople arcade or bazaar, where more than one
trade is plied, this river barber, aproned and slippered,
but rather crusty-looking for the moment, it may be
from being newly out of bed, was throwing open his
premises for the day, and suitably arranging the exterior.
With business-like dispatch, having rattled down his
shutters, and at a palm-tree angle set out in the iron
fixture his little ornamental pole, and this without overmuch tenderness for the elbows and toes of the crowd,
he concluded his operations by bidding people stand still
more aside, when, jumping on a stool, he hung over
his door, on the customary nail, a gaudy sort of illuminated pasteboard sign, skilfully executed by himself, gilt
with the likeness of a razor elbowed in readiness to
shave, and also, for the public benefit, with two words
not unfrequently seen ashore gracing other shops besides
barbers' :—

'No Trust.'*

An inscription which, though in a sense not less in-
trusive than the contrasted ones of the stranger, did
not, as it seemed, provoke any corresponding derision
or surprise, much less indignation ; and still less, to all
appearances, did it gain for the inscriber the repute of
being a simpleton.

Meanwhile, he with the slate continued moving slowly
up and down, not without causing some stares to change
into jeers, and some jeers into pushes, and some pushes
into punches ; when suddenly, in one of his turns, he was

hailed from behind by two porters carrying a large trunk ; but as the summons, though loud, was without effect, they accidentally or otherwise swung their burden against him, nearly overthrowing him ; when, by a quick start, a peculiar inarticulate moan, and a pathetic telegraphing of his fingers, he involuntarily betrayed that he was not alone dumb, but also deaf.

Presently, as if not wholly unaffected by his reception thus far, he went forward, seating himself in a retired spot on the forecastle, nigh the foot of a ladder there leading to a deck above, up and down which ladder some of the boatmen, in discharge of their duties, were occasionally going.

From his betaking himself to this humble quarter, it was evident that, as a deck-passenger, the stranger, simple though he seemed, was not entirely ignorant of his place, though his taking a deck-passage might have been partly for convenience ; as, from his having no luggage, it was probable that his destination was one of the small wayside landings within a few hours' sail. But, though he might not have a long way to go, yet he seemed already to have come from a very long distance.

Though neither soiled nor slovenly, his cream-coloured suit had a tossed look, almost linty, as if, travelling night and day from some far country beyond the prairies, he had long been without the solace of a bed. His aspect was at once gentle and jaded, and, from the moment of seating himself, increasing in tired abstraction and dreaminess. Gradually overtaken by slumber, his flaxen head drooped, his whole lamb-like figure relaxed, and, half reclining against the ladder's foot, lay motionless, as some sugar-snow in March, which, softly stealing down over night, with its white placidity startles the brown farmer peering out from his threshold at daybreak.

CHAPTER II

SHOWING THAT MANY MEN HAVE MANY MINDS

' ODD fish ! '

    ' Poor fellow ! '

    ' Who can he be ? '

    ' Casper Hauser.'*

    ' Bless my soul ! '

    ' Uncommon countenance.'

    ' Green prophet from Utah.'*

    ' Humbug ! '

    ' Singular innocence.'

    ' Means something.'

    ' Spirit-rapper.'*

    ' Moon-calf.'*

    ' Piteous.'

    ' Trying to enlist interest.'

    ' Beware of him.'

    ' Fast asleep here, and, doubtless, pick-pockets on board.'

    ' Kind of daylight Endymion.'*

    ' Escaped convict, worn out with dodging.'

    ' Jacob dreaming at Luz.'*

Such the epitaphic comments, conflictingly spoken or thought, of a miscellaneous company, who, assembled on the overlooking, cross-wise balcony at the forward end of the upper deck near by, had not witnessed preceding occurrences.

Meantime, like some enchanted man in his grave, happily oblivious of all gossip, whether chiselled or chatted, the deaf and dumb stranger still tranquilly slept, while now the boat started on her voyage.

The great ship-canal of Ving-King-Ching,* in the Flowery Kingdom, seems the Mississippi in parts, where, amply flowing between low, vine-tangled banks, flat as tow-paths, it bears the huge toppling steamers, bedizened and lacquered within like imperial junks.

Pierced along its great white bulk with two tiers of small embrasure-like windows, well above the water-line, the *Fidèle*, though, might at distance have been taken by strangers for some whitewashed fort on a floating isle.

Merchants on 'change* seem the passengers that buzz on her decks, while, from quarters unseen, comes a murmur as of bees in the comb. Fine promenades, domed saloons, long galleries, sunny balconies, confidential passages, bridal chambers, state-rooms plenty as pigeon-holes, and out-of-the-way retreats like secret drawers in an escritoire, present like facilities for publicity or privacy. Auctioneer or coiner, with equal ease, might somewhere here drive his trade.

Though her voyage of twelve hundred miles extends from apple to orange, from clime to clime, yet, like any small ferry-boat, to right and left, at every landing, the huge *Fidèle* still receives additional passengers in exchange for those that disembark; so that, though always full of strangers, she continually, in some degree, adds to, or replaces them with strangers still more strange; like Rio Janeiro fountain, fed from the Coco-varde mountains, which is ever overflowing with strange waters, but never with the same strange particles in every part.

Though hitherto, as has been seen, the man in cream-colours had by no means passed unobserved, yet by stealing into retirement, and there going asleep and continuing so, he seemed to have courted oblivion, a boon not often withheld from so humble an applicant as he. Those staring crowds on the shore were now left far behind, seen dimly clustering like swallows on eaves ; while the passengers' attention was soon drawn away to the rapidly shooting high bluffs and shot-towers on the Missouri shore, or the bluff-looking Missourians and towering Kentuckians among the throngs on the decks.

By and by—two or three random stoppages having been made, and the last transient memory of the slumberer vanished, and he himself, not unlikely, waked up and landed ere now—the crowd, as is usual, began in all parts to break up from a concourse into various clusters or squads, which in some cases disintegrated again into quartettes, trios, and couples, or even solitaires ; involuntarily submitting to that natural law which ordains dissolution equally to the mass, as in time to the member.

As among Chaucer's Canterbury pilgrims, or those oriental ones crossing the Red Sea towards Mecca in the festival month, there was no lack of variety. Natives of all sorts, and foreigners ; men of business and men of pleasure ; parlour men and backwoodsmen ; farm-hunters and fame-hunters ; heiress-hunters, gold-hunters, buffalo-hunters, bee-hunters, happiness-hunters, truth-hunters, and still keener hunters after all these hunters. Fine ladies in slippers, and moccasined squaws ; Northern speculators and Eastern philosophers ; English, Irish, German, Scotch, Danes ; Santa Fé traders in striped blankets, and Broadway bucks in cravats of cloth of gold ; fine-looking Kentucky boatmen, and Japanese looking Mississippi cotton-planters ; Quakers in full drab, and United States soldiers in full regimentals ; slaves, black, mulatto, quadroon ; modish young Spanish Creoles, and old-fashioned French Jews ; Mormons and Papists ; Dives and Lazarus ; jesters and mourners, teetotallers and convivialists, deacons and blacklegs*; hard-shell* Baptists and clay-eaters ;* grinning negroes, and Sioux chiefs solemn as high-priests. In short, a piebald parliament, an Anacharsis Cloots congress* of all kinds of that multiform pilgrim species, man.

As pine, beech, birch, ash, hackmatack, hemlock, spruce, basswood, maple, interweave their foliage in the natural wood, so these varieties of mortals blended their varieties of visage and garb. A Tartar-like* picturesqueness ; a sort of pagan abandonment and assurance. Here reigned the dashing and all-fusing spirit of the West, whose type is the Mississippi itself, which, uniting the streams of the most distant and opposite zones, pours them along, helter-skelter, in one cosmopolitan and confident tide.

CHAPTER III

IN WHICH A VARIETY OF CHARACTERS APPEAR

In the forward part of the boat, not the least attractive object, for a time, was a grotesque negro cripple, in tow-cloth attire and an old coal-sifter of a tambourine in his hand, who, owing to something wrong about his legs, was, in effect, cut down to the stature of a Newfoundland dog; his knotted black fleece and good-natured, honest black face rubbing against the upper part of people's thighs as he made shift to shuffle about, making music, such as it was, and raising a smile even from the gravest. It was curious to see him, out of his very deformity, indigence, and houselessness, so cheerily endured, raising mirth in some of that crowd, whose own purses, hearths, hearts, all their possessions, sound limbs included, could not make gay.

' What is your name, old boy ? ' said a purple-faced drover, putting his large purple hand on the cripple's bushy wool, as if it were the curled forehead of a black steer.

' Der Black Guinea dey calls me, sar.'

' And who is your master, Guinea ? '

' Oh, sar, I am der dog widout massa.'

' A free dog, eh ?   Well, on your account, I 'm sorry for that, Guinea.   Dogs without masters fare hard.'

' So dey do, sar ; so dey do.   But you see, sar, dese here legs ?   What ge'mman want to own dese here legs ? '

' But where do you live ? '

' All 'long shore, sar ; dough now I 'se going to see
brodder at der landing ; but chiefly I libs in der city.'

' St. Louis, ah ? Where do you sleep there of nights ? '

' On der floor of der good baker's oven, sar.'

' In an oven ? whose, pray ?   What baker, I should
like to know, bakes such black bread in his oven, alongside of his nice white rolls, too.   Who is that too charitable
baker, pray ? '

' Dar he be,' with a broad grin lifting his tambourine
high over his head.

' The sun is the baker, eh ? '

' Yes, sar, in der city dat good baker warms der stones
for dis ole darkie when he sleeps out on der pabements
o' nights.'

' But that must be in the summer only, old boy.   How
about winter, when the cold Cossacks come clattering
and jingling ?   How about winter, old boy ? '

' Den dis poor old darkie shakes werry bad, I tell you,
sar.   Oh, sar, oh ! don't speak ob der winter,' he added,
with a reminiscent shiver, shuffling off into the thickest
of the crowd, like a half-frozen black sheep nudging itself
a cosy berth in the heart of the white flock.

Thus far not very many pennies had been given him,
and, used at last to his strange looks, the less polite
passengers of those in that part of the boat began to
get their fill of him as a curious object ; when suddenly
the negro more than revived their first interest by an
expedient which, whether by chance or design, was a
singular temptation at once to *diversion* and charity,
though, even more than his crippled limbs, it put him
on a canine footing. In short, as in appearance he
seemed a dog, so now, in a merry way, like a dog he
began to be treated. Still shuffling among the crowd,
now and then he would pause, throwing back his head
and opening his mouth like an elephant for tossed apples

at a menagerie; when, making a space before him, people would have a bout at a strange sort of pitch-penny game, the cripple's mouth being at once target and purse, and he hailing each expertly caught copper with a cracked bravura from his tambourine. To be the subject of alms-giving is trying, and to feel in duty bound to appear cheerfully grateful under the trial, must be still more so; but whatever his secret emotions, he swallowed them, while still retaining each copper this side the œsophagus. And nearly always he grinned, and only once or twice did he wince, which was when certain coins, tossed by more playful almoners, came inconveniently nigh to his teeth, an accident whose un-welcomeness was not unedged by the circumstance that the pennies thus thrown proved buttons.

While this game of charity was yet at its height, a limping, gimlet-eyed, sour-faced person—it may be some discharged custom-house officer, who, suddenly stripped of convenient means of support, had concluded to be avenged on government and humanity by making himself miserable for life, either by hating or suspecting everything and everybody—this shallow unfortunate, after sundry sorry observations of the negro, began to croak out something about his deformity being a sham, got up for financial purposes, which immediately threw a damp upon the frolic benignities of the pitch-penny players.

But that these suspicions came from one who himself on a wooden leg went halt, this did not appear to strike anybody present. That cripples, above all men, should be companionable, or, at least, refrain from picking a fellow-limper to pieces, in short, should have a little sympathy in common misfortune, seemed not to occur to the company.

Meantime, the negro's countenance, before marked

with even more than patient good-nature, drooped into
a heavy-hearted expression, full of the most painful
distress. So far abased beneath its proper physical
level, that Newfoundland-dog face turned in passively
hopeless appeal, as if instinct told it that the right or
the wrong might not have overmuch to do with whatever
wayward mood superior intelligences might yield to.

But instinct, though knowing, is yet a teacher set
below reason, which itself says, in the grave words of
Lysander in the comedy, after Puck has made a sage of
him with his spell :—

'The will of man is by his reason swayed.'*

So that, suddenly change as people may, in their dispositions, it is not always waywardness, but improved
judgment, which, as in Lysander's case, or the present,
operates with them.

Yes, they began to scrutinise the negro curiously
enough ; when, emboldened by this evidence of the
efficacy of his words, the wooden-legged man hobbled
up to the negro, and, with the air of a beadle, would,
to prove his alleged imposture on the spot, have stripped
him and then driven him away, but was prevented by
the crowd's clamour, now taking part with the poor
fellow, against one who had just before turned nearly
all minds the other way. So he with the wooden leg
was forced to retire ; when the rest, finding themselves
left sole judges in the case, could not resist the opportunity of acting the part : not because it is a human
weakness to take pleasure in sitting in judgment upon
one in a box, as surely this unfortunate negro now was,
but that it strangely sharpens human perceptions, when,
instead of standing by and having their fellow-feelings
touched by the sight of an alleged culprit severely
handled by some one justiciary, a crowd suddenly come

to be all justiciaries in the same case themselves; as
in Arkansas once, a man proved guilty, by law, of murder,
but whose condemnation was deemed unjust by the
people, so that they rescued him to try him themselves;
whereupon, they, as it turned out, found him even
guiltier than the court had done, and forthwith proceeded
to execution; so that the gallows presented the truly
warning spectacle of a man hanged by his friends.

But not to such extremities, or anything like them,
did the present crowd come; they, for the time, being
content with putting the negro fairly and discreetly to
the question; among other things, asking him, had he
any documentary proof, any plain paper about him,
attesting that his case was not a spurious one.

' No, no, dis poor ole darkie hain't none o' dem waloable
papers,' he wailed.

' But is there not someone who can speak a good
word for you ? ' here said a person newly arrived from
another part of the boat, a young Episcopal clergyman,
in a long, straight-bodied black coat; small in stature,
but manly; with a clear face and blue eye; innocence,
tenderness, and good sense triumvirate in his air.

' Oh yes, oh yes, ge'mmen,' he eagerly answered, as if
his memory, before suddenly frozen up by cold charity,
as suddenly thawed back into fluidity at the first kindly
word. ' Oh yes, oh yes, dar is aboard here* a werry
nice, good ge'mman wid a weed, and a ge'mman in a
gray coat and white tie, what knows all about me; and
a ge'mman wid a big book, too; and a yarb-doctor;
and a ge'mman in a yaller west; and a ge'mman wid a
brass plate; and a ge'mman in a wiolet robe; and a
ge'mman as is a sodjer; and ever so many good, kind,
honest ge'mmen more aboard what knows me and will
speak for me, God bress 'em; yes, and what knows
me as well as dis poor old darkie knows hisself, God

bress him ! Oh, find 'em, find 'em,' he earnestly added,
' and let 'em come quick, and show you all, ge'mmen,
dat dis poor ole darkie is werry well wordy of all you
kind ge'mmen's kind confidence.'

' But how are we to find all these people in this great
crowd ? ' was the question of a bystander, umbrella in
hand ; a middle-aged person, a country merchant
apparently, whose natural good-feeling had been made
at least cautious by the unnatural ill-feeling of the discharged custom-house officer.

' Where are we to find them ? ' half rebukefully echoed
the young Episcopal clergyman. ' I will go find one
to begin with,' he quickly added, and, with kind haste
suiting the action to the word, away he went.

' Wild goose chase ! ' croaked he with the wooden leg,
now again drawing nigh. ' Don't believe there 's a soul
of them aboard. Did ever beggar have such heaps of
fine friends ? He can walk fast enough when he tries, a
good deal faster than I ; but he can lie yet faster. He 's
some white operator, betwisted and painted up for a
decoy. He and his friends are all humbugs.'

' Have you no charity, friend ? ' here in self-subdued
tones, singularly contrasted with his unsubdued person,
said a Methodist minister, advancing ; a tall, muscular,
martial-looking man, a Tennesseean by birth, who in the
Mexican war had been volunteer chaplain to a volunteer
rifle-regiment.

' Charity is one thing, and truth is another,' rejoined
he with the wooden leg : ' he 's a rascal, I say.'

' But why not, friend, put as charitable a construction as one can upon the poor fellow ? ' said the
soldier-like Methodist, with increased difficulty main-
taining a pacific demeanour toward one whose own
asperity seemed so little to entitle him to it : ' he looks
honest, don't he ? '

' Looks are one thing, and facts are another,' snapped out the other perversely ; ' and as to your constructions, what construction can you put upon a rascal, but that a rascal he is ? '

' Be not such a Canada thistle,' urged the Methodist, with something less of patience than before. ' Charity, man, charity.'

' To where it belongs with your charity ! to heaven with it ! ' again snapped out the other, diabolically ; ' here on earth, true charity dotes, and false charity plots. Who betrays a fool with a kiss, the charitable fool has the charity to believe is in love with him, and the charitable knave on the stand gives charitable testimony for his comrade in the box.'

' Surely, friend,' returned the noble Methodist, with much ado restraining his still waxing indignation— ' surely, to say the least, you forget yourself. Apply it home,' he continued, with exterior calmness tremulous with inkept emotion. ' Suppose, now, I should exercise no charity in judging your own character by the words which have fallen from you ; what sort of vile, pitiless man do you think I would take you for ? '

' No doubt '—with a grin—' some such pitiless man as has lost his piety in much the same way that the jockey loses his honesty.'

' And how is that, friend ? ' still conscientiously holding back the old Adam in him, as if it were a mastiff he had by the neck.

' Never you mind how it is '—with a sneer ; ' but all horses ain't virtuous, no more than all men kind ; and come close to, and much dealt with, some things are catching. When you find me a' virtuous jockey, I will find you a benevolent wise man.'

' Some insinuation there.'

' More fool you that are puzzled by it.'

'Reprobate!' cried the other, his indignation now at last almost boiling over; 'godless reprobate! if charity did not restrain me, I could call you by names you deserve.'

'Could you, indeed?' with an insolent sneer.

'Yea, and teach you charity on the spot,' cried the goaded Methodist, suddenly catching this exasperating opponent by his shabby coat-collar, and shaking him till his timber-toe* clattered on the deck like a ninepin. 'You took me for a non-combatant, did you?—thought, seedy coward that you are, that you could abuse a Christian with impunity. You find your mistake'— with another hearty shake.

'Well said and better done, church militant!' cried a voice.

'The white cravat against the world!' cried another.

'Bravo, bravo!' chorused many voices, with like enthusiasm taking sides with the resolute champion.

'You fools!' cried he with the wooden leg, writhing himself loose and inflamedly turning upon the throng; 'you flock of fools, under this captain of fools, in this ship of fools!'*

With which exclamations, followed by idle threats against his admonisher, this condign victim to justice hobbled away, as disdaining to hold further argument with such a rabble. But his scorn was more than repaid by the hisses that chased him, in which the brave Methodist, satisfied with the rebuke already administered, was, to omit still better reasons, too magnanimous to join. All he said was, pointing toward the departing recusant, 'There he shambles off on his one lone leg, emblematic of his one-sided view of humanity.'

'But trust your painted decoy,' retorted the other from a distance, pointing back to the black cripple, 'and I have my revenge.'

'But we ain't a-going to trust him!' shouted back a voice.

'So much the better,' he jeered back. 'Look you,' he added, coming to a dead halt where he was; 'look you, I have been called a Canada thistle. Very good. And a seedy one: still better. And the seedy Canada thistle has been pretty well shaken among ye: best of all. Dare say some seed has been shaken out; and won't it spring, though? And when it does spring, do you cut down the young thistles, and won't they spring the more? It's encouraging and coaxing 'em. Now, when with my thistles your farms shall be well stocked, why then—you may abandon 'em!'

'What does all that mean, now?' asked the country merchant, staring.

'Nothing; the foiled wolf's parting howl,' said the Methodist. 'Spleen, much spleen, which is the rickety child of his evil heart of unbelief: it has made him mad. I suspect him for one naturally reprobate. Oh, friends,' raising his arms as in the pulpit, 'oh beloved, how are we admonished by the melancholy spectacle of this raver. Let us profit by the lesson; and is it not this: that if, next to mistrusting Providence, there be aught that man should pray against, it is against mistrusting his fellow-man. I have been in mad-houses full of tragic mopers, and seen there the end of suspicion: the cynic, in the moody madness muttering in the corner; for years a barren fixture there; head lopped over, gnawing his own lip, vulture of himself; while, by fits and starts, from the corner opposite came the grimace of the idiot at him.'

'What an example,' whispered one.

'Might deter Timon,'*was the response.

'Oh, oh, good ge'mmen, have you no confidence in dis poor ole darkie?' now wailed the returning negro, who, during the late scene, had stumped apart in alarm.

'Confidence in you?' echoed he who had whispered, with abruptly changed air turning short round; 'that remains to be seen.'

'I tell you what it is, Ebony,' in similarly changed tones said he who had responded to the whisperer, 'yonder churl,' pointing toward the wooden leg in the distance, 'is, no doubt, a churlish fellow enough, and I would not wish to be like him; but that is no reason why you may not be some sort of black Jeremy Diddler.*'

'No confidence in dis poor old darkie, den?'

'Before giving you our confidence,' said a third, 'we will wait the report of the kind gentleman who went in search of one of your friends who was to speak for you.'

'Very likely, in that case,' said a fourth, 'we shall wait here till Christmas. Shouldn't wonder, did we not see that kind gentleman again. After seeking awhile in vain, he will conclude he has been made a fool of, and so not return to us for pure shame. Fact is, I begin to feel a little qualmish about the darkie myself. Something queer about this darkie, depend upon it.'

Once more the negro wailed, and turning in despair from the last speaker, imploringly caught the Methodist by the skirt of his coat. But a change had come over that before impassioned intercessor. With an irresolute and troubled air, he mutely eyed the suppliant; against whom, somehow, by what seemed instinctive influences, the distrusts first set on foot were now generally reviving, and, if anything, with added severity.

'No confidence in dis poor ole darkie,' yet again wailed the negro, letting go the coat-skirts and turning appealingly all round him.

'Yes, my poor fellow, *I* have confidence in you,' now exclaimed the country merchant before named, whom the negro's appeal, coming so piteously on the heel of pitilessness, seemed at last humanely to have decided in his favour. 'And here, here is some proof of my trust,' with which, tucking his umbrella under his arm, and diving down his hand into his pocket, he fished forth a purse, and, accidentally, along with it, his business card, which, unobserved, dropped to the deck. 'Here, here, my poor fellow,' he continued, extending a half-dollar.

Not more grateful for the coin than the kindness, the cripple's face glowed like a polished copper saucepan, and shuffling a pace nigher, with one upstretched hand he received the alms, while, as unconsciously, his one advanced leather stump covered the card.

Done in despite of the general sentiment, the good deed of the merchant was not, perhaps, without its unwelcome return from the crowd, since that good deed seemed somehow to convey to them a sort of reproach. Still again, and more pertinaciously than ever, the cry arose against the negro, and still again he wailed forth his lament and appeal; among other things, repeating that the friends, of whom already he had partially run off the list, would freely speak for him, would anybody go find them.

'Why don't you go find 'em yourself?' demanded a gruff boatman.

'How can I go find 'em myself? Dis poor ole game-legged darkie's friends must come to him. Oh, whar, whar is dat good friend of dis darkie's, dat good man wid de weed?'

At this point, a steward ringing a bell came along, summoning all persons who had not got their tickets to step to the captain's office; an announcement which speedily thinned the throng about the black cripple, who himself soon forlornly stumped out of sight, probably on much the same errand as the rest.

CHAPTER IV

RENEWAL OF OLD ACQUAINTANCE

'How do you do, Mr. Roberts?'

'Eh?'

'Don't you know me?'

'No, certainly.'

The crowd about the captain's office, having in good time melted away, the above encounter took place in one of the side balconies astern, between a man in mourning clean and respectable, but none of the glossiest, a long weed* on his hat, and the country merchant before mentioned, whom, with the familiarity of an old acquaintance, the former had accosted.

'Is it possible, my dear sir,' resumed he with the weed, 'that you do not recall my countenance? Why, yours I recall distinctly as if but half an hour, instead of half an age, had passed since I saw you. Don't you recall me, now? Look harder.'

'In my conscience—truly—I protest,' honestly bewildered, 'bless my soul, sir, I don't know you—really, really. But stay, stay,' he hurriedly added, not without gratification, glancing up at the crape on the stranger's hat, 'stay—yes—seems to me, though I have not the pleasure of personally knowing you, yet I am pretty sure I have at least *heard* of you, and recently too, quite recently. A poor negro aboard here referred to you, among others, for a character, I think.'

'Oh, the cripple. Poor fellow, I know him well. They found me. I have said all I could for him. I think I abated their distrust. Would I could have been of more substantial service. And à propos, sir,' he added, ' now that it strikes me, allow me to ask, whether the circumstance of one man, however humble, referring for a character to another man, however afflicted, does not argue more or less of moral worth in the latter ? '

The good merchant looked puzzled.

' Still you don't recall my countenance ? '

' Still does truth compel me to say that I cannot, despite my best efforts,' was the reluctantly candid reply.

' Can I be so changed ? Look at me. Or is it I who am mistaken ?—Are you not, sir, Henry Roberts, for-warding merchant, of Wheeling, Pennsylvania ? Pray, now, if you use the advertisement of business cards, and happen to have one with you, just look at it, and see whether you are not the man I take you for.'

' Why,' a bit chafed, perhaps, ' I hope I know myself.'

' And yet self-knowledge is thought by some not so easy. Who knows, my dear sir, but for a time you may have taken yourself for somebody else ? Stranger things have happened.'

The good merchant stared.

' To come to particulars, my dear sir, I met you, now some six years back, at Brade Brothers & Co.'s office, I think. I was travelling for a Philadelphia house. The senior Brade introduced us, you remember ; some business chat followed, then you forced me home with you to a family tea, and a family time we had. Have you forgotten about the urn, and what I said about Werter's Charlotte,* and the bread and butter, and that capital story you told of the large loaf. A hundred times since, I have laughed over it. At least you must recall my name—Ringman, John Ringman.'

' Large loaf ? Invited you to tea ? Ringman ? Ringman ? Ring ? Ring ? '

'Ah, sir,' sadly smiling, 'don't ring the changes that way. I see you have a faithless memory, Mr. Roberts. But trust in the faithfulness of mine.'

'Well, to tell the truth, in some things my memory ain't of the very best,' was the honest rejoinder. 'But still,' he perplexedly added, 'still I——'

'Oh, sir, suffice it that it is as I say. Doubt not that we are all well acquainted.'

'But—but I don't like this going dead against my own memory; I——'

'But didn't you admit, my dear sir, that in some things this memory of yours is a little faithless? Now, those who have faithless memories, should they not have some little confidence in the less faithless memories of others?'

'But, of this friendly chat and tea, I have not the slightest——'

'I see, I see; quite erased from the tablet. Pray, sir,' with a sudden illumination, 'about six years back, did it happen to you to receive any injury on the head? Surprising effects have arisen from such a cause. Not alone unconsciousness as to events for a greater or less time immediately subsequent to the injury, but likewise—strange to add—oblivion, entire and incurable, as to events embracing a longer or shorter period immediately preceding it; that is, when the mind at the time was perfectly sensible of them, and fully competent also to register them in the memory, and did in fact so do; but all in vain, for all was afterwards bruised out by the injury.'

After the first start, the merchant listened with what appeared more than ordinary interest. The other proceeded :—

'In my boyhood I was kicked by a horse, and lay insensible for a long time. Upon recovering, what a blank ! No faintest trace in regard to how I had come near the horse, or what horse it was, or where it was, or that it was a horse at all that had brought me to that pass. For the knowledge of those particulars I am indebted solely to my friends, in whose statements, I need not say, I place implicit reliance, since particulars of some sort there must have been, and why should they deceive me ? You see, sir, the mind is ductile, very much so : but images, ductilely received into it, need a certain time to harden and bake in their impressions, otherwise such a casualty as I speak of will in an instant obliterate them, as though they had never been. We are but clay,* sir, potter's clay, as the good book says, clay, feeble, and too-yielding clay. But I will not philosophise. Tell me, was it your misfortune to receive any concussion upon the brain about the period I speak of ? If so, I will with pleasure supply the void in your memory by more minutely rehearsing the circumstances of our acquaintance.'

The growing interest betrayed by the merchant had not relaxed as the other proceeded. After some hesitation, indeed, something more than hesitation, he confessed that, though he had never received any injury of the sort named, yet, about the time in question, he had in fact been taken with a brain fever, losing his mind completely for a considerable interval. He was continuing, when the stranger with much animation exclaimed :—

'There now, you see, I was not wholly mistaken. That brain fever accounts for it all.'

'Nay ; but——'

'Pardon me, Mr. Roberts,' respectfully interrupting him, ' but time is short, and I have something private and particular to say to you. Allow me.'

Mr. Roberts, good man, could but acquiesce, and the

two having silently walked to a less public spot, the
manner of the man with the weed suddenly assumed a
seriousness almost painful. What might be called a
writhing expression stole over him. He seemed struggling
with some disastrous necessity inkept. He made one or
two attempts to speak, but words seemed to choke
him. His companion stood in humane surprise,
wondering what was to come. At length, with an
effort mastering his feelings, in a tolerably composed
tone he spoke :—

'If I remember, you are a mason,* Mr. Roberts ? '

'Yes, yes.'

Averting himself a moment, as to recover from a
return of agitation, the stranger grasped the other's
hand ; 'and would you not loan a brother a shilling if
he needed it ? '

The merchant started, apparently, almost as if to
retreat.

'Ah, Mr. Roberts, I trust you are not one of those
business men, who make a business of never having to
do with unfortunates. For God's sake don't leave me.
I have something on my heart—on my heart. Under
deplorable circumstances thrown among strangers, utter
strangers. I want a friend in whom I may confide.
Yours, Mr. Roberts, is almost the first known face I 've
seen for many weeks.'

It was so sudden an outburst ; the interview offered
such a contrast to the scene around, that the merchant,
though not used to be very indiscreet, yet, being not
entirely inhumane, remained not entirely unmoved.

The other, still tremulous, resumed :—

'I need not say, sir, how it cuts me to the soul, to
follow up a social salutation with such words as have
just been mine. I know that I jeopardise your good
opinion. But I can't help it : necessity knows no law,

and heeds no risk. Sir, we are masons, one more step aside; I will tell you my story.'

In a low, half-suppressed tone, he began it. Judging from his auditor's expression, it seemed to be a tale of singular interest, involving calamities against which no integrity, no forethought, no energy, no genius, no piety, could guard.

At every disclosure, the hearer's commiseration increased. No sentimental pity. As the story went on, he drew from his wallet a bank-note, but after a while, at some still more unhappy revelation, changed it for another, probably of a somewhat larger amount; which, when the story was concluded, with an air studiously disclamatory of alms-giving, he put into the stranger's hands; who, on his side, with an air studiously disclamatory of alms-taking, put it into his pocket.

Assistance being received, the stranger's manner assumed a kind and degree of decorum which, under the circumstances, seemed almost coldness. After some words, not over ardent, and yet not exactly inappropriate, he took leave, making a bow which had one knows not what of a certain chastened independence about it; as if misery, however burdensome, could not break down self-respect, nor gratitude, however deep, humiliate a gentleman.

He was hardly yet out of sight, when he paused as if thinking; then with hastened steps returning to the merchant, 'I am just reminded that the president, who is also transfer-agent, of the Black Rapids Coal Company, happens to be on board here, and, having been subpœnaed as witness in a stock case on the docket in Kentucky, has his transfer-book with him. A month since, in a panic contrived by artful alarmists, some credulous stock-holders sold out; but, to frustrate the aim of the alarmists, the Company, previously advised of their scheme, so managed it as to get into its own hands those sacrificed shares, resolved that, since a spurious panic must be, the panic-makers should be no gainers by it. The Company, I hear, is now ready, but not anxious, to redispose of those shares; and having obtained them at their depressed value, will now sell them at par, though, prior to the panic, they were held at a handsome figure above. That the readiness of the Company to do this is not generally known, is shown by the fact that the stock still stands on the transfer-book in the Company's name, offering to one in funds a rare chance for investment. For, the panic subsiding more and more every day, it will daily be seen how it originated; confidence will be more than restored; there will be a reaction; from the stock's descent its rise will be higher than from no fall, the holders trusting themselves to fear no second fate."

Having listened at first with curiosity, at last with interest, the merchant replied to the effect, that some time since, through friends concerned with it, he had heard of the company, and heard well of it, but was ignorant that there had latterly been fluctuations. He added that he was no speculator; that hitherto he had avoided having to do with stocks of any sort, but in the present case he really felt something like being tempted. 'Pray,' in conclusion, 'do you think that upon a pinch anything could be transacted on board here with the transfer-agent? Are you acquainted with him?'

'Not personally. I but happened to hear that he was a passenger. For the rest, though it might be somewhat informal, the gentleman might not object to doing a little business on board. Along the Mississippi, you know, business is not so ceremonious as at the East.'

'True,' returned the merchant, and looked down a

moment in thought, then, raising his head quickly, said, in a tone not so benign as his wonted one, ' This would seem a rare chance, indeed ; why, upon first hearing it, did you not snatch at it ?   I mean for yourself ! '

' I ?—would it had been possible ! '

Not without some emotion was this said, and not without some embarrassment was the reply. ' Ah, yes, I had forgotten.'

Upon this, the stranger regarded him with mild gravity, not a little disconcerting ; the more so, as there was in it what seemed the aspect not alone of the superior, but, as it were, the rebuker ; which sort of bearing, in a beneficiary toward his benefactor, looked strangely enough ; none the less, that, somehow, it sat not altogether unbecomingly upon the beneficiary, being free from anything like the appearance of assumption, and mixed with a kind of painful conscientiousness, as though nothing but a proper sense of what he owed to himself swayed him. At length he spoke :—

' To reproach a penniless man with remissness in not availing himself of an opportunity for pecuniary investment—but, no, no ; it was forgetfulness ; and this, charity will impute to some lingering effect of that unfortunate brain fever, which, as to occurrences dating yet further back, disturbed Mr. Roberts's memory still more seriously.'

' As to that,' said the merchant, rallying, ' I am not——'

' Pardon me, but you must admit, that just now, an unpleasant distrust, however vague, was yours. Ah, shallow as it is, yet, how subtle a thing is suspicion, which at times can invade the humanest of hearts and wisest of heads. But, enough. My object, sir, in calling your attention to this stock, is by way of acknowledgment of your goodness. I but seek to be grateful ; if my information leads to nothing, you must remember the motive.'

He bowed, and finally retired, leaving Mr. Roberts not wholly without self-reproach, for having momentarily indulged injurious thoughts against one who, it was evident, was possessed of a self-respect which forbade his indulging them himself.

CHAPTER V

THE MAN WITH THE WEED MAKES IT AN EVEN QUESTION
WHETHER HE BE A GREAT SAGE OR A GREAT SIMPLETON

WELL, there is sorrow in the world, but goodness
too ; and goodness that is not greenness, either, no
more than sorrow is. Dear good man. Poor beating
heart ! '

It was the man with the weed, not very long after
quitting the merchant, murmuring to himself with his
hand to his side like one with the heart-disease.

Meditation over kindness received seemed to have
softened him something, too, it may be, beyond what
might, perhaps, have been looked for from one whose
unwonted self-respect in the hour of need, and in the
act of being aided, might have appeared to some not
wholly unlike pride out of place ; and pride, in any
place, is seldom very feeling. But the truth, perhaps,
is, that those who are at least touched with that vice,
besides being not unsusceptible to goodness, are sometimes the ones whom a ruling sense of propriety makes
appear cold, if not thankless, under a favour. For, at
such a time, to be full of warm, earnest words, and
heart-felt protestations, is to create a scene ; and well-
bred people dislike few things more than that ; which
would seem to look as if the world did not relish earnestness ; but, not so ; because the world, being earnest
itself, likes an earnest scene, and an earnest man, very
well, but only in their place—the stage. See what sad

work they make of it, who, ignorant of this, flame out
in Irish enthusiasm and with Irish sincerity, to a benefactor, who, if a man of sense and respectability, as
well as kindliness, can but be more or less annoyed by
it ; and, if of a nervously fastidious nature, as some are,
may be led to think almost as much less favourably of
the beneficiary paining him by his gratitude, as if he had
been guilty of its contrary, instead only of an indiscretion.
But, beneficiaries who know better, though they may
feel as much, if not more, neither inflict such pain,
nor are inclined to run any risk of so doing. And these,
being wise, are the majority. By which one sees how
inconsiderate those persons are, who, from the absence
of its officious manifestations in the world, complain
that there is not much gratitude extant ; when the
truth is, that there is as much of it as there is of modesty ;
but, both being for the most part votarists of the shade,
for the most part keep out of sight.

What started this was, to account, if necessary, for
the changed air of the man with the weed, who, throwing
off in private the cold garb of decorum, and so giving
warmly loose to his genuine heart, seemed almost transformed into another being. This subdued air of softness,
too, was toned with melancholy, melancholy unreserved ;
a thing which, however at variance with propriety, still
the more attested his earnestness ; for one knows not
how it is, but it sometimes happens that, where earnestness is, there, also, is melancholy.

At the time, he was leaning over the rail at the boat's
side, in his pensiveness, unmindful of another pensive
figure near—a young gentleman with a swan-neck,
wearing a lady-like open shirt collar, thrown back, and
tied with a black ribbon. From a square, tableted
brooch, curiously engraved with Greek characters, he
seemed a collegian—not improbably, a sophomore*—on

his travels ; possibly, his first. A small book bound in
Roman vellum was in his hand.

Overhearing his murmuring neighbour, the youth
regarded him with some surprise, not to say interest.
But, singularly for a collegian, being apparently of a
retiring nature, he did not speak ; when the other still
more increased his diffidence by changing from soliloquy
to colloquy, in a manner strangely mixed of familiarity
and pathos.

' Ah, who is this ? You did not hear me, my young
friend, did you ? Why, you, too, look sad. My melancholy is not catching ! '

' Sir, sir,' stammered the other.

' Pray, now,' with a sort of sociable sorrowfulness,
slowly sliding along the rail,—' pray, now, my young
friend, what volume have you there ? Give me leave,'
gently drawing it from him. ' Tacitus ! '* Then opening it at random, read : ' In general a black and shameful
period lies before me.' ' Dear young sir,' touching his
arm alarmedly, ' don't read this book. It is poison,
moral poison. Even were there truth in Tacitus, such
truth would have the operation of falsity, and so still
be poison, moral poison. Too well I know this Tacitus.
In my college days he came near souring me into
cynicism. Yes, I began to turn down my collar, and go
about with a disdainfully joyless expression.'

' Sir, sir, I—I——'

' Trust me. Now, young friend, perhaps you think
that Tacitus, like me, is only melancholy ; but he 's
more—he 's ugly. A vast difference, young sir, between
the melancholy view and the ugly. The one may show
the world still beautiful, not so the other. The one
may be compatible with benevolence, the other not.
The one may deepen insight, the other shallows it. Drop
Tacitus. Phrenologically, my young friend, you would

seem to have a well-developed head, and large ; but cribbed within the ugly view, the Tacitus view, your large brain, like your large ox in the contracted field, will but starve the more. And don't dream, as some of you students may, that, by taking this same ugly view, the deeper meanings of the deeper books will so alone become revealed to you. Drop Tacitus. His subtlety is falsity. To him, in his double-refined anatomy of human nature, is well applied the Scripture saying— " There is a subtle man,* and the same is deceived." Drop Tacitus. Come, now, let me throw the book over- board.'

' Sir, I—I——'

' Not a word ; I know just what is in your mind, and that is just what I am speaking to. Yes, learn from me that, though the sorrows of the world are great, its wickedness—that is, its ugliness—is small. Much cause to pity man, little to distrust him. I myself have known adversity, and know it still. But for that, do I turn cynic ? No, no : it is small beer that sours. To my fellow-creatures I owe alleviations. So, whatever I may have undergone, it but deepens my confidence in my kind. Now, then ' (winningly), ' this book—will you let me drown it for you ? '

' Really, sir—I——'

' I see, I see. But of course you read Tacitus in order to aid you in understanding human nature—as if truth was ever got at by libel. My young friend, if to know human nature is your object, drop Tacitus and go north to the cemeteries of Auburn and Greenwood.'*

' Upon my word, I—I——'

' Nay, I foresee all that. But you carry Tacitus, that shallow Tacitus. What do *I* carry ? See '—producing a pocket-volume—' Akenside*—his *Pleasures of Imagina- tion*. One of these days you will know it. Whatever

our lot, we should read serene and cheery books, fitted
to inspire love and trust. But Tacitus! I have long
been of opinion that these classics are the bane of
colleges; for—not to hint of the immorality of Ovid,
Horace, Anacreon,* and the rest, and the dangerous
theology of Æschylus* and others—where will one find
views so injurious to human nature as in Thucydides,
Juvenal, Lucian, but more particularly Tacitus ?* When
I consider that, ever since the revival of learning, these
classics have been the favourites of successive generations of students and studious men, I tremble to think
of that mass of unsuspected heresy on every vital topic
which for centuries must have simmered unsurmised in
the heart of Christendom. But Tacitus—he is the most
extraordinary example of a heretic; not one iota of
confidence in his kind. What a mockery that such an
one should be reputed wise, and Thucydides be esteemed
the statesman's manual! But Tacitus—I hate Tacitus;
not, though, I trust, with the hate that sins, but a
righteous hate. Without confidence himself, Tacitus
destroys it in all his readers. Destroys confidence,
paternal confidence, of which God knows that there is
in this world none to spare. For, comparatively inexperienced as you are, my dear friend, did you never
observe how little, very little, confidence, there is ? I
mean between man and man—more particularly between
stranger and stranger. In a sad world it is the saddest
fact. Confidence! I have sometimes almost thought
that confidence is fled; that confidence is the New
Astrea*—emigrated—vanished—gone.' Then softly sliding nearer, with the softest air, quivering down and
looking up, ' Could you now, my dear young sir, under
such circumstances, by way of experiment, simply have
confidence in *me* ? '

From the outset, the sophomore, as has been seen,

had struggled with an ever-increasing embarrassment, arising, perhaps, from such strange remarks coming from a stranger—such persistent and prolonged remarks, too. In vain had he more than once sought to break the spell by venturing a deprecatory or leave-taking word. In vain. Somehow, the stranger fascinated him. Little wonder, then, that, when the appeal came, he could hardly speak, but, as before intimated, being apparently of a retiring nature, abruptly retired from the spot, leaving the chagrined stranger to wander away in the opposite direction.

CHAPTER VI

—'You—pish! Why will the captain suffer these begging fellows on board?'

These pettish words were breathed by a well-to-do gentleman in a ruby-coloured velvet vest, and with a ruby-coloured cheek, a ruby-headed cane in his hand, to a man in a gray coat and white tie, who, shortly after the interview last described, had accosted him for contributions to a Widow and Orphan Asylum recently founded among the Seminoles.* Upon a cursory view, this last person might have seemed, like the man with the weed, one of the less unrefined children of misfortune; but, on a closer observation, his countenance revealed little of sorrow, though much of sanctity.

With added words of touchy disgust, the well-to-do gentleman hurried away. But, though repulsed, and rudely, the man in gray did not reproach, for a time patiently remaining in the chilly loneliness to which he had been left, his countenance, however, not without token of latent though chastened reliance.

At length an old gentleman, somewhat bulky, drew nigh, and from him also a contribution was sought.

'Look, you,' coming to a dead halt, and scowling upon him. 'Look, you,' swelling his bulk out before him like a swaying balloon, 'look, you, you on others' behalf ask for money; you, a fellow with a face as long as my arm. Hark ye, now : there is such a thing as gravity, and in condemned felons it may be genuine ; but of long faces there are three sorts : that of grief's drudge, that of the lantern-jawed man, and that of the impostor. You know best which yours is.'

'Heaven give you more charity, sir.'

'And you less hypocrisy, sir.'

With which words, the hard-hearted old gentleman marched off.

While the other still stood forlorn, the young clergyman, before introduced, passing that way, catching a chance sight of him, seemed suddenly struck by some recollection ; and, after a moment's pause, hurried up with : 'Your pardon, but shortly since I was all over looking for you.'

'For me ? ' as marvelling that one of so little account should be sought for.

'Yes, for you ; do you know anything about the negro, apparently a cripple, aboard here ? Is he, or is he not, what he seems to be ? '

'Ah, poor Guinea ! have you, too, been distrusted ? you, upon whom nature has placarded the evidence of your claims ? '

'Then you do really know him, and he is quite worthy ? It relieves me to hear it—much relieves me. Come, let us go find him, and see what can be done.'

'Another instance that confidence may come too late. I am sorry to say that at the last landing I myself—just happening to catch sight of him on the gangway-plank— assisted the cripple ashore. No time to talk, only to help. He may not have told you, but he has a brother in that vicinity.'

'Really, I regret his going without my seeing him again ; regret it, more, perhaps, than you can readily think. You see, shortly after leaving St. Louis, he was on the forecastle, and there, with many others, I saw him, and put trust in him ; so much so, that, to convince those who did not, I, at his entreaty, went in search of you, you being one of several individuals he mentioned, and whose personal appearance he more or less described, individuals who he said would willingly speak for him. But, after diligent search, not finding you, and catching no glimpse of any of the others he had enumerated, doubts were at last suggested ; but doubts indirectly originating, as I can but think, from prior distrust unfeelingly proclaimed by another. Still, certain it is, I began to suspect.'

' Ha, ha, ha ! '

A sort of laugh more like a groan than a laugh ; and yet, somehow, it seemed intended for a laugh.

Both turned, and the young clergyman started at seeing the wooden-legged man close behind him, morosely grave as a criminal judge with a mustard-plaster on his back. In the present case the mustard-plaster might have been the memory of certain recent biting rebuffs and mortifications.

' Wouldn't think it was I who laughed, would you ? '

' But who was it you laughed at ? or rather, tried to laugh at ? ' demanded the young clergyman, flushing— ' me ? '

' Neither you nor anyone within a thousand miles of you. But perhaps you don't believe it.'

' If he were of a suspicious temper, he might not,' interposed the man in gray calmly ; ' it is one of the imbecilities of the suspicious person to fancy that every stranger, however absent-minded, he sees so much as smiling or gesturing to himself in any odd sort of way, is secretly making him his butt. In some moods, the movements of an entire street, as the suspicious man walks down it, will seem an express pantomimic jeer

at him. In short, the suspicious man kicks himself
with his own foot.'

'Whoever can do that, ten to one he saves other folks'
sole-leather,' said the wooden-legged man with a crusty
attempt at humour. But with augmented grin and
squirm, turning directly upon the young clergyman, ' You
still think it was *you* I was laughing at, just now. To
prove your mistake, I will tell you what I *was* laughing
at ; a story I happened to call to mind just then.'

Whereupon, in his porcupine way, and with sarcastic
details, unpleasant to repeat, he related a story, which
might, perhaps, in a good-natured version, be rendered
as follows :—

A certain Frenchman of New Orleans, an old man,
less slender in purse than limb, happening to attend the
theatre one evening, was so charmed with the character
of a faithful wife, as there represented to the life, that
nothing would do but he must marry upon it. So,
marry he did, a beautiful girl from Tennessee, who had
first attracted his attention by her liberal mould, and
was subsequently recommended to him through her kin,
for her equally liberal education and disposition. Though
large, the praise proved not too much. For, ere long,
rumour more than corroborated it, by whispering that
the lady was liberal to a fault. But though various
circumstances, which by most Benedicts* would have
been deemed all but conclusive, were duly recited to the
old Frenchman by his friends, yet such was his confidence
that not a syllable would he credit, till, chancing one
night to return unexpectedly from a journey, upon
entering his apartment, a stranger burst from the alcove :
' Begar ! ' cried he, ' now I *begin* to suspec'.'

His story told, the wooden-legged man threw back
his head, and gave vent to a long, gasping, rasping sort
of taunting cry, intolerable as that of a high-pressure

engine jeering off steam ; and that done, with apparent
satisfaction hobbled away.

'Who is that scoffer ? ' said the man in gray, not
without warmth. 'Who is he, who even were truth on
his tongue, his way of speaking it would make truth
almost offensive as falsehood. Who is he ? '

'He who I mentioned to you as having boasted his
suspicion of the negro,' replied the young clergyman,
recovering from disturbance ; 'in short, the person to
whom I ascribe the origin of my own distrust ; he maintained that Guinea was some white scoundrel, betwisted
and painted up for a decoy. Yes, these were his very
words, I think.'

'Impossible ! he could not be so wrong-headed. Pray,
will you call him back, and let me ask him if he were
really in earnest ? '

The other complied ; and, at length, after no few
surly objections, prevailed upon the one-legged individual
to return for a moment. Upon which, the man in gray
thus addressed him : 'This reverend gentleman tells me,
sir, that a certain cripple, a poor negro, is by you considered an ingenious impostor. Now, I am not unaware
that there are some persons in this world, who, unable
to give better proof of being wise, take a strange delight
in showing what they think they have sagaciously read
in mankind by uncharitable suspicions of them. I hope
you are not one of these. In short, would you tell me
now, whether you were not merely joking in the notion
you threw out about the negro. Would you be so
kind ? '

'No, I won't be so kind, I 'll be so cruel.'

'As you please about that.'

'Well, he 's just what I said he was.'

'A white masquerading as a black ? '

'Exactly.'

The man in gray glanced at the young clergyman a moment, then quietly whispered to him, ' I thought you represented your friend here as a very distrustful sort of person, but he appears endued with a singular credulity. —Tell me, sir, do you really think that a white could look the negro so ? For one, I should call it pretty good acting.'

' Not much better than any other man acts.'

' How ? Does all the world act ? Am *I*, for instance, an actor ? Is my reverend friend here, too, a performer ? '

' Yes, don't you both perform acts ? To do, is to act ; so all doers are actors.'

' You trifle.—I ask again, if a white, how could he look the negro so ? '

' Never saw the negro minstrels, I suppose ? '

' Yes, but they are apt to overdo the ebony ; exemplifying the old saying, not more just than charitable, that " the devil is never so black as he is painted." But his limbs, if not a cripple, how could he twist his limbs so ? '

' How do other hypocritical beggars twist theirs ? Easy enough to see how they are hoisted up.'

' The sham is evident, then ? '

' To the discerning eye,' with a horrible screw of his gimlet one.

' Well, where is Guinea ? ' said the man in gray ; ' where is he ? Let us at once find him, and refute beyond cavil this injurious hypothesis.'

' Do so,' cried the one-eyed man, ' I 'm just in the humour now for having him found, and leaving the streaks of these fingers on his paint, as the lion leaves the streaks of his nails on a Caffre.* They wouldn't let me touch him before. Yes, find him, I 'll make wool fly, and him after.'

' You forget,' here said the young clergyman to the man in gray, ' that yourself helped poor Guinea ashore.'

'So I did, so I did; how unfortunate. But look now,' to the other, ' I think that without personal proof I can convince you of your mistake. For I put it to you, is it reasonable to suppose that a man with brains, sufficient to act such a part as you say, would take all that trouble, and run all that hazard, for the mere sake of those few paltry coppers, which, I hear, was all he got for his pains, if pains they were ? '

'That puts the case irrefutably,' said the young clergyman, with a challenging glance toward the one-legged man.

'You two green-horns ! Money, you think, is the sole motive to pains and hazard, deception and deviltry, in this world. How much money did the devil make by gulling Eve ? '

Whereupon he hobbled off again with a repetition of his intolerable jeer.

The man in gray stood silently eyeing his retreat a while, and then, turning to his companion, said : ' A bad man, a dangerous man ; a man to be put down in any Christian community.—And this was he who was the means of begetting your distrust ? Ah, we should shut our ears to distrust, and keep them open only for its opposite.'

'You advance a principle, which, if I had acted upon it this morning, I should have spared myself what I now feel.—That but one man, and he with one leg, should have such ill power given him ; his one sour word leavening into congenial sourness (as, to my know-ledge, it did) the dispositions, before sweet enough, of a numerous company. But, as I hinted, with me at the time his ill words went for nothing ; the same as now ; only afterwards they had effect ; and I confess, this puzzles me.'

'It should not. With humane minds, the spirit of

distrust works something as certain potions do ; it is a spirit which may enter such minds, and yet, for a time, longer or shorter, lie in them quiescent ; but only the more deplorable its ultimate activity.'

' An uncomfortable solution ; for, since that baneful man did but just now anew drop on me his bane, how shall I be sure that my present exemption from its effects will be lasting ? '

' You cannot be sure, but you can strive against it.'

' How ? '

' By strangling the least symptom of distrust, of any sort, which hereafter, upon whatever provocation, may arise in you.'

' I will do so.' Then added as in soliloquy, ' Indeed, indeed, I was to blame in standing passive under such influences as that one-legged man's. My conscience upbraids me.—The poor negro : you see him occasionally, perhaps ? '

' No, not often ; though in a few days, as it happens, my engagements will call me to the neighbourhood of his present retreat ; and, no doubt, honest Guinea, who is a grateful soul, will come to see me there.'

' Then you have been his benefactor ? '

' His benefactor ? I did not say that. I have known him.'

' Take this mite. Hand it to Guinea when you see him ; say it comes from one who has full belief in his honesty, and is sincerely sorry for having indulged, however transiently, in a contrary thought.'

' I accept the trust. And, by the way, since you are of this truly charitable nature, you will not turn away an appeal in behalf of the Seminole Widow and Orphan Asylum ? '

' I have not heard of that charity.'

' But recently founded.'

After a pause, the clergyman was irresolutely putting his hand in his pocket, when, caught by something in his companion's expression, he eyed him inquisitively, almost uneasily.

'Ah, well,' smiled the other wanly, 'if that subtle bane, we were speaking of but just now, is so soon beginning to work, in vain my appeal to you. Good-bye.'

'Nay,' not untouched, 'you do me injustice; instead of indulging present suspicions, I had rather make amends for previous ones. Here is something for your asylum. Not much; but every drop helps. Of course you have papers?'

'Of course,' producing a memorandum book and pencil. 'Let me take down name and amount. We publish these names. And now let me give you a little history of our asylum, and the providential way in which it was started.'

CHAPTER VII

A GENTLEMAN WITH GOLD SLEEVE-BUTTONS

At an interesting point of the narration, and at the moment when, with much curiosity, indeed, urgency, the narrator was being particularly questioned upon that point, he was, as it happened, altogether diverted both from it and his story, by just then catching sight of a gentleman who had been standing in sight from the beginning, but, until now, as it seemed, without being observed by him.

'Pardon me,' said he, rising, 'but yonder is one who I know will contribute, and largely. Don't take it amiss if I quit you.'

'Go: duty before all things,' was the conscientious reply.

The stranger was a man of more than winsome aspect. There he stood apart and in repose, and yet, by his mere look, lured the man in gray from his story, much as, by its graciousness of bearing, some full-leaved elm, alone in a meadow, lures the noon sickleman to throw down his sheaves, and come and apply for the alms of its shade.

But, considering that goodness is no such rare thing among men—the world familiarly know the noun; a common one in every language—it was curious that what so signalised the stranger, and made him look like a kind of foreigner, among the crowd (as to some it make him appear more or less unreal in this portraiture), was but the expression of so prevalent a quality. Such

goodness seemed his, allied with such fortune, that, so
far as his own personal experience could have gone,
scarcely could he have known ill, physical or moral;
and as for knowing or suspecting the latter in any serious
degree (supposing such degree of it to be), by observation or philosophy; for that, probably, his nature, by
its opposition, imperfectly qualified, or from it wholly
exempted. For the rest, he might have been five-and-
fifty, perhaps sixty, but tall, rosy, between plump and
portly, with a primy, palmy air, and for the time and
place, not to hint of his years, dressed with a strangely
festive finish and elegance. The inner side of his coat-
skirts was of white satin, which might have looked
especially inappropriate, had it not seemed less a bit of
mere tailoring than something of an emblem, as it were;
an involuntary emblem, let us say, that what seemed
so good about him was not all outside; no, the fine
covering had a still finer lining. Upon one hand he
wore a white kid glove, but the other hand, which was
ungloved, looked hardly less white. Now, as the *Fidèle*,
like most steamboats, was upon deck a little soot-
streaked here and there, especially about the railings,
it was a marvel how, under such circumstances, these
hands retained their spotlessness. But, if you watched
them a while, you noticed that they avoided touching
anything; you noticed, in short, that a certain negro
body-servant, whose hands nature had dyed black,
perhaps with the same purpose that millers wear white,
this negro servant's hands did most of his master's
handling for him; having to do with dirt on his account,
but not to his prejudices. But if, with the same unde-
filedness of consequences to himself, a gentleman could
also sin by deputy, how shocking would that be! But
it is not permitted to be; and even if it were, no judicious
moralist would make proclamation of it.

This gentleman, therefore, there is reason to affirm, was one who, like the Hebrew governor,* knew how to keep his hands clean, and who never in his life happened to be run suddenly against by hurrying house-painter, or sweep ; in a word, one whose very good luck it was to be a very good man.

Not that he looked as if he were a kind of Wilberforce* at all ; that superior merit, probably, was not his ; nothing in his manner bespoke him righteous, but only good, and though to be good is much below being righteous, and though there is a difference between the two, yet not, it is to be hoped, so incompatible as that a righteous man cannot be a good man ; though, conversely, in the pulpit it has been with much cogency urged, that a merely good man, that is, one good merely by his nature, is so far from there by being righteous, that nothing short of a total change and conversion can make him so ; which is something which no honest mind, well read in the history of righteousness, will care to deny ; nevertheless, since St. Paul himself, agreeing in a sense with the pulpit distinction, though not altogether in the pulpit deduction, and also pretty plainly intimating which of the two qualities in question enjoys his apostolic preference ; I say, since St. Paul has so meaningly said, that, ' scarcely for a righteous man* will one die, yet peradventure for a good man some would even dare to die ' ; therefore, when we repeat of this gentleman, that he was only a good man, whatever else by severe censors may be objected to him, it is still to be hoped that his goodness will not at least be considered criminal in him. At all events, no man, not even a righteous man, would think it quite right to commit this gentleman to prison for the crime, extraordinary as he might deem it ; more especially, as, until everything could be known, there would be some chance that

the gentleman might after all be quite as innocent of it
as he himself.

It was pleasant to mark the good man's reception of
the salute of the righteous man, that is, the man in
gray; his inferior, apparently, not more in the social
scale than in stature. Like the benign elm again, the
good man seemed to wave the canopy of his goodness
over that suitor, not in conceited condescension, but
with that even amenity of true majesty, which can be
kind to anyone without stooping to it.

To the plea in behalf of the Seminole widows and
orphans, the gentleman, after a question or two duly
answered, responded by producing an ample pocket-
book in the good old capacious style, of fine green French
morocco and workmanship, bound with silk of the same
colour, not to omit bills crisp with newness, fresh from
the bank, no muckworms' grime upon them. Lucre
those bills might be, but as yet having been kept un-
spotted from the world, not of the filthy sort. Placing
now three of those virgin bills in the applicant's hands,
he hoped that the smallness of the contribution would
be pardoned; to tell the truth, and this at last accounted
for his toilet, he was bound but a short run down the
river, to attend, in a festive grove, the afternoon wedding
of his niece: so did not carry much money with him.

The other was about expressing his thanks when the
gentleman in his pleasant way checked him: the gratitude was on the other side. To him, he said, charity
was in one sense not an effort, but a luxury; against too
great indulgence in which his steward, a humorist, had
sometimes admonished him.

In some general talk which followed, relative to
organised modes of doing good, the gentleman expressed
his regrets that so many benevolent societies as there
were, here and there isolated in the land, should not

act in concert by coming together, in the way that already in each society the individuals composing it had done, which would result, he thought, in like advantages upon a larger scale. Indeed, such a confederation might, perhaps, be attended with as happy results as politically attended that of the states.

Upon his hitherto moderate enough companion, this suggestion had an effect illustrative in a sort of that notion of Socrates,* that the soul is a harmony ; for as the sound of a flute, in any particular key, will, it is said, audibly affect the corresponding chord of any harp in good tune, within hearing, just so now did some string in him respond, and with animation.

Which animation, by the way, might seem more or less out of character in the man in gray, considering his unsprightly manner when first introduced, had he not already, in certain after colloquies, given proof, in some degree, of the fact, that, with certain natures, a soberly continent air at times, so far from arguing emptiness of stuff, is good proof it is there, and plenty of it, because unwasted, and may be used the more effectively, too, when opportunity offers. What now follows on the part of the man in gray will still further exemplify, perhaps somewhat strikingly, the truth, or what appears to be such, of this remark.

' Sir,' said he eagerly, ' I am before you. A project, not dissimilar to yours, was by me thrown out at the World's Fair in London.'*

' World's Fair ? You there ? Pray how was that ? '

' First, let me—— '

' Nay, but first tell me what took you to the Fair ? '

' I went to exhibit an invalid's easy-chair I had invented.'

' Then you have not always been in the charity business ? '

' Is it not charity to ease human suffering ? I am, and always have been, as I always will be, I trust, in the charity business, as you call it ; but charity is not like a pin, one to make the head, and the other the point ; charity is a work to which a good workman may be competent in all its branches. I invented my Protean* easy-chair in odd intervals stolen from meals and sleep.'

' You call it the Protean easy-chair ; pray describe it.'

' My Protean easy-chair is a chair so all over bejointed, behinged, and bepadded, every way so elastic, springy, and docile to the airiest touch, that in some one of its endlessly changeable accommodations of back, seat, foot-board, and arms, the most restless body, the body most racked, nay, I had almost added the most tormented conscience must, somehow and somewhere, find rest. Believing that I owed it to suffering humanity to make known such a chair to the utmost, I scraped together my little means and off to the World's Fair with it.'

' You did right. But your scheme ; how did you come to hit upon that ? '

' I was going to tell you. After seeing my invention duly catalogued and placed, I gave myself up to pondering the scene about me. As I dwelt upon that shining pageant of arts, and moving concourse of nations, and reflected that here was the pride of the world glorying in a glass house, a sense of the fragility of worldly grandeur profoundly impressed me. And I said to myself, I will see if this occasion of vanity cannot supply a hint toward a better profit than was designed. Let some world-wide good to the world-wide cause be now done. In short, inspired by the scene, on the fourth day I issued at the World's Fair my prospectus of the World's Charity.'

' Quite a thought. But, pray explain it.'

' The World's Charity is to be a society whose members shall comprise deputies from every charity and mission extant; the one object of the society to be the methodisation of the world's benevolence; to which end, the present system of voluntary and promiscuous contribution to be done away, and the society to be empowered by the various governments to levy, annually, one grand benevolence tax upon all mankind; as in Augustus Cæsar's time, the whole world to come up to be taxed; a tax which, for the scheme of it, should be something like the income-tax in England, a tax, also, as before hinted, to be a consolidation-tax of all possible benevolence taxes; as in America here, the state-tax, and the county-tax, and the town-tax, and the poll-tax, are by the assessors rolled into one. This tax, according to my tables, calculated with care, would result in the yearly raising of a fund little short of eight hundred millions; this fund to be annually applied to such objects, and in such modes, as the various charities and missions, in general congress represented, might decree; whereby, in fourteen years, as I estimate, there would have been devoted to good works the sum of eleven thousand two hundred millions; which would warrant the dissolution of the society, as that fund judiciously expended, not a pauper or heathen could remain the round world over.'

' Eleven thousand two hundred millions! And all by passing round a *hat*, as it were.'

' Yes, I am no Fourier,* the projector of an impossible scheme, but a philanthropist and a financier setting forth a philanthropy and a finance which are practicable.'

' Practicable ? '

' Yes. Eleven thousand two hundred millions; it will frighten none but a retail philanthropist. What is it but eight hundred millions for each of fourteen years ?

Now eight hundred millions—what is that, to average it, but one little dollar a head for the population of the planet ? And who will refuse, what Turk or Dyak even, his own little dollar for sweet charity's sake ? Eight hundred millions ! More than that sum is yearly expended by mankind, not only in vanities, but miseries. Consider that bloody spendthrift, War. And are mankind so stupid, so wicked, that, upon the demonstration of these things, they will not, amending their ways, devote their superfluities to blessing the world instead of cursing it ? Eight hundred millions ! They have not to make it, it is theirs already ; they have but to direct it from ill to good. And to this, scarce a self-denial is demanded. Actually, they would not in the mass be one farthing the poorer for it ; as certainly would they be all the better and happier. Don't you see ? But admit, as you must, that mankind is not mad, and my project is practicable. For, what creature but a madman would not rather do good than ill, when it is plain that, good or ill, it must return upon himself ? '

'Your sort of reasoning,' said the good gentleman, adjusting his gold sleeve-buttons, ' seems all reasonable enough, but with mankind it won't do.'

'Then mankind are not reasoning beings, if reason won't do with them.'

'That is not to the purpose. By the way, from the manner in which you alluded to the world's census, it would appear that, according to your world-wide scheme, the pauper not less than the nabob is to contribute to the relief of pauperism, and the heathen not less than the Christian to the conversion of heathenism. How is that ? '

'Why, that—pardon me—is quibbling. Now, no philanthropist likes to be opposed with quibbling.'

'Well, I won't quibble any more. But, after all, if

I understand your project, there is little specially new in it, further than the magnifying of means now in operation.'

'Magnifying and energising. For one thing, missions I would thoroughly reform. Missions I would quicken with the Wall Street spirit.'

'The Wall Street spirit ? '

'Yes; for if, confessedly, certain spiritual ends are to be gained but through the auxiliary agency of worldly means, then, to the surer gaining of such spiritual ends, the example of worldly policy in worldly projects should not by spiritual projectors be slighted. In brief, the conversion of the heathen, so far, at least, as depending on human effort, would, by the world's charity, be let out on contract. So much by bid for converting India, so much for Borneo, so much for Africa. Competition allowed, stimulus would be given. There would be no lethargy of monopoly. We should have no mission-house or tract-house of which slanderers could, with any plausibility, say that it had degenerated in its clerkships into a sort of custom-house. But the main point is the Archimedean* money-power that would be brought to bear.'

'You mean the eight hundred million power ? '

'Yes. You see, this doing good to the world by driblets amounts to just nothing. I am for doing good to the world with a will. I am for doing good to the world once for all and having done with it. Do but think, my dear sir, of the eddies and maelstroms of pagans in China. People here have no conception of it. Of a frosty morning in Hong-Kong, pauper pagans are found dead in the streets like so many nipped peas in a bin of peas. To be an immortal being in China is no more distinction than to be a snow-flake in a snow-squall. What are a score or two of missionaries to such

a people ?   A pinch of snuff to the kraken.* I am for
sending ten thousand missionaries in a body and converting the Chinese *en masse* within six months of the
debarkation.   The thing is then done, and turn to something else.'

' I fear you are too enthusiastic.'

' A philanthropist is necessarily an enthusiast ; for
without enthusiasm what was ever achieved but commonplace ?   But again : consider the poor in London.   To
that mob of misery, what is a joint here and a loaf there ?
I am for voting to them twenty thousand bullocks and
one hundred thousand barrels of flour to begin with.
They are then comforted, and no more hunger for one
while among the poor of London.   And so all round.'

' Sharing the character of your general project, these
things, I take it, are rather examples of wonders that
were to be wished, than wonders that will happen.'

' And is the age of wonders past ?   Is the world too
old ?   Is it barren ?   Think of Sarah.'

' Then I am Abraham reviling the angel*(with a smile).
But still, as to your design at large, there seems a certain
audacity.'

' But if to the audacity of the design there be brought
a commensurate circumspectness of execution, how then ?'

' Why, do you really believe that your world's charity
will ever go into operation ?'

' I have confidence that it will.'

' But may you not be over-confident ?'

' For a Christian to talk so ! '

' But think of the obstacles ! '

' Obstacles ?   I have confidence to remove obstacles,
though mountains.   Yes, confidence in the world's
charity to that degree, that, as no better person offers to
supply the place, I have nominated myself provisional
treasurer, and will be happy to receive subscriptions, for

the present to be devoted to striking off a million more
of my prospectuses.'

The talk went on ; the man in gray revealed a spirit
of benevolence which, mindful of the millennial promise,*
had gone abroad over all the countries of the globe,
much as the diligent spirit of the husbandman, stirred
by forethought of the coming seed-time, leads him, in
March reveries at his fireside, over every field of his
farm. The master chord of the man in gray had been
touched, and it seemed as if it would never cease vibrating.
A not unsilvery tongue, too, was his, with gestures that
were a Pentecost*of added ones, and persuasiveness before
which granite hearts might crumble into gravel.

Strange, therefore, how his auditor, so singularly good-
hearted as he seemed, remained proof to such eloquence ;
though not, as it turned out, to such pleadings. For,
after listening a while longer with pleasant incredulity,
presently, as the boat touched his place of destination,
the gentleman, with a look half humour, half pity, put
another bank-note into his hands ; charitable to the
last, if only to the dreams of enthusiasm.

CHAPTER VIII

A CHARITABLE LADY

IF a drunkard in a sober fit is the dullest of mortals,
an enthusiast in a reason fit is not the most lively. And
this, without prejudice to his greatly improved understanding ; for, if his elation was the height of his
madness, his despondency is but the extreme of his
sanity. Something thus now, to all appearance, with
the man in gray. Society his stimulus, loneliness was
his lethargy. Loneliness, like the sea-breeze, blowing
off from a thousand leagues of blankness, he did not
find, as veteran solitaires do, if anything, too bracing.
In short, left to himself, with none to charm forth his
latent lymphatic, he insensibly resumes his original air,
a quiescent one, blended of sad humility and demureness.

Ere long he goes laggingly into the ladies' saloon, as
in spiritless quest of somebody ; but, after some disappointed glances about him, seats himself upon a sofa
with an air of melancholy exhaustion and depression.

At the sofa's further end sits a plump and pleasant
person, whose aspect seems to hint that, if she have
any weak point, it must be anything rather than her
excellent heart. From her twilight dress, neither dawn
nor dark, apparently she is a widow just breaking the
chrysalis of her mourning. A small gilt testament is in
her hand, which she has just been reading. Half
relinquished, she holds the book in revery, her finger
inserted at the xiii. of 1st Corinthians, to which chapter
possibly her attention might have recently been turned,

by witnessing the scene of the monitory mute and his slate.

The sacred page no longer meets her eye ; but, as at evening, when for a time the western hills shine on though the sun be set, her thoughtful face retains its tenderness though the teacher is forgotten.

Meantime, the expression of the stranger is such as ere long to attract her glance. But no responsive one. Presently, in her somewhat inquisitive survey, her volume drops. It is restored. No encroaching politeness in the act, but kindness, unadorned. The eyes of the lady sparkle. Evidently, she is not now unprepossessed. Soon, bending over, in a low, sad tone, full of deference, the stranger breathes, ' Madam, pardon my freedom, but there is something in that face which strangely draws me. May I ask, are you a sister of the Church ? '

' Why—really—you—— '

In concern for her embarrassment, he hastens to relieve it, but without seeming so to do. ' It is very solitary for a brother here,' eyeing the showy ladies brocaded in the background, ' I find none to mingle souls with. It may be wrong—I *know* it is—but I cannot force myself to be easy with the people of the world. I prefer the company, however silent, of a brother or sister in good standing. By the way, madam, may I ask if you have confidence ? '*

' Really, sir—why, sir—really—I—— '

' Could you put confidence in *me*, for instance ? '

' Really, sir—as much—I mean, as one may wisely put in a—a—stranger, an entire stranger, I had almost said,' rejoined the lady, hardly yet at ease in her affability, drawing aside a little in body, while at the same time her heart might have been drawn as far the other way. A natural struggle between charity and prudence.

'Entire stranger !' with a sigh. 'Ah, who would be a stranger ? In vain, I wander ; no one will have confidence in me.'

'You interest me,' said the good lady, in mild surprise. 'Can I any way befriend you ?'

'No one can befriend me, who has not confidence.'

'But I—I have—at least to that degree—I mean that——'

'Nay, nay, you have none—none at all. Pardon, I see it. No confidence. Fool, fond fool that I am to seek it !'

'You are unjust, sir,' rejoins the good lady with heightened interest ; 'but it may be that something untoward in your experiences has unduly biased you. Not that I would cast reflections. Believe me, I—yes, yes—I may say—that—that——'

'That you have confidence ? Prove it. Let me have twenty dollars.'

'Twenty dollars !'

'There, I told you, madam, you had no confidence.'

The lady was, in an extraordinary way, touched. She sat in a sort of restless torment, knowing not which way to turn. She began twenty different sentences, and left off at the first syllable of each. At last, in desperation, she hurried out, 'Tell me, sir, for what you want the twenty dollars ?'

'And did I not——' Then glancing at her half-mourning, 'for the widow and the fatherless. I am travelling agent of the Widow and Orphan Asylum, recently founded among the Seminoles.'

'And why did you not tell me your object before ?' As not a little relieved. 'Poor souls—Indians, too— those cruelly used Indians. Here, here ; how could I hesitate. I am so sorry it is no more.'

'Grieve not for that, madam,' rising and folding up

the bank-notes. 'This is an inconsiderable sum, I admit, but,' taking out his pencil and book, 'though I here but register the amount, there is another register, where is set down the motive. Good-bye; you have confidence. Yea, you can say to me as the apostle said to the Corinthians, "I rejoice that I have confidence* in you in all things."'

CHAPTER IX

TWO BUSINESS MEN TRANSACT A LITTLE BUSINESS

—'PRAY, sir, have you seen a gentleman with a weed hereabouts, rather a saddish gentleman ? Strange where he can have gone to. I was talking with him not twenty minutes since.'

By a brisk, ruddy-cheeked man in a tasselled travelling-cap, carrying under his arm a ledger-like volume, the above words were addressed to the collegian before introduced, suddenly accosted by the rail to which not long after his retreat, as in a previous chapter recounted, he had returned, and there remained.

'Have you seen him, sir ? '

Rallied from his apparent diffidence by the genial jauntiness of the stranger, the youth answered with unwonted promptitude : 'Yes, a person with a weed was here not very long ago.'

'Saddish ? '

'Yes, and a little cracked, too, I should say.'

'It was he. Misfortune, I fear, has disturbed his brain. Now quick, which way did he go ? '

'Why, just in the direction from which you came, the gangway yonder.'

'Did he ? Then the man in the gray coat, whom I just met, said right : he must have gone ashore. How unlucky ! '

He stood vexedly twitching at his cap-tassel, which fell over by his whisker, and continued : 'Well, I am very sorry. In fact, I had something for him here.'—

Then drawing nearer, ' You see, he applied to me for
relief, no, I do him injustice, not that, but he began to
intimate, you understand. Well, being very busy just
then, I declined ; quite rudely, too, in a cold, morose,
unfeeling way, I fear. At all events, not three minutes
afterward I felt self-reproach, with a kind of prompting,
very peremptory, to deliver over into that unfortunate
man's hands a ten-dollar bill. You smile. Yes, it may
be superstition, but I can't help it ; I have my weak
side, thank God. Then again,' he rapidly went on, ' we
have been so very prosperous lately in our affairs—by
we, I mean the Black Rapids Coal Company—that,
really, out of my abundance, associative and individual,
it is but fair that a charitable investment or two should
be made, don't you think so ? '

' Sir,' said the collegian without the least embarrassment, ' do I understand that you are officially connected
with the Black Rapids Coal Company ? '

' Yes, I happen to be president and transfer-agent.'

' You are ? '

' Yes, but what is it to you ? You don't want to
invest ? '

' Why, do you sell the stock ? '

' Some might be bought, perhaps ; but why do you
ask ? you don't want to invest ? '

' But supposing I did,' with cool self-collectedness,
' could you do up the thing for me, and here ? '

' Bless my soul,' gazing at him in amaze, ' really, you
are quite a business man. Positively, I feel afraid of
you.'

' Oh, no need of that.—You could sell me some of that
stock, then ? '

' I don't know, I don't know. To be sure, there are a
few shares under peculiar circumstances bought in by
the Company ; but it would hardly be the thing to

convert this boat into the Company's office. I think you had better defer investing. So,' with an indifferent air, ' you have seen the unfortunate man I spoke of ? '

' Let the unfortunate man go his ways.—What is that large book you have with you ? '

' My transfer-book. I am subpœnaed with it to court.'

' Black Rapids Coal Company,' obliquely reading the gilt inscription on the back ; ' I have heard much of it. Pray, do you happen to have with you any statement of the condition of your company.'

' A statement has lately been printed.'

' Pardon me, but I am naturally inquisitive. Have you a copy with you ? '

' I tell you again, I do not think that it would be suitable to convert this boat into the Company's office. —' That unfortunate man, did you relieve him at all ? '

' Let the unfortunate man relieve himself.—Hand me the statement.'

' Well, you are such a business man, I can hardly deny you. Here,' handing a small, printed pamphlet. The youth turned it over sagely.

' I hate a suspicious man,' said the other, observing him ; ' but I must say I like to see a cautious one.'

' I can gratify you there,' languidly returning the pamphlet ; ' for, as I said before, I am naturally inquisitive ; I am also circumspect. No appearances can deceive me. Your statement,' he added, ' tells a very fine story ; but pray, was not your stock a little heavy a while ago ? downward tendency ? Sort of low spirits among holders on the subject of that stock ? '

' Yes, there was a depression. But how came it ? who devised it ? The " bears," sir.* The depression of our stock was solely owing to the growling, the hypo-critical growling, of the bears.'

' How, hypocritical ? '

'Why, the most monstrous of all hypocrites are these bears : hypocrites by inversion ; hypocrites in the simulation of things dark instead of bright ; souls that thrive, less upon depression, than the fiction of depression ; professors of the wicked art of manufacturing depressions ; spurious Jeremiahs ; sham Heraclituses* who, the lugubrious day done, return, like sham Lazaruses* among the beggars, to make merry over the gains got by their pretended sore heads—scoundrelly bears ! '

'You are warm against these bears ? '

'If I am, it is less from the remembrance of their stratagems as to our stock, than from the persuasion that these same destroyers of confidence, and gloomy philosophers of the stock-market, though false in themselves, are yet true types of most destroyers of confidence and gloomy philosophers, the world over. Fellows who, whether in stocks, politics, bread-stuffs, morals, metaphysics, religion—be it what it may—trump up their black panics in the naturally quiet brightness, solely with a view to some sort of covert advantage. That corpse of calamity which the gloomy philosopher parades, is but his Good-Enough-Morgan.'*

'I rather like that,' knowingly drawled the youth. 'I fancy these gloomy souls as little as the next one. Sitting on my sofa after a champagne dinner, smoking my plantation cigar, if a gloomy fellow come to me—what a bore ! '

'You tell him it 's all stuff, don't you ? '

'I tell him it ain't natural. I say to him, you are happy enough, and you know it ; and everybody else is as happy as you, and you know that, too ; and we shall all be happy after we are no more, and you know that, too ; but no, still you must have your sulk.'

'And do you know whence this sort of fellow gets his sulk ? not from life ; for he 's often too much of a

recluse, or else too young, to have seen anything of it.
No, he gets it from some of those old plays he sees on the
stage, or some of those old books he finds up in garrets.
Ten to one, he has lugged home from auction a musty
old Seneca,* and sets about stuffing himself with that
stale old hay ; and, thereupon, thinks it looks wise and
antique to be a croaker,* thinks it 's taking a standway
above his kind.'

'Just so,' assented the youth. 'I 've lived some, and
seen a good many such ravens at second-hand. By the
way, strange how that man with the weed, you were
inquiring for, seemed to take me for some soft senti-
mentalist, only because I kept quiet, and thought,
because I had a copy of Tacitus with me, that I was
reading him for his gloom, instead of his gossip. But I
let him talk. And, indeed, by my manner humoured him.'

'You shouldn't have done that, now. Unfortunate
man, you must have made quite a fool of him.'

'His own fault if I did. But I like prosperous fellows,
comfortable fellows ; fellows that talk comfortably and
prosperously, like you. Such fellows are generally
honest. And, I say now, I happen to have a superfluity
in my pocket, and I 'll just——'

'—Act the part of a brother to that unfortunate
man ?'

'Let the unfortunate man be his own brother. What
are you dragging him in for all the time ? One would
think you didn't care to register any transfers, or dispose
of any stock—mind running on something else. I say
I will invest.'

'Stay, stay, here come some uproarious fellows—this
way, this way.'

And with off-handed politeness the man with the book
escorted his companion into a private little haven removed from the brawling swells without.

Business transacted, the two came forth, and walked the deck.

' Now tell me, sir,' said he with the book, ' how comes it that a young gentleman like you, a sedate student at the first appearance, should dabble in stocks and that sort of thing ? '

' There are certain sophomorean errors in the world,' drawled the sophomore, deliberately adjusting his shirt-collar, ' not the least of which is the popular notion touching the nature of the modern scholar, and the nature of the modern scholastic sedateness.'

' So it seems, so it seems. Really, this is quite a new leaf in my experience.'

' Experience, sir,' originally observed the sophomore, ' is the only teacher.'

' Hence am I your pupil ; for it 's only when experience speaks, that I can endure to listen to speculation.'

' My speculations, sir,' dryly drawing himself up, ' have been chiefly governed by the maxim of Lord Bacon ; I speculate in those philosophies which come home to my business and bosom*—pray, do you know of any other good stocks ? '

' You wouldn't like to be concerned in the New Jerusalem,* would you ? '

' New Jerusalem ? '

' Yes, the new and thriving city, so called, in northern Minnesota. It was originally founded by certain fugitive Mormons. Hence the name. It stands on the Mississippi. Here, here is the map,' producing a roll. ' There—there, you see are the public buildings—here the landing—there the park—yonder the botanic gardens—and this, this little dot here, is a perpetual fountain, you understand. You observe there are twenty asterisks. Those are for the lyceums.* They have lignum-vitae rostrums.'

' And are all these buildings now standing ? '

'All standing—*bona fide.*'

'These marginal squares here, are they the water-lots ?'

'Water-lots in the city of New Jerusalem ? All terra firma—you don't seem to care about investing, though ?'

'Hardly think I should read my title clear, as the law students say,' yawned the collegian.

'Prudent—you are prudent. Don't know that you are wholly out, either. At any rate, I would rather have one of your shares of coal stock than two of this other. Still, considering that the first settlement was by two fugitives, who had swum over*naked from the opposite shore—it 's a surprising place. It is, *bona fide.*— But dear me, I must go. Oh, if by possibility you should come across that unfortunate man——'

'—In that case,' with drawling impatience, 'I will send for the steward, and have him and his misfortunes consigned overboard.'

'Ha, ha !—now were some gloomy philosopher here, some theological bear, forever taking occasion to growl down the stock of human nature (with ulterior views, d' ye see, to a fat benefice in the gift of the worshippers of Ariamius),* he would pronounce that the sign of a hardening heart and a softening brain. Yes, that would be his sinister construction. But it 's nothing more than the oddity of a genial humour—genial but dry. Confess it. Good-bye.'

CHAPTER X

IN THE CABIN

STOOLS, settees, sofas, divans, ottomans ; occupying them are clusters of men, old and young, wise and simple ; in their hands are cards spotted with diamonds, spades, clubs, hearts ; the favourite games are whist, cribbage, and brag. Lounging in arm-chairs or sauntering among the marble-topped tables, amused with the scene, are the comparatively few, who, instead of having hands in the games, for the most part keep their hands in their pockets. These may be the philosophes. But here and there, with a curious expression, one is reading a small sort of handbill of anonymous poetry, rather wordily entitled :—

'ODE

ON THE INTIMATIONS

OF

DISTRUST IN MAN,*

UNWILLINGLY INFERRED FROM REPEATED REPULSES,

IN DISINTERESTED ENDEAVOURS

TO PROCURE HIS

CONFIDENCE.'

On the floor are many copies, looking as if fluttered down from a balloon. The way they came there was this : A somewhat elderly person, in the quaker dress, had quietly passed through the cabin, and, much in the manner of those railway book-peddlers who precede their proffers of sale by a distribution of puffs, direct or indirect, of the volumes to follow, had, without speaking, handed about the odes, which, for the most part, after a cursory glance, had been disrespectfully tossed aside, as no doubt the moonstruck production of some wandering rhapsodist.

In due time, book under arm, in trips the ruddy man with the travelling-cap, who, lightly moving to and fro, looks animatedly about him, with a yearning sort of gratulatory affinity and longing, expressive of the very soul of sociality ; as much as to say, ' Oh, boys, would that I were personally acquainted with each mother's son of you, since what a sweet world, to make sweet acquaintance in, is ours, my brothers ; yea, and what dear, happy dogs are we all ! '

And just as if he had really warbled it forth, he makes fraternally up to one lounging stranger or another, exchanging with him some pleasant remark.

' Pray, what have you there ? ' he asked of one newly accosted, a little, dried-up man, who looked as if he never dined.

' A little ode, rather queer, too,' was the reply, ' of the same sort you see strewn on the floor here.'

' I did not observe them. Let me see ' ; picking one up and looking it over. ' Well now, this is pretty ; plaintive, especially the opening :—

> " Alas for man, he hath small sense
> Of genial trust and confidence."

—If it be so, alas for him, indeed. Runs off very smoothly, sir. Beautiful pathos. But do you think the sentiment just ? '

' As to that,' said the little dried-up man, ' I think it a kind of queer thing altogether, and yet I am almost ashamed to add, it really has set me to thinking ; yes, and to feeling. Just now, somehow, I feel as it were trustful and genial. I don't know that ever I felt so much so before. I am naturally numb in my sensibilities; but this ode, in its way, works on my numbness not unlike a sermon, which by lamenting over my lying dead in trespasses and sins, thereby stirs me up to be all alive in well-doing.'

' Glad to hear it, and hope you will do well, as the doctors say. But who snowed the odes about here ? '

' I cannot say; I have not been here long.'

' Wasn't an angel, was it ? Come, you say you feel genial : let us do as the rest, and have cards.'

' Thank you, I never play cards.'

' A bottle of wine ? '

' Thank you, I never drink wine.'

' Cigars ? '

' Thank you, I never smoke cigars.'

'Tell stories ? '

' To speak truly, I hardly think I know one worth telling.'

' Seems to me, then, this geniality you say you feel waked in you, is as water-power in a land without mills. Come, you had better take a genial hand at the cards. To begin, we will play for as small a sum as you please; just enough to make it interesting.'

' Indeed, you must excuse me. Somehow I distrust cards.'

' What, distrust cards ? Genial cards ? Then for once I join with our sad Philomel*here :—

" Alas for man, he hath small sense
    Of genial trust and confidence."

Good-bye ! '

Sauntering and chatting here and there, again, he with the book at length seems fatigued, looks round for a seat, and spying a partly vacant settee drawn up against the side, drops down there ; soon, like his chance neighbour, who happens to be the good merchant, becoming not a little interested in the scene more immediately before him ; a party at whist ; two cream-faced, giddy, unpolished youths, the one in a red cravat, the other in a green, opposed to two bland, grave, handsome, self-possessed men of middle age, decorously dressed in a sort of professional black, and apparently doctors of some eminence in the civil law.

By and by, after a preliminary scanning of the newcomer next him, the good merchant, sideways leaning over, whispers behind a crumpled copy of the Ode which he holds : ' Sir, I don't like the looks of those two, do you ? '

' Hardly,' was the whispered reply ; ' those coloured cravats are not in the best taste, at least not to mine ; but my taste is no rule for all.'

' You mistake ; I mean the other two, and I don't refer to dress, but countenance. I confess I am not familiar with such gentry any further than reading about them in the papers—but those two are—are sharpers, ain't they ? '

' Far be from us the captious and fault-finding spirit, my dear sir.'

' Indeed, sir, I would not find fault ; I am little given that way ; but certainly, to say the least, these two youths can hardly be adepts, while the opposed couple may be even more.'

' You would not hint that the coloured cravats would be so bungling as to lose, and the dark cravats so dextrous as to cheat ?—Sour imaginations, my dear sir.   Dismiss them. To little purpose have you read the Ode you have there. Years and experience, I trust, have not sophisticated you. A fresh and liberal construction would teach us to regard those four players—indeed, this whole cabinful of players—as playing at games in which every player plays fair, and not a player but shall win.'

'Now, you hardly mean that; because games in which all may win, such games remain as yet in this world uninvented, I think.'

'Come, come,' luxuriously laying himself back, and casting a free glance upon the players, 'fares all paid; digestion sound; care, toil, penury, grief, unknown; lounging on this sofa, with waistband relaxed, why not be cheerfully resigned to one's fate, nor peevishly pick holes in the blessed fate of the world?'

Upon this, the good merchant, after staring long and hard, and then rubbing his forehead, fell into meditation, at first uneasy, but at last composed, and in the end, once more addressed his companion: 'Well, I see it's good to out with one's private thoughts now and then. Somehow, I don't know why, a certain misty suspiciousness seems inseparable from most of one's private notions about some men and some things; but once out with these misty notions, and their mere contact with other men's soon dissipates, or, at least, modifies them.'

'You think I have done you good, then? maybe I have. But don't thank me, don't thank me. If by words, casually delivered in the social hour, I do any good to right or left, it is but involuntary influence—locust-tree* sweetening the herbage under it; no merit at all; mere wholesome accident, of a wholesome nature.—Don't you see?'

Another stare from the good merchant, and both were silent again.

Finding his book, hitherto resting on his lap, rather irksome there, the owner now places it edgewise on the settee, between himself and neighbour; in so doing, chancing to expose the lettering on the back—'*Black*

Rapids Coal Company '—which the good merchant,
scrupulously honourable, had much ado to avoid reading,
so directly would it have fallen under his eye, had he
not conscientiously averted it. On a sudden, as if just
reminded of something, the stranger starts up, and
moves away, in his haste leaving his book ; which the
merchant observing, without delay takes it up, and,
hurrying after, civilly returns it ; in which act he could
not avoid catching sight by an involuntary glance of
part of the lettering.

'Thank you, thank you, my good sir,' said the other,
receiving the volume, and was resuming his retreat, when
the merchant spoke : ' Excuse me, but are you not in
some way connected with the—the Coal Company I
have heard of ? '

'There is more than one Coal Company that may be
heard of, my good sir,' smiled the other, pausing with
an expression of painful impatience, disinterestedly
mastered.

'But you are connected with one in particular—the
" Black Rapids," are you not ? '

'How did you find that out ? '

'Well, sir, I have heard rather tempting information
of your Company.'

'Who is your informant, pray,' somewhat coldly.

'A—a person by the name of Ringman.'

'Don't know him. But, doubtless, there are plenty
who know our Company, whom our Company does not
know ; in the same way that one may know an individual, yet be unknown to him.—Known this Ringman
long ? Old friend, I suppose.—But pardon, I must
leave you.'

'Stay, sir, that—that stock.'

'Stock ? '

'Yes, it 's a little irregular, perhaps, but——'

'Dear me, you don't think of doing any business with me, do you ? In my official capacity I have not been authenticated to you. This transfer-book, now,' holding it up so as to bring the lettering in sight, ' how do you know that it may not be a bogus one ? And I, being personally a stranger to you, how can you have confidence in me ? '

'Because,' knowingly smiled the good merchant, ' if you were other than I have confidence that you are, hardly would you challenge distrust that way.'

'But you have not examined my book.'

'What need to, if already I believe that it is what it is lettered to be ? '

'But you had better. It might suggest doubts.'

'Doubts, maybe, it might suggest, but not knowledge ; for how, by examining the book, should I think I knew any more than I now think I do ; since, if it be the true book, I think it so already ; and since if it be otherwise, then I have never seen the true one, and don't know what that ought to look like.'

'Your logic I will not criticise, but your confidence I admire, and earnestly, too, jocose as was the method I took to draw it out. Enough, we will go to yonder table, and if there be any business which, either in my private or official capacity, I can help you do, pray command me.'

CHAPTER XI

ONLY A PAGE OR SO

THE transaction concluded, the two still remained seated, falling into familiar conversation, by degrees verging into that confidential sort of sympathetic silence, the last refinement and luxury of unaffected good feeling. A kind of social superstition, to suppose that to be truly friendly one must be saying friendly words all the time, any more than be doing friendly deeds continually. True friendliness, like true religion, being in a sort independent of works.

At length, the good merchant, whose eyes were pensively resting upon the gay tables in the distance, broke the spell by saying that, from the spectacle before them, one would little divine what other quarters of the boat might reveal. He cited the case, accidentally encountered but an hour or two previous, of a shrunken old miser, clad in shrunken old moleskin, stretched out, an invalid, on a bare plank in the emigrants' quarters, eagerly clinging to life and lucre, though the one was gasping for outlet, and about the other he was in torment lest death, or some other unprincipled cut-purse, should be the means of his losing it; by like feeble tenure holding lungs and pouch, and yet knowing and desiring nothing beyond them; for his mind, never raised above mould, was now all but mouldered away. To such a degree, indeed, that he had no trust in anything, not even in his parchment bonds, which, the better to preserve from the tooth of time, he had packed down and sealed up, like brandy peaches, in a tin case of spirits.

The worthy man proceeded at some length with these dispiriting particulars. Nor would his cheery companion wholly deny that there might be a point of view from which such a case of extreme want of confidence might, to the humane mind, present features not altogether welcome as wine and olives after dinner. Still, he was not without compensatory considerations, and, upon the whole, took his companion to task for evincing what, in a good-natured, round-about way, he hinted to be a somewhat jaundiced sentimentality. Nature, he added, in Shakespeare's words, had meal and bran*; and, rightly regarded, the bran in its way was not to be condemned.

The other was not disposed to question the justice of Shakespeare's thought, but would hardly admit the propriety of the application in this instance, much less of the comment. So, after some further temperate discussion of the pitiable miser, finding that they could not entirely harmonise, the merchant cited another case, that of the negro cripple. But his companion suggested whether the alleged hardships of that alleged unfortunate might not exist more in the pity of the observer than the experience of the observed. He knew nothing about the cripple, nor had seen him, but ventured to surmise that, could one but get at the real state of his heart, he would be found about as happy as most men, if not, in fact, full as happy as the speaker himself. He added that negroes were by nature a singularly cheerful race; no one ever heard of a native-born African Zimmermann* or Torquemada*; that even from religion they dismissed all gloom; in their hilarious rituals they danced, so to speak, and, as it were, cut pigeon-wings. It was improbable, therefore, that a negro, however reduced to his stumps by fortune, could be ever thrown off the legs of a laughing philosophy.

Foiled again, the good merchant would not desist, but ventured still a third case, that of the man with the weed, whose story, as narrated by himself, and confirmed and filled out by the testimony of a certain man in a gray coat, whom the merchant had afterwards met, he now proceeded to give ; and that, without holding back those particulars disclosed by the second informant, but which delicacy had prevented the unfortunate man himself from touching upon.

But as the good merchant could, perhaps, do better justice to the man than the story, we shall venture to tell it in other words than his, though not to any other effect.

CHAPTER XII

STORY OF THE UNFORTUNATE MAN, FROM WHICH MAY BE
GATHERED WHETHER OR NO HE HAS BEEN JUSTLY
SO ENTITLED

IT appeared that the unfortunate man had had for a
wife one of those natures, anomalously vicious, which
would almost tempt a metaphysical lover of our species
to doubt whether the human form be, in all cases, conclusive evidence of humanity, whether, sometimes, it
may not be a kind of unpledged and indifferent tabernacle,
and whether, once for all to crush the saying of Thrasea*
(an unaccountable one, considering that he himself was
so good a man), that ' he who hates vice, hates humanity,'
it should not, in self-defence, be held for a reasonable
maxim, that none but the good are human.

Goneril* was young, in person lithe and straight, too
straight, indeed, for a woman, a complexion naturally
rosy, and which would have been charmingly so, but
for a certain hardness and bakedness, like that of the
glazed colours on stone-ware. Her hair was of a deep,
rich chestnut, but worn in close, short curls all round
her head. Her Indian figure was not without its impairing effect on her bust, while her mouth would have
been pretty but for a trace of moustache. Upon the
whole, aided by the resources of the toilet, her appearance at distance was such, that some might have thought
her, if anything, rather beautiful, though of a style of
beauty rather peculiar and cactus-like.

It was happy for Goneril that her more striking peculiarities were less of the person than of temper and taste. One hardly knows how to reveal, that, while having a natural antipathy to such things as the breast of chicken, or custard, or peach, or grape, Goneril could yet in private make a satisfactory lunch on hard crackers and brawn of ham. She liked lemons, and the only kind of candy she loved were little dried sticks of blue clay, secretly carried in her pocket. Withal she had hard, steady health like a squaw's, with as firm a spirit and resolution. Some other points about her were likewise such as pertain to the women of savage life. Lithe though she was, she loved supineness, but upon occasion could endure like a stoic. She was taciturn, too. From early morning till about three o'clock in the afternoon she would seldom speak—it taking that time to thaw her, by all accounts, into but talking terms with humanity. During the interval she did little but look, and keep looking out of her large, metallic eyes, which her enemies called cold as a cuttle-fish's, but which by her were esteemed gazelle-like ; for Goneril was not without vanity. Those who thought they best knew her, often wondered what happiness such a being could take in life, not considering the happiness which is to be had by some natures in the very easy way of simply causing pain to those around them. Those who suffered from Goneril's strange nature, might, with one of those hyberboles to which the resentful incline, have pronounced her some kind of toad ; but her worst slanderers could never, with any show of justice, have accused her of being a toady. In a large sense she possessed the virtue of independence of mind. Goneril held it flattery to hint praise even of the absent, and even if merited ; but honesty, to fling people's imputed faults into their faces. This was thought malice, but it certainly was not passion. Passion is human. Like an icicle-dagger, Goneril at once stabbed

and froze ; so at least they said ; and when she saw
frankness and innocence tyrannised into sad nervousness
under her spell, according to the same authority, inly
she chewed her blue clay, and you could mark that she
chuckled. These peculiarities were strange and unpleasing ; but another was alleged, one really incompre-
hensible. In company she had a strange way of touching, as by accident, the arm or hand of comely young
men, and seemed to reap a secret delight from it, but
whether from the humane satisfaction of having given
the evil-touch, as it is called, or whether it was something else in her, not equally wonderful, but quite as
deplorable, remained an enigma.

Needless to say what distress was the unfortunate
man's, when, engaged in conversation with company,
he would suddenly perceive his Goneril bestowing her
mysterious touches, especially in such cases where the
strangeness of the thing seemed to strike upon the
touched person, notwithstanding good-breeding forbade
his proposing the mystery, on the spot, as a subject of
discussion for the company. In these cases, too, the
unfortunate man could never endure so much as to look
upon the touched young gentleman afterward, fearful of
the mortification of meeting in his countenance some
kind of more or less quizzingly-knowing expression. He
would shudderingly shun the young gentleman. So that
here, to the husband, Goneril's touch had the dread
operation of the heathen taboo. Now Goneril brooked
no chiding. So, at favourable times, he, in a wary
manner, and not indelicately, would venture in private
interviews gently to make distant allusions to this
questionable propensity. She divined him. But, in her
cold loveless way, said it was witless to be telling one's
dreams, especially foolish ones ; but if the unfortunate
man liked connubially to rejoice his soul with such

chimeras, much connubial joy might they give him. All this was sad—a touching case—but all might, perhaps, have been borne by the unfortunate man—conscientiously mindful of his vow—for better or for worse—to love and cherish his dear Goneril so long as kind heaven might spare her to him—but when, after all that had happened, the devil of jealousy entered her, a calm, clayey, cakey devil, for none other could possess her, and the object of that deranged jealousy, her own child, a little girl of seven, her father's consolation and pet; when he saw Goneril artfully torment the little innocent, and then play the maternal hypocrite with it, the unfortunate man's patient long-suffering gave way. Knowing that she would neither confess nor amend, and might, possibly, become even worse than she was, he thought it but duty as a father, to withdraw the child from her; but, loving it as he did, he could not do so without accompanying it into domestic exile himself. Which, hard though it was, he did. Whereupon the whole female neighbour-hood, who till now had little enough admired dame Goneril, broke out in indignation against a husband, who, without assigning a cause, could deliberately abandon the wife of his bosom, and sharpen the sting to her, too, by depriving her of the solace of retaining her offspring. To all this, self-respect, with Christian charity toward Goneril, long kept the unfortunate man dumb. And well had it been had he continued so; for when, driven to desperation, he hinted something of the truth of the case, not a soul would credit it; while for Goneril, she pronounced all he said to be a malicious invention. Ere long, at the suggestion of some woman's-rights women, the injured wife began a suit, and, thanks to able counsel and accommodating testimony, succeeded in such a way, as not only to recover custody of the child, but to get such a settlement awarded upon a

separation, as to make penniless the unfortunate man (so
he averred), besides, through the legal sympathy she
enlisted, effecting a judicial blasting of his private
reputation. What made it yet more lamentable was,
that the unfortunate man, thinking that, before the
court, his wisest plan, as well as the most Christian,
besides being, as he deemed, not at variance with the
truth of the matter, would be to put forth the plea of
the mental derangement of Goneril, which done, he
could, with less of mortification to himself, and odium
to her, reveal in self-defence those eccentricities which
had led to his retirement from the joys of wedlock,
had much ado in the end to prevent this charge of
derangement from fatally recoiling upon himself—especially, when, among other things, he alleged her mysterious
touchings. In vain did his counsel, striving to make
out the derangement to be where, in fact, if anywhere,
it was, urge that, to hold otherwise, to hold that such a
being as Goneril was sane, this was constructively a
libel upon womankind. Libel be it. And all ended by
the unfortunate man's subsequently getting wind of
Goneril's intention to procure him to be permanently
committed for a lunatic. Upon which he fled, and was
now an innocent outcast, wandering forlorn in the great
valley of the Mississippi, with a weed on his hat for the
loss of his Goneril ; for he had lately seen by the papers
that she was dead, and thought it but proper to comply
with the prescribed form of mourning in such cases.
For some days past he had been trying to get money
enough to return to his child, and was but now started
with inadequate funds.

Now all of this, from the beginning, the good merchant
could not but consider rather hard for the unfortunate
man.

CHAPTER XIII

THE MAN WITH THE TRAVELLING-CAP EVINCES MUCH HUMANITY, AND IN A WAY WHICH WOULD SEEM TO SHOW HIM TO BE ONE OF THE MOST LOGICAL OF OPTIMISTS

YEARS ago, a grave American savant,* being in London, observed at an evening party there, a certain coxcombical fellow, as he thought, an absurd ribbon in his lapel, and full of smart persiflage, whisking about to the admiration of as many as were disposed to admire. Great was the savant's disdain; but, chancing ere long to find himself in a corner with the jackanapes, got into conversation with him, when he was somewhat ill-prepared for the good sense of the jackanapes, but was altogether thrown aback, upon subsequently being whispered by a friend that the jackanapes was almost as great a savant as himself, being no less a personage than Sir Humphry Davy.*

The above anecdote is given just here by way of an anticipative reminder to such readers as, from the kind of jaunty levity, or what may have passed for such, hitherto for the most part appearing in the man with the travelling-cap, may have been tempted into a more or less hasty estimate of him; that such readers, when they find the same person, as they presently will, capable of philosophic and humanitarian discourse—no mere casual sentence or two as heretofore at times, but solidly sustained throughout an almost entire sitting; that they may not, like the American savant, be thereupon betrayed into any surprise incompatible with their own good opinion of their previous penetration.

The merchant's narration being ended, the other would not deny but that it did in some degree affect him. He hoped he was not without proper feeling for the unfortunate man. But he begged to know in what spirit he bore his alleged calamities. Did he despond or have confidence ?

The merchant did not, perhaps, take the exact import of the last member of the question ; but answered, that, if whether the unfortunate man was becomingly resigned under his affliction or no, was the point, he could say for him that resigned he was, and to an exemplary degree : for not only, so far as known, did he refrain from any one-sided reflections upon human goodness and human justice, but there was observable in him an air of chastened reliance, and at times tempered cheerfulness.

Upon which the other observed, that since the unfortunate man's alleged experience could not be deemed very conciliatory toward a view of human nature better than human nature was, it largely redounded to his fair-mindedness, as well as piety, that under the alleged dissuasives, apparently so, from philanthropy, he had not, in a moment of excitement, been warped over to the ranks of misanthropes. He doubted not, also, that with such a man his experience would, in the end, act by a complete and beneficent inversion, and so far from shaking his confidence in his kind, confirm it, and rivet it. Which would the more surely be the case, did he (the unfortunate man) at last become satisfied (as sooner or later he probably would be) that in the distraction of his mind his Goneril had not in all respects had fair play. At all events, the description of the lady, charity could not but regard as more or less exaggerated, and so far unjust. The truth probably was that she was a wife with some blemishes mixed with some beauties. But when the blemishes were displayed, her husband, no adept in the female nature, had tried to use reason with her, instead of something far more persuasive. Hence his failure to convince and convert. The act of withdrawing from her, seemed, under the circumstances, abrupt. In brief, there were probably small faults on both sides, more than balanced by large virtues ; and one should not be hasty in judging.

When the merchant, strange to say, opposed views so calm and impartial, and again, with some warmth, deplored the case of the unfortunate man, his companion, not without seriousness, checked him, saying, that this would never do ; that, though but in the most exceptional case, to admit the existence of unmerited misery, more particularly if alleged to have been brought about by unhindered arts of the wicked, such an admission was, to say the least, not prudent ; since, with some, it might unfavourably bias their most important persuasions. Not that those persuasions were legitimately servile to such influences. Because, since the common occurrences of life could never, in the nature of things, steadily look one way and tell one story, as flags in the trade-wind ; hence, if the conviction of a Providence, for instance, were in any way made dependent upon such variabilities as everyday events, the degree of that conviction would, in thinking minds, be subject to fluctuations akin to those of the stock-exchange during a long and uncertain war. Here he glanced aside at his transfer-book, and after a moment's pause continued. It was of the essence of a right conviction of the divine nature, as with a right conviction of the human, that, based less on experience than intuition, it rose above the zones of weather.

When now the merchant, with all his heart, coincided

with this (as being a sensible, as well as religious person, he could not but do), his companion expressed satisfaction, that, in an age of some distrust on such subjects, he could yet meet with one who shared with him, almost to the full, so sound and sublime a confidence.

Still, he was far from the illiberality of denying that philosophy duly bounded was not permissible. Only he deemed it at least desirable that, when such a case as that alleged of the unfortunate man was made the subject of philosophic discussion, it should be so philosophised upon, as not to afford handles to those unblessed with the true light. For, but to grant that there was so much as a mystery about such a case, might by those persons be held for a tacit surrender of the question. And as for the apparent licence temporarily permitted sometimes, to the bad over the good (as was by implication alleged with regard to Goneril and the unfortunate man), it might be injudicious there to lay too much polemic stress upon the doctrine of future retribution as the vindication of present impunity. For though, indeed, to the right-minded that doctrine was true, and of sufficient solace, yet with the perverse the polemic mention of it might but provoke the shallow, though mischievous conceit, that such a doctrine was but tantamount to the one which should affirm that Providence was not now, but was going to be. In short, with all sorts of cavillers, it was best, both for them and everybody, that whoever had the true light should stick behind the secure Malakoff* of confidence, nor be tempted forth to hazardous skirmishes on the open ground of reason. Therefore, he deemed it unadvisable in the good man, even in the privacy of his own mind, or in communion with a congenial one, to indulge in too much latitude of philosophising, or, indeed, of compassionating, since this might beget an indiscreet habit of thinking and feeling which might unexpectedly betray him upon unsuitable occasions. Indeed, whether in private or public, there was nothing which a good man was more bound to guard himself against than, on some topics, the emotional unreserve of his natural heart ; for, that the natural heart, in certain points, was not what it might be, men had been authoritatively admonished.

But he thought he might be getting dry.

The merchant, in his good-nature, thought otherwise, and said that he would be glad to refresh himself with such fruit all day. It was sitting under a ripe pulpit, and better such a seat than under a ripe peach-tree.

The other was pleased to find that he had not, as he feared, been prosing ; but would rather not be considered in the formal light of a preacher ; he preferred being still received in that of the equal and genial companion. To which end, throwing still more of sociability into his manner, he again reverted to the unfortunate man. Take the very worst view of that case ; admit that his Goneril was, indeed, a Goneril ; how fortunate to be at last rid of this Goneril, both by nature and by law ? If he were acquainted with the unfortunate man, instead of condoling with him, he would congratulate him. Great good fortune had this unfortunate man. Lucky dog, he dared say, after all.

To which the merchant replied, that he earnestly hoped it might be so, and at any rate he tried his best to comfort himself with the persuasion that, if the unfortunate man was not happy in this world, he would, at least, be so in another.

His companion made no question of the unfortunate man's happiness in both worlds ; and, presently calling for some champagne, invited the merchant to partake, upon the playful plea that, whatever notions other than felicitous ones he might associate with the unfortunate man, a little champagne would readily bubble away.

At intervals they slowly quaffed several glasses in silence and thoughtfulness. At last the merchant's expressive face flushed, his eye moistly beamed, his lips trembled with an imaginative and feminine sensibility. Without sending a single fume to his head, the wine seemed to shoot to his heart, and begin soothsaying there. ' Ah,' he cried, pushing his glass from him, ' Ah, wine is good, and confidence is good ; but can wine or confidence percolate down through all the stony strata of hard considerations, and drop warmly and ruddily into the cold cave of truth ? Truth will *not* be comforted. Led by dear charity, lured by sweet hope, fond fancy essays this feat ; but in vain ; mere dreams and ideals, they explode in your hand, leaving naught but the scorching behind ! '

' Why, why, why ! ' in amaze, at the burst ; ' bless me, if *In vino veritas** be a true saying, then, for all the fine confidence you professed with me, just now, distrust, deep distrust, underlies it ; and ten thousand strong, like the Irish Rebellion,* breaks out in you now. That wine, good wine, should do it ! Upon my soul,' half seriously, half humorously, securing the bottle, ' you shall drink no more of it. Wine was meant to gladden the heart, not grieve it ; to heighten confidence, not depress it.'

Sobered, shamed, all but confounded by this raillery, the most telling rebuke under such circumstances, the merchant stared about him, and then, with altered mien, stammeringly confessed, that he was almost as much surprised as his companion, at what had escaped him. He did not understand it ; was quite at a loss to account for such a rhapsody popping out of him unbidden. It could hardly be the champagne ; he felt his brain unaffected ; in fact, if anything, the wine had acted upon it something like white of egg in coffee, clarifying and brightening.'

'Brightening ? brightening it may be, but less the white of egg in coffee, than like stove-lustre on a stove—black, brightening seriously. I repent calling for the champagne. To a temperament like yours, champagne is not to be recommended. Pray, my dear sir, do you feel quite yourself again ?   Confidence restored ? '

' I hope so ; I think I may say it is so.   But we have had a long talk, and I think I must retire now.'

So saying, the merchant rose, and making his adieus, left the table with the air of one, mortified at having been tempted by his own honest goodness, accidentally stimulated into making mad disclosures—to himself as to another—of the queer, unaccountable caprices of his natural heart.

CHAPTER XIV

WORTH THE CONSIDERATION OF THOSE TO WHOM
IT MAY PROVE WORTH CONSIDERING

As the last chapter was begun with a reminder looking forward, so the present must consist of one glancing backward.

To some, it may raise a degree of surprise that one so full of confidence, as the merchant has throughout shown himself, up to the moment of his late sudden impulsiveness, should, in that instance, have betrayed such a depth of discontent. He may be thought inconsistent, and even so he is. But for this, is the author to be blamed ? True, it may be urged that there is nothing a writer of fiction should more carefully see to, as there is nothing a sensible reader will more carefully look for, than that, in the depiction of any character, its consistency should be preserved. But this, though at first blush seeming reasonable enough, may, upon a closer view, prove not so much so. For how does it couple with another requirement—equally insisted upon, perhaps—that, while to all fiction is allowed some play of invention, yet, fiction based on fact should never be contradictory to it ; and is it not a fact, that, in real life, a consistent character is a *rara avis* ?* Which being so, the distaste of readers to the contrary sort in books, can hardly arise from any sense of their untrueness. It may rather be from perplexity as to understanding them. But if the acutest sage be often at his wits' ends to understand living character, shall those who are not sages

expect to run and read*character in those mere phantoms
which flit along a page, like shadows along a wall ?   That
fiction, where every character can, by reason of its consistency, be comprehended at a glance, either exhibits
but sections of character, making them appear for wholes,
or else is very untrue to reality ; while, on the other
hand, that author who draws a character, even though
to common view incongruous in its parts, as the flying-
squirrel, and, at different periods, as much at variance
with itself as the caterpillar is with the butterfly* into
which it changes, may yet, in so doing, be not false but
faithful to facts.

If reason be judge, no writer has produced such inconsistent characters as nature herself has.   It must call
for no small sagacity in a reader unerringly to discriminate
in a novel between the inconsistencies of conception and
those of life as elsewhere.   Experience is the only guide
here ; but as no one man can be coextensive with *what is*,
it may be unwise in every case to rest upon it.   When
the duck-billed beaver of Australia was first brought
stuffed to England, the naturalists, appealing to their
classifications, maintained that there was, in reality, no
such creature ; the bill in the specimen must needs be,
in some way, artificially stuck on.

But let nature, to the perplexity of the naturalists,
produce her duck-billed beavers as she may, lesser
authors, some may hold, have no business to be per-
plexing readers with duck-billed characters. Always,
they should represent human nature not in obscurity,
but transparency, which, indeed, is the practice with
most novelists, and is, perhaps, in certain cases, some way
felt to be a kind of honour rendered by them to their
kind.   But whether it involve honour or otherwise might
be mooted, considering that, if these waters of human
nature can be so readily seen through, it may be either

that they are very pure or very shallow. Upon the whole, it might rather be thought, that he, who, in view of its inconsistencies, says of human nature the same that, in view of its contrasts, is said of the divine nature, that it is past finding out, thereby evinces a better appreciation of it than he who, by always representing it in a clear light, leaves it to be inferred that he clearly knows all about it.

But though there is a prejudice against inconsistent characters in books, yet the prejudice bears the other way, when what seemed at first their inconsistency, afterward, by the skill of the writer, turns out to be their good keeping. The great masters excel in nothing so much as in this very particular. They challenge astonishment at the tangled web of some character, and then raise admiration still greater at their satisfactory unravelling of it ; in this way throwing open, sometimes to the understanding even of school misses, the last complications of that spirit which is affirmed by its Creator to be fearfully and wonderfully made.*

At least, something like this is claimed for certain psychological novelists ; nor will the claim be here disputed. Yet, as touching this point, it may prove suggestive, that all those sallies of ingenuity, having for their end the revelation of human nature on fixed principles, have, by the best judges, been excluded with contempt from the ranks of the sciences—palmistry, physiognomy, phrenology, psychology. Likewise, the fact, that in all ages such conflicting views have, by the most eminent minds, been taken of mankind, would, as with other topics, seem some presumption of a pretty general and pretty thorough ignorance of it. Which may appear the less improbable if it be considered that, after poring over the best novels professing to portray human nature, the studious youth will still run risk of

being too often at fault upon actually entering the
world; whereas, had he been furnished with a true
delineation, it ought to fare with him something as with
a stranger entering, map in hand, Boston town; the
streets may be very crooked, he may often pause; but,
thanks to his true map, he does not hopelessly lose his
way. Nor, to this comparison, can it be an adequate
objection, that the twistings of the town are always the
same, and those of human nature subject to variation.
The grand points of human nature are the same to-day
they were a thousand years ago. The only variability
in them is in expression, not in feature.

But as, in spite of seeming discouragement, some
mathematicians are yet in hopes of hitting upon an
exact method of determining the longitude, the more
earnest psychologists may, in the face of previous failures,
still cherish expectations with regard to some mode of
infallibly discovering the heart of man.

But enough has been said by way of apology for
whatever may have seemed amiss or obscure in the
character of the merchant; so nothing remains but to
turn to our comedy, or, rather, to pass from the comedy
of thought to that of action.

CHAPTER XV

THE merchant having withdrawn, the other remained
seated alone for a time, with the air of one who, after
having conversed with some excellent man, carefully
ponders what fell from him, however intellectually
inferior it may be, that none of the profit may be lost ;
happy if from any honest word he has heard he can
derive some hint, which, besides confirming him in the
theory of virtue, may, likewise, serve for a finger-post to
virtuous action.

Ere long his eye brightened, as if some such hint was
now caught. He rises, book in hand, quits the cabin,
and enters upon a sort of corridor, narrow and dim, a
by-way to a retreat less ornate and cheery than the
former ; in short, the emigrants' quarters ; but which,
owing to the present trip being a down-river one, will
doubtless be found comparatively tenantless. Owing to
obstructions against the side windows, the whole place
is dim and dusky ; very much so, for the most part ;
yet, by starts, haggardly lit here and there by narrow,
capricious skylights in the cornices. But there would
seem no special need for light, the place being designed
more to pass the night in, than the day ; in brief, a pine
barrens* dormitory, of knotty pine bunks, without
bedding. As with the nests in the geometrical towns of
the associate penguin and pelican, these bunks were dis-

posed with Philadelphian regularity,* but, like the cradle of the oriole, they were pendulous, and, moreover, were, so to speak, three-story cradles; the description of one of which will suffice for all.

Four ropes, secured to the ceiling, passed downwards through auger-holes bored in the corners of three rough planks, which at equal distances rested on knots vertically tied in the ropes, the lowermost plank but an inch or two from the floor, the whole affair resembling, on a large scale, rope book-shelves; only, instead of hanging firmly against a wall, they swayed to and fro at the least suggestion of motion, but were more especially lively upon the provocation of a green emigrant sprawling into one, and trying to lay himself out there, when the cradling would be such as almost to toss him back whence he came. In consequence, one less inexperienced, essaying repose on the uppermost shelf, was liable to serious disturbance, should a raw beginner select a shelf beneath. Sometimes a throng of poor emigrants, coming at night in a sudden rain to occupy these oriole nests, would—through ignorance of their peculiarity—bring about such a rocking uproar of carpentry, joining to it such an uproar of exclamations, that it seemed as if some luckless ship, with all its crew, was being dashed to pieces among the rocks. They were beds devised by some sardonic foe of poor travellers, to deprive them of that tranquillity which should precede, as well as accompany, slumber.—Procrustean beds,* on whose hard grain humble worth and honesty writhed, still invoking repose, while but torment responded. Ah, did anyone make such a bunk for himself, instead of having it made for him, it might be just, but how cruel, to say, You must lie on it!

But, purgatory as the place would appear, the stranger advances into it; and, like Orpheus in his gay descent* to Tartarus, lightly hums to himself an opera snatch.

Suddenly there is a rustling, then a creaking, one of the cradles swings out from a murky nook, a sort of wasted penguin-flipper is supplicatingly put forth, while a wail like that of Dives* is heard :—
'Water, water ! '

It was the miser of whom the merchant had spoken.

Swift as a sister-of-charity, the stranger hovers over him :—

'My poor, poor sir, what can I do for you ? '

'Ugh, ugh—water ! '

Darting out, he procures a glass, returns, and, holding it to the sufferer's lips, supports his head while he drinks : 'And did they let you lie here, my poor sir, racked with this parching thirst ? '

The miser, a lean old man, whose flesh seemed salted codfish, dry as combustibles ; head, like one whittled by an idiot out of a knot ; flat, bony mouth, nipped between buzzard nose and chin ; expression, flitting between hunks*and imbecile—now one, now the other—he made no response. His eyes were closed, his cheek lay upon an old white moleskin coat, rolled under his head like a wizened apple upon a grimy snow-bank.

Revived at last, he inclined toward his ministrant, and, in a voice disastrous with a cough, said : 'I am old and miserable, a poor beggar, not worth a shoe-string— how can I repay you ? '

'By giving me your confidence.'

'Confidence ! ' he squeaked, with changed manner, while the pallet swung ; 'little left at my age, but take the stale remains, and welcome.'

'Such as it is, though, you give it. Very good. Now give me a hundred dollars.'

Upon this the miser was all panic. His hands groped

toward his waist, then suddenly flew upward beneath his moleskin pillow, and there lay clutching something out of sight. Meantime, to himself he incoherently mumbled : ' Confidence ? Cant, gammon !* Confidence ? hum, bubble !—Confidence ? fetch, gouge !—Hundred dollars ?—hundred devils ! '

Half spent, he lay mute awhile, then feebly raising himself, in a voice for the moment made strong by the sarcasm, said : ' A hundred dollars ? rather high price to put upon confidence. But don't you see I am a poor, old rat here, dying in the wainscot ? You have served me ; but, wretch that I am, I can but cough you my thanks,—ugh, ugh, ugh ! '

This time his cough was so violent that its convulsions were imparted to the plank, which swung him about like a stone in a sling preparatory to its being hurled.

' Ugh, ugh, ugh ! '

' What a shocking cough. I wish, my friend, the herb-doctor was here now ; a box of his Omni-Balsamic Reinvigorator would do you good.'

' Ugh, ugh, ugh ! '

' I 've a good mind to go find him. He 's aboard somewhere. I saw his long, snuff-coloured surtout. Trust me, his medicines are the best in the world.'

' Ugh, ugh, ugh ! '

' Oh, how sorry I am.'

' No doubt of it,' squeaked the other again, ' but go, get your charity out on deck. There parade the pursy peacocks ; they don't cough down here in desertion and darkness, like poor old me. Look how scaly a pauper I am, clove with this churchyard cough. Ugh, ugh, ugh ! '

' Again, how sorry I feel, not only for your cough, but your poverty. Such a rare chance made unavailable. Did you have but the sum named, how I could invest it for you. Treble profits. But confidence—I fear that, even had you the precious cash, you would not have the more precious confidence I speak of.'

'Ugh, ugh, ugh!' flightily raising himself. 'What's that? How, how? Then you don't want the money for yourself?'

'My dear, *dear* sir, how could you impute to me such preposterous self-seeking? To solicit out of hand, for my private behoof, an hundred dollars from a perfect stranger? I am not mad, my dear sir.'

'How, how?' still more bewildered, 'do you, then, go about the world, gratis, seeking to invest people's money for them?'

'My humble profession, sir. I live not for myself; but the world will not have confidence in me, and yet confidence in me were great gain.'

'But, but,' in a kind of vertigo, 'what do—do you do—do with people's money? Ugh, ugh! How is the gain made?'

'To tell that would ruin me. That known, everyone would be going into the business, and it would be overdone. A secret, a mystery—all I have to do with you is to receive your confidence, and all you have to do with me is, in due time, to receive it back, thrice paid in trebling profits.'

'What, what?' imbecility in the ascendant once more; 'but the vouchers, the vouchers,' suddenly hunkish again.

'Honesty's best voucher is honesty's face.'

'Can't see yours, though,' peering through the obscurity.

From this last alternating flicker of rationality, the miser fell back, sputtering, into his previous gibberish, but it took now an arithmetical turn. Eyes closed, he lay muttering to himself :—

'One hundred, one hundred—two hundred, two hundred—three hundred, three hundred.'

He opened his eyes, feebly stared, and still more feebly said :—

'It's a little dim here, ain't it ? Ugh, ugh ! But, as well as my poor old eyes can see, you look honest.'

'I am glad to hear that.'

'If—if, now, I should put '—trying to raise himself, but vainly, excitement having all but exhausted him— 'if, if now, I should put, put——'

'No ifs. Downright confidence, or none. So help me heaven, I will have no half-confidences.'

He said it with an indifferent and superior air, and seemed moving to go.

'Don't, don't leave me, friend ; bear with me ; age can't help some distrust ; it can't, friend, it can't. Ugh, ugh, ugh ! Oh, I am so old and miserable. I ought to have a guardeean. Tell me, if——'

'If ? No more ! '

'Stay ! how soon—ugh, ugh !—would my money be trebled ? How soon, friend ? '

'You won't confide. Good-bye ! '

'Stay, stay,' falling back now like an infant, 'I confide, I confide ; help, friend, my distrust ! '*

From an old buckskin pouch, tremulously dragged forth, ten hoarded eagles, tarnished into the appearance of ten old horn-buttons, were taken, and half eagerly, half reluctantly, offered.

'I know not whether I should accept this slack confidence,' said the other coldly, receiving the gold, 'but an eleventh-hour confidence, a sick-bed confidence, a distempered, death-bed confidence, after all. Give me the healthy confidence of healthy men, with their healthy wits about them. But let that pass. All right. Good-bye ! '

'Nay, back, back—receipt, my receipt! Ugh, ugh, ugh! Who are you? What have I done? Where go you? My gold, my gold! Ugh, ugh, ugh!'

But, unluckily for this final flicker of reason, the stranger was now beyond earshot, nor was anyone else within hearing of so feeble a call.

CHAPTER XVI

A SICK MAN, AFTER SOME IMPATIENCE, IS INDUCED TO BECOME A PATIENT

THE sky slides into blue, the bluffs into bloom; the rapid Mississippi expands; runs sparkling and gurgling, all over in eddies; one magnified wake of a seventy-four.* The sun comes out, a golden hussar, from his tent, flashing his helm on the world. All things, warmed in the landscape, leap. Speeds the daedal* boat as a dream.

But, withdrawn in a corner, wrapped about in a shawl, sits an unparticipating man, visited, but not warmed, by the sun—a plant whose hour seems over, while buds are blowing and seeds are astir. On a stool at his left sits a stranger in a snuff-coloured surtout,* the collar thrown back; his hand waving in persuasive gesture, his eye beaming with hope. But not easily may hope be awakened in one long tranced into hopelessness by a chronic complaint.

To some remark the sick man, by word or look, seemed to have just made an impatiently querulous answer, when, with a deprecatory air, the other resumed :—

'Nay, think not I seek to cry up my treatment by crying down that of others. And yet, when one is confident he has truth on his side, and that it is not on the other, it is no very easy thing to be charitable; not that temper is the bar, but conscience; for charity would beget toleration, you know, which is a kind of implied permitting, and in effect a kind of countenan-

cing ; and that which is countenanced is so far furthered.
But should untruth be furthered ? Still, while for the
world's good I refuse to further the cause of these mineral
doctors, I would fain regard them, not as wilful wrong-
doers, but good Samaritans* erring. And is this—I put
it to you, sir—is this the view of an arrogant rival
and pretender ? '

His physical power all dribbled and gone, the sick
man replied not by voice or by gesture ; but, with feeble
dumb-show of his face, seemed to be saying, ' Pray leave
me ; who was ever cured by talk ? '

But the other, as if not unused to make allowances
for such despondency, proceeded ; and kindly, yet
firmly :—

' You tell me, that by advice of an eminent physiologist
in Louisville, you took tincture of iron. For what ? To
restore your lost energy. And how ? Why, in healthy
subjects iron is naturally found in the blood, and iron
in the bar is strong ; ergo, iron is the source of animal
invigoration. But you being deficient in vigour, it
follows that the cause is deficiency of iron. Iron, then,
must be put into you ; and so your tincture. Now as to
the theory here, I am mute. But in modesty assuming
its truth, and then, as a plain man viewing that theory
in practice, I would respectfully question your eminent
physiologist : " Sir," I would say, " though by natural
processes, lifeless natures taken as nutriment become
vitalised, yet is a lifeless nature, under any circumstances, capable of a living transmission, with all its
qualities as a lifeless nature unchanged ? If, sir, nothing
can be incorporated with the living body but by assimila-
tion, and if that implies the conversion of one thing to
a different thing (as, in a lamp, oil is assimilated into
flame), is it, in this view, likely, that by banqueting on
fat, Calvin Edson* will fatten ? That is, will what is

fat on the board prove fat on the bones ? If it will,
then, sir, what is iron in the vial will prove iron in the
vein." Seems that conclusion too confident ? '

But the sick man again turned his dumb-show look,
as much as to say, ' Pray leave me. Why, with painful
words, hint the vanity of that which the pains of this
body have too painfully proved ? ' But the other, as if
unobservant of that querulous look, went on :—

' But this notion, that science can play farmer to the
flesh, making there what living soil it pleases, seems not
so strange as that other conceit—that science is nowadays
so expert that, in consumptive cases, as yours, it can,
by prescription of the inhalation of certain vapours,
achieve the sublimest act of omnipotence, breathing into
all but lifeless dust the breath of life. For did you not
tell me, my poor sir, that by order of the great chemist
in Baltimore, for three weeks you were never driven out
without a respirator, and for a given time of every day
sat bolstered up in a sort of gasometer, inspiring vapours
generated by the burning of drugs ? as if this concocted
atmosphere of man were an antidote to the poison of
God's natural air. Oh, who can wonder at that old
reproach against science, that it is atheistical ? And
here is my prime reason for opposing these chemical
practitioners, who have sought out so many inventions.
For what do their inventions indicate, unless it be that
kind and degree of pride in human skill, which seems
scarce compatible with reverential dependence upon the
power above ? Try to rid my mind of it as I may, yet
still these chemical practitioners with their tinctures,
and fumes, and braziers, and occult incantations, seem
to me like Pharaoh's vain sorcerers,* trying to beat down
the will of heaven. Day and night, in all charity, I
intercede for them, that heaven may not, in its own
language, be provoked to anger with their inventions*;

may not take vengeance of their inventions. A thousand
pities that you should ever have been in the hands of
these Egyptians.'

But again came nothing but the dumb-show look, as
much as to say, ' Pray, leave me ; quacks, and indignation against quacks, both are vain.'

But, once more, the other went on : ' How different
we herb-doctors ! who claim nothing, invent nothing ;
but staff in hand, in glades, and upon hillsides, go about
in nature, humbly seeking her cures. True Indian doctors,
though not learned in names, we are not unfamiliar with
essences—successors of Solomon the Wise, who knew
all vegetables, from the cedar of Lebanon, to the hyssop
on the wall.* Yes, Solomon was the first of herb-doctors.
Nor were the virtues of herbs unhonoured by yet older
ages. Is it not writ, that on a moonlight night,

> " Medea gathered the enchanted herbs,
> That did renew old Æson."*

Ah, would you but have confidence, you should be the
new Æson, and I your Medea.* A few vials of my Omni-
Balsamic Reinvigorator would, I am certain, give you
some strength.'

Upon this, indignation and abhorrence seemed to
work by their excess the effect promised of the balsam.
Roused from that long apathy of impotence, the cadaver-
ous man started, and, in a voice that was as the sound
of obstructed air gurgling through a maze of broken
honey-combs, cried : ' Begone ! You are all alike. The
name of doctor, the dream of helper, condemns you.
For years I have been but a gallipot for you experiment-
isers to rinse your experiments into, and now, in this
livid skin, partake of the nature of my contents. Begone ! I hate ye.'

' I were inhuman, could I take affront at a want of

confidence, born of too bitter an experience of betrayers.
Yet, permit one who is not without feeling——'

'Begone! Just in that voice talked to me, not six
months ago, the German doctor at the water cure, from
which I now return, six months and sixty pangs nigher
my grave.'

'The water cure? Oh, fatal delusion of the well-
meaning Preisnitz !*—Sir, trust me——'

'Begone!'

'Nay, an invalid should not always have his own way.
Ah, sir, reflect how untimely this distrust in one like
you. How weak you are; and weakness, is it not the
time for confidence? Yes, when through weakness everything bids despair, then is the time to get strength by
confidence.'*

Relenting in his air, the sick man cast upon him a
long glance of beseeching, as if saying, 'With confidence
must come hope; and how can hope be?'

The herb-doctor took a sealed paper box from his
surtout pocket, and holding it toward him, said solemnly,
'Turn not away. This may be the last time of health's
asking. Work upon yourself; invoke confidence, though
from ashes; rouse it; for your life, rouse it, and invoke
it, I say.'

The other trembled, was silent; and then, a little
commanding himself, asked the ingredients of the
medicine.

'Herbs.'

'What herbs? And the nature of them? And the
reason for giving them?'

'It cannot be made known.'

'Then I will none of you.'

Sedately observant of the juiceless, joyless form before
him, the herb-doctor was mute a moment, then said:
'I give up.'

' How ? '

' You are sick, and a philosopher.'

' No, no ;—not the last.'

' But to demand the ingredient, with the reason for
giving, is the mark of a philosopher ; just as the consequence is the penalty of a fool. A sick philosopher is
incurable ? '

' Why ? '

' Because he has no confidence.'

' How does that make him incurable ? '

' Because either he spurns his powder, or, if he take
it, it proves a blank cartridge, though the same given to
a rustic in like extremity, would act like a charm. I am
no materialist ; but the mind so acts upon the body,
that if the one have no confidence, neither has the other.'

Again, the sick man appeared not unmoved. He
seemed to be thinking what in candid truth could be
said to all this. At length, ' You talk of confidence.
How comes it that when brought low himself, the herb-
doctor, who was most confident to prescribe in other
cases, proves least confident to prescribe in his own ;
having small confidence in himself for himself ? '

' But he has confidence in the brother he calls in.
And that he does so, is no reproach to him, since he
knows that when the body is prostrated, the mind is
not erect. Yes, in this hour the herb-doctor does distrust himself, but not his art.'

The sick man's knowledge did not warrant him to
gainsay this. But he seemed not grieved at it ; glad
to be confuted in a way tending toward his wish.

' Then you give me hope ? ' his sunken eye turned up.

' Hope is proportioned to confidence. How much
confidence you give me, so much hope do I give you.
For this,' lifting the box, ' if all depended upon this, I
should rest. It is nature's own.'

' Nature ! '

' Why do you start ? '

' I know not,' with a sort of shudder, ' but I have heard of a book entitled *Nature in Disease.*'*

' A title I cannot approve ; it is suspiciously scientific. *Nature in Disease ?* As if nature, divine nature, were aught but health ; as if through nature disease is decreed ! But did I not before hint of the tendency of science, that forbidden tree ? Sir, if despondency is yours from recalling that title, dismiss it. Trust me, nature is health ; for health is good, and nature cannot work ill. As little can she work error. Get nature, and you get well. Now, I repeat, this medicine is nature's own.'

Again the sick man could not, according to his light, conscientiously disprove what was said. Neither, as before, did he seem over-anxious to do so ; the less, as in his sensitiveness it seemed to him, that hardly could he offer so to do without something like the appearance of a kind of implied irreligion ; nor in his heart was he ungrateful, that since a spirit opposite to that pervaded all the herb-doctor's hopeful words, therefore, for hopefulness, he (the sick man) had not alone medical warrant, but also doctrinal.

' Then you do really think,' hectically, ' that if I take this medicine,' mechanically reaching out for it, ' I shall regain my health ? '

' I will not encourage false hopes,' relinquishing to him the box, ' I will be frank with you. Though frankness is not always the weakness of the mineral practitioner, yet the herb doctor must be frank, or nothing. Now then, sir, in your case, a radical cure—such a cure, understand, as should make you robust—such a cure, sir, I do not and cannot promise.'

' Oh, you need not ! only restore me the power of being

something else to others than a burdensome care, and to myself a droning grief. Only cure me of this misery of weakness; only make me so that I can walk about in the sun and not draw the flies to me, as lured by the coming of decay. Only do that—but that.'

'You ask not much; you are wise; not in vain have you suffered. That little you ask, I think, can be granted. But remember, not in a day, nor a week, nor perhaps a month, but sooner or later; I say not exactly when, for I am neither prophet nor charlatan. Still, if, according to the directions in your box there, you take my medicine steadily, without assigning an especial day, near or remote, to discontinue it, then may you calmly look for some eventual result of good. But again I say, you must have confidence.'

Feverishly he replied that he now trusted he had, and hourly should pray for its increase. When suddenly relapsing into one of those strange caprices peculiar to some invalids, he added: 'But to one like me, it is so hard, so hard. The most confident hopes so often have failed me, and as often have I vowed never, no, never, to trust them again. Oh,' feebly wringing his hands, 'you do not know, you do not know.'

'I know this, that never did a right confidence come to naught. But time is short; you hold your cure, to retain or reject.'

'I retain,' with a clinch, 'and now how much ?'

'As much as you can evoke from your heart and heaven.'

'How ?—the price of this medicine ?'

'I thought it was confidence you meant; how much confidence you should have. The medicine,—that is half a dollar a vial. Your box holds six.'

The money was paid.

'Now, sir,' said the herb-doctor, 'my business calls

me away, and it may so be that I shall never see you
again ; if then——'

He paused, for the sick man's countenance fell
blank.

' Forgive me,' cried the other, ' forgive that imprudent
phrase " never see you again." Though I solely intended
it with reference to myself, yet I had forgotten what
your sensitiveness might be. I repeat, then, that it
may be that we shall not soon have a second interview,
so that hereafter, should another of my boxes be needed,
you may not be able to replace it except by purchase at
the shops ; and, in so doing, you may run more or less
risk of taking some not salutary mixture. For such is
the popularity of the Omni-Balsamic Reinvigorator—
thriving not by the credulity of the simple, but the trust
of the wise—that certain contrivers have not been idle,
though I would not, indeed, hastily affirm of them that
they are aware of the sad consequences to the public.
Homicides and murderers, some call those contrivers ;
but I do not ; for murder (if such a crime be possible)
comes from the heart, and these men's motives come
from the purse. Were they not in poverty, I think
they would hardly do what they do. Still, the public
interests forbid that I should let their needy device for
a living succeed. In short, I have adopted precautions.
Take the wrapper from any of my vials and hold it to
the light, you will see water-marked in capitals the
word " confidence," which is the countersign of the
medicine, as I wish it was of the world. The wrapper
bears that mark or else the medicine is counterfeit.
But if still any lurking doubt should remain, pray
enclose the wrapper to this address,' handing a card,
' and by return mail I will answer.'

At first the sick man listened, with the air of vivid
interest, but gradually, while the other was still talking,

another strange caprice came over him, and he presented
the aspect of the most calamitous dejection.

' How now ? ' said the herb-doctor.

' You told me to have confidence, said that confidence
was indispensable, and here you preach to me distrust.
Ah, truth will out ! '

' I told you, you must have confidence, unquestioning
confidence, I meant confidence in the genuine medicine,
and the genuine *me*.'

' But in your absence, buying vials purporting to be
yours, it seems I cannot have unquestioning confidence.'

' Prove all the vials ;* trust those which are true.'

' But to doubt, to suspect, to prove—to have all this
wearing work to be doing continually—how opposed to
confidence.   It is evil ! '

' From evil comes good.   Distrust is a stage to confidence.   How has it proved in our interview ?   But your
voice is husky ; I have let you talk too much.   You
hold your cure ; I leave you.   But stay—when I hear
that health is yours, I will not, like some I know, vainly
make boasts ; but, giving glory where all glory is due,
say, with the devout herb-doctor, Japus in Virgil,* when,
in the unseen but efficacious presence of Venus, he with
simples healed the wound of Æneas :—

> " This is no mortal work, no cure of mine,
>   Nor art's effect, but done by power divine." '

CHAPTER XVII

TOWARD THE END OF WHICH THE HERB-DOCTOR
PROVES HIMSELF A FORGIVER OF INJURIES

IN a kind of ante-cabin, a number of respectable-looking people, male and female, way-passengers, recently come on board, are listlessly sitting in a mutually shy sort of silence.

Holding up a small, square bottle, ovally labelled with the engraving of a countenance full of soft pity as that of the Romish-painted Madonna, the herb-doctor passes slowly among them, benignly urbane, turning this way and that, saying :—

'Ladies and gentlemen, I hold in my hand here the Samaritan Pain Dissuader, thrice-blessed discovery of that disinterested friend of humanity whose portrait you see. Pure vegetable extract. Warranted to remove the acutest pain within less than ten minutes. Five hundred dollars to be forfeited on failure. Especially efficacious in heart disease and tic-douloureux.* Observe the expression of this pledged friend of humanity.—Price only fifty cents.'

In vain. After the first idle stare, his auditors—in pretty good health, it seemed—instead of encouraging his politeness, appeared, if anything, impatient of it ; and, perhaps, only diffidence, or some small regard for his feelings, prevented them from telling him so. But, insensible to their coldness, or charitably overlooking it, he more wooingly than ever resumed : ' May I venture

upon a small supposition ? Have I your kind leave,
ladies and gentlemen ? '

To which modest appeal, no one had the kindness to
answer a syllable.

' Well,' said he, resignedly, ' silence is at least not
denial, and may be consent. My supposition is this :
possibly some lady, here present, has a dear friend at
home, a bed-ridden sufferer from spinal complaint. If
so, what gift more appropriate to that sufferer than this
tasteful little bottle of Pain Dissuader ? '

Again he glanced about him, but met much the same
reception as before. Those faces, alien alike to sympathy
or surprise, seemed patiently to say, ' We are travellers ;
and, as such, must expect to meet, and quietly put up
with, many antic fools, and more antic quacks.'

' Ladies and gentlemen ' (deferentially fixing his eyes
upon their now self-complacent faces), ' ladies and gentlemen, might I, by your kind leave, venture upon one
other small supposition ?   It is this : that there is scarce
a sufferer, this noon-day, writhing on his bed, but in
his hour he sat satisfactorily healthy and happy ; that
the Samaritan Pain Dissuader is the one only balm for
that to which each living creature—who knows ?—may
be a draughted victim, present or prospective. In
short :—Oh, Happiness on my right hand, and oh,
Security on my left, can ye wisely adore a Providence,
and not think it wisdom to provide ?—Provide ! ' (Uplifting the bottle.)

What immediate effect, if any, this appeal might have
had, is uncertain. For just then the boat touched at a
houseless landing, scooped, as by a land-slide, out of
sombre forests ; back through which led a road, the
sole one, which, from its narrowness, and its being walled
up with story on story of dusk, matted foliage, presented
the vista of some cavernous old gorge in a city, like

haunted Cock Lane* in London. Issuing from that road,
and crossing that landing, there stooped his shaggy form
in the doorway, and entered the ante-cabin, with a step
so burdensome that shot seemed in his pockets, a kind of
invalid Titan* in homespun ; his beard blackly pendent,
like the Carolina-moss, and dank with cypress dew ; his
countenance tawny and shadowy as an iron-ore country
in a clouded day. In one hand he carried a heavy
walking-stick of swamp-oak ; with the other, led a puny
girl, walking in moccasins, not improbably his child,
but evidently of alien maternity, perhaps Creole, or even
Camanche. Her eye would have been large for a woman,
and was inky as the pools of falls among mountain pines.
An Indian blanket, orange-hued, and fringed with lead
tassel-work, appeared that morning to have shielded the
child from heavy showers. Her limbs were tremulous ;
she seemed a little Cassandra,* in nervousness.

No sooner was the pair spied by the herb-doctor, than
with a cheerful air, both arms extended like a host's,
he advanced, and taking the child's reluctant hand,
said, trippingly : ' On your travels, ah, my little May
Queen ? Glad to see you. What pretty moccasins.
Nice to dance in.' Then with a half-caper sang—

> ' " Hey diddle, diddle, the cat and the fiddle,
>   The cow jumped over the moon."

Come, chirrup, chirrup, my little robin ! '

Which playful welcome drew no responsive playful-
ness from the child, nor appeared to gladden or conciliate the father ; but rather, if anything, to dash the
dead weight of his heavy-hearted expression with a
smile hypochondriacally scornful.

Sobering down now, the herb-doctor addressed the
stranger in a manly, business-like way—a transition
which, though it might seem a little abrupt, did not

appear constrained, and, indeed, served to show that
his recent levity was less the habit of a frivolous nature,
than the frolic condescension of a kindly heart.

' Excuse me,' said he, ' but, if I err not, I was speaking
to you the other day ;—on a Kentucky boat, wasn't it ? '

' Never to me,' was the reply ; the voice deep and
lonesome enough to have come from the bottom of an
abandoned coal-shaft.

' Ah !—But am I again mistaken (his eye falling on the
swamp-oak stick), or don't you go a little lame, sir ? '

' Never was lame in my life.'

' Indeed ? I fancied I had perceived not a limp, but
a hitch, a slight hitch ; some experience in these things—
divined some hidden cause of the hitch—buried bullet,
maybe—some dragoons in the Mexican war discharged
with such, you know.—Hard fate ! ' he sighed, ' little
pity for it, for who sees it ?—have you dropped anything ? '

Why, there is no telling, but the stranger was bowed
over, and might have seemed bowing for the purpose of
picking up something, were it not that, as arrested in the
imperfect posture, he for the moment so remained ;
slanting his tall stature like a mainmast yielding to the
gale, or Adam to the thunder.

The little child pulled him. With a kind of a surge he
righted himself, for an instant looked toward the herb-
doctor ; but, either from emotion or aversion, or both
together, withdrew his eyes, saying nothing. Presently,
still stooping, he seated himself, drawing his child between his knees, his massy hands tremulous, and still
averting his face, while up into the compassionate one
of the herb-doctor the child turned a fixed, melancholy
glance of repugnance.

The herb-doctor stood observant a moment, then
said :—

'Surely you have pain, strong pain, somewhere; in strong frames pain is strongest. Try, now, my specific' (holding it up). 'Do but look at the expression of this friend of humanity. Trust me, certain cure for any pain in the world. Won't you look?'

'No,' choked the other.

'Very good. Merry time to you, little May Queen.'

And so, as if he would intrude his cure upon no one, moved pleasantly off, again crying his wares, nor now at last without result. A newcomer, not from the shore, but another part of the boat, a sickly young man, after some questions, purchased a bottle. Upon this, others of the company began a little to wake up, as it were; the scales of indifference or prejudice fell from their eyes; now, at last, they seemed to have an inkling that here was something not undesirable which might be had for the buying.

But while, ten times more briskly bland than ever, the herb-doctor was driving his benevolent trade, accompanying each sale with added praises of the thing traded, all at once the dusk giant, seated at some distance, unexpectedly raised his voice with—

'What was that you last said?'

The question was put distinctly, yet resonantly, as when a great clock-bell—stunning admonisher—strikes one; and the stroke, though single, comes bedded in the belfry clamour.

All proceedings were suspended. Hands held forth for the specific were withdrawn, while every eye turned toward the direction whence the question came. But, no way abashed, the herb-doctor, elevating his voice with even more than wonted self-possession, replied—

'I was saying what, since you wish it, I cheerfully repeat, that the Samaritan Pain Dissuader, which I here hold in my hand, will either cure or ease any pain you please, within ten minutes after its application.'

' Does it produce insensibility ? '

' By no means. Not the least of its merits is, that it is not an opiate. It kills pain without killing feeling.'

' You lie ! Some pains cannot be eased but by producing insensibility, and cannot be cured but by producing death.'

Beyond this the dusk giant said nothing ; neither, for impairing the other's market, did there appear much need to. After eyeing the rude speaker a moment with an expression of mingled admiration and consternation, the company silently exchanged glances of mutual sympathy under unwelcome conviction. Those who had purchased looked sheepish or ashamed ; and a cynical-looking little man, with a thin flaggy beard, and a countenance ever wearing the rudiments of a grin, seated alone in a corner commanding a good view of the scene, held a rusty hat before his face.

But, again, the herb-doctor, without noticing the retort, overbearing though it was, began his panegyrics anew, and in a tone more assured than before, going so far now as to say that his specific was sometimes almost as effective in cases of mental suffering as in cases of physical ; or rather, to be more precise, in cases when, through sympathy, the two sorts of pain co-operated into a climax of both—in such cases, he said, the specific had done very well. He cited an example : Only three bottles, faithfully taken, cured a Louisiana widow (for three weeks sleepless in a darkened chamber) of neuralgic sorrow for the loss of husband and child, swept off in one night by the last epidemic. For the truth of this, a printed voucher was produced, duly signed.

While he was reading it aloud, a sudden side-blow all but felled him.

It was the giant, who, with a countenance lividly epileptic with hypochondriac mania, exclaimed—

'Profane fiddler on heart-strings ! Snake ! '

More he would have added, but, convulsed, could not ; so, without another word, taking up the child, who had followed him, went with a rocking pace out of the cabin.

'Regardless of decency, and lost to humanity ! ' exclaimed the herb-doctor, with much ado recovering himself. Then, after a pause, during which he examined his bruise, not omitting to apply externally a little of his specific, and with some success, as it would seem, plained to himself :

'No, no, I won't seek redress ; innocence is my redress. But,' turning upon them all, 'if that man's wrathful blow provokes me to no wrath, should his evil distrust arouse you to distrust ? I do devoutly hope,' proudly raising voice and arm, 'for the honour of humanity— hope that, despite this coward assault, the Samaritan Pain Dissuader stands unshaken in the confidence of all who hear me ! '

But, injured as he was, and patient under it, too, somehow his case excited as little compassion as his oratory now did enthusiasm. Still, pathetic to the last, he continued his appeals, notwithstanding the frigid regard of the company, till, suddenly interrupting himself, as if in reply to a quick summons from without, he said hurriedly, 'I come, I come,' and so, with every token of precipitate dispatch, out of the cabin the herb-doctor went.

CHAPTER XVIII

INQUEST INTO THE TRUE CHARACTER OF THE HERB-DOCTOR

'Shan't see that fellow again in a hurry,' remarked an auburn-haired gentleman, to his neighbour with a hook-nose. 'Never knew an operator so completely unmasked.'

'But do you think it the fair thing to unmask an operator that way?'

'Fair? It is right.'

'Supposing that at high 'change on the Paris Bourse,* Asmodeus* should lounge in, distributing hand-bills, revealing the true thoughts and designs of all the operators present—would that be the fair thing in Asmodeus? Or, as Hamlet says,* were it " to consider the thing too curiously "?'

'We won't go into that. But since you admit the fellow to be a knave——'

'I don't admit it. Or, if I did, I take it back. Shouldn't wonder if, after all, he is no knave at all, or, but little of one. What can you prove against him?'

'I can prove that he makes dupes.'

'Many held in honour do the same; and many, not wholly knaves, do it too.'

'How about that last?'

'He is not wholly at heart a knave, I fancy, among whose dupes is himself. Did you not see our quack friend apply to himself his own quackery? A fanatic quack; essentially a fool, though effectively a knave.'

Bending over, and looking down between his knees

on the floor, the auburn-haired gentleman meditatively scribbled there awhile with his cane, then, glancing up, said :—

'I can't conceive how you, in any way, can hold him a fool. How he talked—so glib, so pat, so well.'

'A smart fool always talks well ; takes a smart fool to be tonguey.'

In much the same strain the discussion continued—the hook-nosed gentleman talking at large and excellently, with a view of demonstrating that a smart fool always talks just so. Ere long he talked to such purpose as almost to convince.

Presently, back came the person of whom the auburn-haired gentleman had predicted that he would not return. Conspicuous in the doorway he stood, saying, in a clear voice, 'Is the agent of the Seminole Widow and Orphan Asylum within here ? '

No one replied.

'Is there within here any agent or any member of any charitable institution whatever ? '

No one seemed competent to answer, or, no one thought it worth while to.

'If there be within here any such person, I have in my hand two dollars for him.'

Some interest was manifested.

'I was called away so hurriedly, I forgot this part of my duty. With the proprietor of the Samaritan Pain Dissuader it is a rule, to devote, on the spot, to some benevolent purpose, the half of the proceeds of sales. Eight bottles were disposed of among this company. Hence, four half-dollars remain to charity. Who, as steward, takes the money ? '

One or two pair of feet moved upon the floor, as with a sort of itching ; but nobody rose.

'Does diffidence prevail over duty ? If, I say, there

be any gentleman, or any lady, either, here present, who
is in any connection with any charitable institution
whatever, let him or her come forward. He or she
happening to have at hand no certificate of such connection, makes no difference. Not of a suspicious temper,
thank God, I shall have confidence in whoever offers to
take the money.'

A demure-looking woman, in a dress rather tawdry
and rumpled, here drew her veil well down and rose ;
but, marking every eye upon her, thought it advisable,
upon the whole, to sit down again.

'Is it to be believed that, in this Christian company,
there is no one charitable person ?   I mean, no one connected with any charity ?   Well, then, is there no object
of charity here ? '

Upon this, an unhappy-looking woman, in a sort of
mourning, neat, but sadly worn, hid her face behind a
meagre bundle, and was heard to sob. Meantime, as
not seeing or hearing her, the herb-doctor again spoke,
and this time not unpathetically :—

'Are there none here who feel in need of help, and
who, in accepting such help, would feel that they, in
their time, have given or done more than may ever be
given or done to them ?   Man or woman, is there none
such here ? '

The sobs of the woman were more audible, though she
strove to repress them. While nearly everyone's attention was bent upon her, a man of the appearance of a
day-labourer, with a white bandage across his face,
concealing the side of the nose, and who, for coolness'
sake, had been sitting in his red-flannel shirt-sleeves, his
coat thrown across one shoulder, the darned cuffs droop-
ing behind—this man shufflingly rose, and with a pace
that seemed the lingering memento of the lock-step of
convicts, went up for a duly-qualified claimant.

'Poor wounded hussar!' sighed the herb-doctor, and dropping the money into the man's clam-shell of a hand turned and departed.

The recipient of the alms was about moving after, when the auburn-haired gentleman stayed him: 'Don't be frightened, you; but I want to see those coins. Yes, yes; good silver, good silver. There, take them again, and while you are about it, go bandage the rest of yourself behind something. D' ye hear? Consider yourself, wholly, the scar of a nose, and be off with yourself.'

Being of a forgiving nature, or else from emotion not daring to trust his voice, the man silently, but not without some precipitancy, withdrew.

'Strange,' said the auburn-haired gentleman, returning to his friend, 'the money was good money.'

'Ay, and where your fine knavery now? Knavery to devote the half of one's receipts to charity? He 's a fool, I say again.'

'Others might call him an original genius.'

'Yes, being original in his folly. Genius? His genius is a cracked pate, and, as this age goes, not much originality about that.'

'May he not be knave, fool, and genius altogether?'

'I beg pardon,' here said a third person with a gossiping expression who had been listening, 'but you are somewhat puzzled by this man, and well you may be.'

'Do you know anything about him?' asked the hooked-nosed gentleman.

'No, but I suspect him for something.'

'Suspicion. We want knowledge.'

'Well, suspect first and know next. True knowledge comes but by suspicion or revelation. That 's my maxim.'

'And yet,' said the auburn-haired gentleman, 'since a wise man will keep even some certainties to himself,

much more some suspicions, at least he will at all events
so do till they ripen into knowledge.'

'Do you hear that about the wise man ? ' said the
hook-nosed gentleman, turning upon the newcomer.
' Now what is it you suspect of this fellow ? '

' I shrewdly suspect him,' was the eager response, ' for
one of those Jesuit emissaries prowling all over our
country.* The better to accomplish their secret designs,
they assume, at times, I am told, the most singular
masques ; sometimes, in appearance, the absurdest.'

This, though indeed for some reason causing a droll
smile upon the face of the hook-nosed gentleman, added
a third angle to the discussion, which now became a
sort of triangular duel, and ended, at last, with but a
triangular result.

CHAPTER XIX

A SOLDIER OF FORTUNE

' MEXICO ?   Molino del Rey ?   Resaca de la Palma ? '*
' Resaca de la *Tombs* ! '*

Leaving his reputation to take care of itself, since, as
is not seldom the case, he knew nothing of its being in
debate, the herb-doctor, wandering toward the forward
part of the boat, had there espied a singular character
in a grimy old regimental coat, a countenance at once
grim and wizened, interwoven paralysed legs, stiff as
icicles, suspended between rude crutches, while the whole
rigid body, like a ship's long barometer on gimbals,
swung to and fro, mechanically faithful to the motion
of the boat. Looking downward while he swung, the
cripple seemed in a brown study.

As moved by the sight, and conjecturing that here
was some battered hero from the Mexican battle-fields,
the herb-doctor had sympathetically accosted him as
above, and received the above rather dubious reply.
As, with a half-moody, half-surly sort of air that reply
was given, the cripple, by a voluntary jerk, nervously
increased his swing (his custom when seized by emotion),
so that one would have thought some squall had suddenly rolled the boat and with it the barometer.

' Tombs ? my friend,' exclaimed the herb-doctor in
mild surprise. ' You have not descended to the dead,
have you ? I had imagined you a scarred campaigner,
one of the noble children of war, for your dear country
a glorious sufferer. But you are Lazarus, it seems.'

' Yes, he who had sores.'

' Ah, the *other* Lazarus.* But I never knew that either of them was in the army,' glancing at the dilapidated regimentals.

' That will do now. Jokes enough.'

' Friend,' said the other reproachfully, ' you think amiss. On principle, I greet unfortunates with some pleasant remark, the better to call off their thoughts from their troubles. The physician who is at once wise and humane seldom unreservedly sympathises with his patient. But come, I am a herb-doctor, and also a natural bone-setter. I may be sanguine, but I think I can do something for you. You look up now. Give me your story. Ere I undertake a cure, I require a full account of the case.'

' You can't help me,' returned the cripple gruffly. ' Go away.'

' You seem sadly destitute of——'

' No, I ain't destitute ; to-day, at least. I can pay my way.'

' The Natural Bone-setter is happy, indeed, to hear that. But you were premature. I was deploring your destitution, not of cash, but of confidence. You think the Natural Bone-setter can't help you. Well, suppose he can't, have you any objection to telling him your story. You, my friend, have, in a signal way, experienced adversity. Tell me, then, for my private good, how, without aid from the noble cripple, Epictetus,* you have arrived at his heroic sang-froid in misfortune.'

At these words the cripple fixed upon the speaker the hard ironic eye of one toughened and defiant in misery, and, in the end, grinned upon him with his unshaven face like an ogre.

' Come, come, be sociable—be human, my friend. Don't make that face ; it distresses me.'

'I suppose,' with a sneer, 'you are the man I 've long heard of—The Happy Man.'

'Happy? my friend. Yes, at least I ought to be. My conscience is peaceful. I have confidence in everybody. I have confidence that, in my humble profession, I do some little good to the world. Yes, I think that, without presumption, I may venture to assent to the proposition that I am the Happy Man—the Happy Bone-setter.'

'Then you shall hear my story. Many a month I have longed to get hold of the Happy Man, drill him, drop the powder, and leave him to explode at his leisure.'

'What a demoniac unfortunate,' exclaimed the herb-doctor, retreating. 'Regular infernal machine!'

'Look ye,' cried the other, stumping after him, and with his horny hand catching him by a horn button, 'my name is Thomas Fry. Until my——'

—'Any relation of Mrs. Fry*?' interrupted the other. 'I still correspond with that excellent lady on the subject of prisons. Tell me, are you any way connected with *my* Mrs. Fry?'

'Blister Mrs. Fry! What do them sentimental souls know of prisons or any other black fact? I 'll tell ye a story of prisons. Ha, ha!'

The herb-doctor shrank, and with reason, the laugh being strangely startling.

'Positively, my friend,' said he, 'you must stop that; I can't stand that; no more of that. I hope I have the milk of kindness, but your thunder will soon turn it.'

'Hold, I haven't come to the milk-turning part yet. My name is Thomas Fry. Until my twenty-third year I went by the nickname of Happy Tom—happy—ha, ha! They called me Happy Tom, d' ye see? because I was so good-natured and laughing all the time, just as I am now—ha, ha!'

Upon this the herb-doctor would, perhaps, have run, but once more the hyaena clawed him. Presently, sobering down, he continued :—

'Well, I was born in New York, and there I lived a steady, hard-working man, a cooper by trade. One evening I went to a political meeting in the Park—for you must know, I was in those days a great patriot. As bad luck would have it, there was trouble near, between a gentleman who had been drinking wine, and a pavior* who was sober. The pavior chewed tobacco, and the gentleman said it was beastly in him, and pushed him, wanting to have his place. The pavior chewed on and pushed back. Well, the gentleman carried a sword-cane, and presently the pavior was down—skewered.'

'How was that ? '

'Why, you see the pavior undertook something above his strength.'

'The other must have been a Samson, then. " Strong as a pavior," is the proverb.'

'So it is, and the gentleman was in body a rather weakly man, but, for all that, I say again, the pavior undertook something above his strength.'

'What are you talking about. He tried to maintain his rights, didn't he ? '

'Yes ; but, for all that, I say again, he undertook something above his strength.'

'I don't understand you. But go on.'

'Along with the gentleman, I, with other witnesses, was taken to the Tombs. There was an examination, and, to appear at the trial, the gentleman and witnesses all gave bail—I mean all but me.'

'And why didn't you ? '

'Couldn't get it.'

'Steady, hard-working cooper like you ; what was the reason you couldn't get bail ? '

'Steady, hard-working cooper hadn't no friends. Well, souse I went into a wet cell, like a canal-boat splashing into the lock; locked up in pickle, d'ye see? against the time of the trial.'

'But what had you done?'

'Why, I hadn't got any friends, I tell ye. A worse crime than murder, as ye'll see afore long.'

'Murder? Did the wounded man die?'

'Died the third night.'

'Then the gentleman's bail didn't help him. Imprisoned now, wasn't he?'

'Had too many friends. No, it was *I* that was imprisoned.—But I was going on: They let me walk about the corridor by day; but at night I must into lock. There the wet and the damp struck into my bones. They doctored me, but no use. When the trial came, I was boosted up and said my say.'

'And what was that?'

'My say was that I saw the steel go in, and saw it sticking in.'

'And that hung the gentleman.'

'Hung him with a gold chain! His friends called a meeting in the Park, and presented him with a gold watch and chain upon his acquittal.'

'Acquittal?'

'Didn't I say he had friends?'

There was a pause, broken at last by the herb-doctor's saying: 'Well, there is a bright side to everything. If this speak prosaically for justice, it speaks romantically for friendship! But go on, my fine fellow.'

'My say being said, they told me I might go. I said I could not without help. So the constables helped me, asking *where* would I go? I told them back to the "Tombs." I knew no other place. "But where are your friends?" said they. "I have none." So they

put me into a hand-barrow with an awning to it, and
wheeled me down to the dock and on board a boat, and
away to Blackwell's Island to the Corporation Hospital.
There I got worse—got pretty much as you see me now.
Couldn't cure me. After three years, I grew sick of
lying in a grated iron bed alongside of groaning thieves
and mouldering burglars. They gave me five silver
dollars, and these crutches, and I hobbled off. I had an
only brother who went to Indiana, years ago. I begged
about, to make up a sum to go to him; got to Indiana
at last, and they directed me to his grave. It was on a
great plain, in a log-church yard with a stump fence, the
old gray roots sticking all ways like moose-antlers. The
bier, set over the grave, it being the last dug, was of green
hickory; bark on, and green twigs sprouting from it.
Someone had planted a bunch of violets on the mound,
but it was a poor soil (always choose the poorest soils
for graveyards), and they were all dried to tinder. I was
going to sit and rest myself on the bier and think about
my brother in heaven, but the bier broke down, the
legs being only tacked. So, after driving some hogs out
of the yard that were rooting there, I came away, and,
not to make too long a story of it, here I am, drifting
down stream like any other bit of wreck.'

The herb-doctor was silent for a time, buried in
thought. At last, raising his head, he said : ' I have
considered your whole story, my friend, and strove to
consider it in the light of a commentary on what I
believe to be the system of things; but it so jars withal,
is so incompatible withal, that you must pardon me,
if I honestly tell you, I cannot believe it.'

' That don't surprise me.'

' How ? '

' Hardly anybody believes my story, and so to most I
tell a different one.'

'How, again ? '

'Wait here a bit and I 'll show ye.'

With that, taking off his rag of a cap, and arranging his tattered regimentals the best he could, off he went stumping among the passengers in an adjoining part of the deck, saying with a jovial kind of air : ' Sir, a shilling for Happy Tom, who fought at Buena Vista. Lady, something for General Scott's soldier, crippled in both pins at glorious Contreras.'*

Now, it so chanced that, unbeknown to the cripple, a prim-looking stranger had overheard part of his story. Beholding him, then, on his present begging adventure, this person, turning to the herb-doctor, indignantly said : ' Is it not too bad, sir, that yonder rascal should lie so ? '

'Charity never faileth, my good sir,' was the reply. ' The vice of this unfortunate is pardonable. Consider, he lies not out of wantonness.'

'Not out of wantonness. I never heard more wanton lies. In one breath to tell you what would appear to be his true story, and, in the next, away and falsify it.'

' For all that, I repeat he lies not out of wantonness. A ripe philosopher, turned out of the great Sorbonne of hard times, he thinks that woes, when told to strangers for money, are best sugared. Though the inglorious lockjaw of his knee-pans in a wet dungeon is a far more pitiable ill than to have been crippled at glorious Contreras, yet he is of opinion that this lighter and false ill shall attract, while the heavier and real one might repel.'

'Nonsense ; he belongs to the Devil's regiment ; and I have a great mind to expose him.'

' Shame upon you. Dare to expose that poor unfortunate, and by heaven—don't you do it, sir.'

Noting something in his manner, the other thought it more prudent to retire than retort. By and by, the cripple came back, and with glee, having reaped a pretty good harvest.

'There,' he laughed, 'you know now what sort of soldier I am.'

'Ay, one that fights not the stupid Mexican, but a foe worthy your tactics—Fortune!'

'Hi, hi!' clamoured the cripple, like a fellow in the pit of a sixpenny theatre, then said, 'Don't know much what you meant, but it went off well.'

This over, his countenance capriciously put on a morose ogreness. To kindly questions he gave no kindly answers. Unhandsome notions were thrown out about 'free Ameriky,' as he sarcastically called his country. These seemed to disturb and pain the herb-doctor, who, after an interval of thoughtfulness, gravely addressed him in these words :—

'You, my worthy friend, to my concern, have reflected upon the government under which you live and suffer. Where is your patriotism? Where your gratitude? True, the charitable may find something in your case, as you put it, partly to account for such reflections as coming from you. Still, be the facts how they may, your reflections are none the less unwarrantable. Grant, for the moment, that your experiences are as you give them; in which case I would admit that government might be thought to have more or less to do with what seems undesirable in them. But it is never to be forgotten that human government, being subordinate to the divine, must needs, therefore, in its degree, partake of the characteristics of the divine. That is, while in general efficacious to happiness, the world's law may yet, in some cases, have, to the eye of reason, an unequal operation, just as, in the same imperfect view, some inequalities may appear in the operations of heaven's law; nevertheless, to one who has a right confidence, final benignity is, in every instance, as sure with the one law as the other. I expound the point at some length, because these are the considerations, my poor fellow, which, weighed as they merit, will enable you to sustain with unimpaired trust the apparent calamities which are yours.'

'What do you talk your hog-latin to me for ? ' cried the cripple, who, throughout the address, betrayed the most illiterate obduracy ; and, with an incensed look, anew he swung himself.

Glancing another way till the spasm passed, the other continued :—

'Charity marvels not that you should be somewhat hard of conviction, my friend, since you, doubtless, believe yourself hardly dealt by ; but forget not that those who are loved are chastened.'*

'Mustn't chasten them too much, though, and too long, because their skin and heart get hard, and feel neither pain nor tickle.'

'To mere reason, your case looks something piteous, I grant. But never despond ; many things—the choicest— yet remain. You breathe this bounteous air, are warmed by this gracious sun, and, though poor and friendless, indeed, nor so agile as in your youth, yet, how sweet to roam, day by day, through the groves, plucking the bright mosses and flowers, till forlornness itself becomes a hilarity, and, in your innocent independence, you skip for joy.'

'Fine skipping with these 'ere horse-posts—ha, ha ! '

'Pardon ; I forgot the crutches. My mind, figuring you after receiving the benefit of my art, overlooked you as you stand before me.'

'Your art ? You call yourself a bone-setter—a natural bone-setter, do ye ? Go, bone-set the crooked world, and then come bone-set crooked me.'

'Truly, my honest friend, I thank you for again recalling me to my original object. Let me examine you,' bending down ; ' ah, I see, I see ; much such a case as the negro's. Did you see him ? Oh no, you came aboard since. Well, his case was a little something like yours. I prescribed for him, and I shouldn't wonder at all if, in a very short time, he were able to walk almost as well as myself. Now, have you no confidence in my art ? '

' Ha, ha ! '

The herb-doctor averted himself ; but, the wild laugh dying away, resumed :—

' I will not force confidence on you. Still, I would fain do the friendly thing by you. Here, take this box ; just rub that liniment on the joints night and morning. Take it. Nothing to pay. God bless you. Good-bye.'

' Stay,' pausing in his swing, not untouched by so unexpected an act ; ' stay—thank 'ee—but will this really do me good ? Honour bright, now ; will it ? Don't deceive a poor fellow,' with changed mien and glistening eye.

' Try it. Good-bye.'

' Stay, stay ! *Sure* it will do me good ? '

' Possibly, possibly ; no harm in trying. Good-bye.'

' Stay, stay ; give me three more boxes, and here 's the money.'

' My friend,' returning toward him with a sadly pleased sort of air, ' I rejoice in the birth of your confidence and hopefulness. Believe me that, like your crutches, confidence and hopefulness will long support a man when his own legs will not. Stick to confidence and hopefulness, then, since how mad for the cripple to throw his crutches away. You ask for three more boxes of my liniment. Luckily, I have just that number remaining. Here they are. I sell them at half a dollar apiece. But

I shall take nothing from you. There; God bless you again; good-bye.'

'Stay,' in a convulsed voice, and rocking himself, 'stay, stay! You have made a better man of me. You have borne with me like a good Christian, and talked to me like one, and all that is enough without making me a present of these boxes. Here is the money. I won't take nay. There, there; and may Almighty goodness go with you.'

As the herb-doctor withdrew, the cripple gradually subsided from his hard rocking into a gentle oscillation. It expressed, perhaps, the soothed mood of his revery.

CHAPTER XX

REAPPEARANCE OF ONE WHO MAY BE REMEMBERED

THE herb-doctor had not moved far away, when, in
advance of him, this spectacle met his eye. A dried-up
old man, with the stature of a boy of twelve, was tottering
about like one out of his mind, in rumpled clothes of
old moleskin, showing recent contact with bedding, his
ferret eyes blinking in the sunlight of the snowy boat,
as imbecilely eager, and, at intervals, coughing, he peered
hither and thither as if in alarmed search for his nurse.
He presented the aspect of one who, bed-rid, has, through
overruling excitement, like that of a fire, been stimulated
to his feet.

'You seek someone,' said the herb-doctor, accosting
him. 'Can I assist you?'

'Do, do; I am so old and miserable,' coughed the old
man. 'Where is he? This long time I've been trying
to get up and find him. But I haven't any friends,
and couldn't get up till now. Where is he?'

'Who do you mean?' drawing closer, to stay the
further wanderings of one so weakly.

'Why, why, why,' now marking the other's dress,
'why you, yes you—you, you—ugh, ugh, ugh!'

'I?'

'Ugh, ugh, ugh!—you are the man he spoke of. Who
is he?'

'Faith, that is just what I want to know.'

'Mercy, mercy!' coughed the old man, bewildered,
'ever since seeing him, my head spins round so. I

ought to have a guardeean. Is this a snuff-coloured surtout of yours, or ain't it ? Somehow, can't trust my senses any more, since trusting him—ugh, ugh, ugh ! '

' Oh, you have trusted somebody ? Glad to hear it. Glad to hear of any instance of that sort. Reflects well upon all men. But you inquire whether this is a snuff-coloured surtout. I answer it is ; and will add that a herb-doctor wears it.'

Upon this the old man, in his broken way, replied that then he (the herb-doctor) was the person he sought—the person spoken of by the other person as yet unknown. He then, with flighty eagerness, wanted to know who this last person was, and where he was, and whether he could be trusted with money to treble it.

' Ay, now, I begin to understand ; ten to one you mean my worthy friend, who, in pure goodness of heart, makes people's fortunes for them—their everlasting fortunes, as the phrase goes—only charging his one small commission of confidence. Ay, ay ; before entrusting funds with my friend, you want to know about him. Very proper—and, I am glad to assure you, you need have no hesitation ; none, none, just none in the world ; *bona fide*, none. Turned me in a trice a hundred dollars the other day into as many eagles.'*

' Did he ? did he ? But where is he ? Take me to him.'

' Pray, take my arm ! The boat is large ! We may have something of a hunt ! Come on ! Ah, is that he ? '

' Where ? where ? '

' Oh, no ; I took yonder coat-skirts for his. But no, my honest friend would never turn tail that way. Ah !——'

' Where ? where ? '

' Another mistake. Surprising resemblance. I took yonder clergyman for him. Come on ! '

Having searched that part of the boat without success, they went to another part, and, while exploring that, the boat sided up to a landing, when, as the two were passing by the open guard, the herb-doctor suddenly rushed toward the disembarking throng, crying out : 'Mr. Truman, Mr. Truman ! There he goes—that 's he. Mr. Truman, Mr. Truman !—Confound that steam-pipe. Mr. Truman ! for God's sake, Mr. Truman !—No, no.—There, the plank 's in—too late—we 're off.'

With that, the huge boat, with a mighty, walrus wallow, rolled away from the shore, resuming her course.

'How vexatious ! ' exclaimed the herb-doctor, return-ing. 'Had we been but one single moment sooner.—There he goes, now, toward yon hotel, his portmanteau following. You see him, don't you ? '

'Where ? where ? '

'Can't see him any more. Wheel-house shot between. I am very sorry. I should have so liked you to have let him have a hundred or so of your money. You would have been pleased with the investment, believe me.'

'Oh, I *have* let him have some of my money,' groaned the old man.

'You have ? My dear sir,' seizing both the miser's hands in both his own and heartily shaking them—'my dear sir, how I congratulate you. You don't know.'

'Ugh, ugh ! I fear I don't,' with another groan. 'His name is Truman, is it ? '

'John Truman.'

'Where does he live ? '

'In St. Louis.'

'Where 's his office ? '

'Let me see. Jones Street, number one hundred and—no, no—anyway, it 's somewhere or other upstairs in Jones Street.'

'Can't you remember the number ? Try, now.'

'One hundred—two hundred—three hundred——'

'Oh, my hundred dollars! I wonder whether it will be one hundred, two hundred, three hundred, with them! Ugh, ugh! Can't remember the number?'

'Positively, though I once knew, I have forgotten, quite forgotten it. Strange. But never mind. You will easily learn in St. Louis. He is well known there.'

'But I have no receipt—ugh, ugh! Nothing to show—don't know where I stand—ought to have a guardeean—ugh, ugh! Don't know anything. Ugh, ugh!'

'Why, you know that you gave him your confidence, don't you?'

'Oh, yes.'

'Well, then?'

'But what, what—how, how—ugh, ugh!'

'Why, didn't he tell you?'

'No.'

'What! Didn't he tell you that it was a secret, a mystery?'

'Oh—yes.'

'Well, then?'

'But I have no bond.'

'Don't need any with Mr. Truman. Mr. Truman's word is his bond.'

'But how am I to get my profits—ugh, ugh!—and my money back? Don't know anything. Ugh, ugh!'

'Oh, you must have confidence.'

'Don't say that word again. Makes my head spin so. Oh, I'm so old and miserable, nobody caring for me, everybody fleecing me, and my head spins so—ugh, ugh! —and this cough racks me so. I say again, I ought to have a guardeean.'

'So you ought; and Mr. Truman is your guardian to the extent you invested with him. Sorry we missed him just now. But you'll hear from him, all right.

It 's imprudent, though, to expose yourself this way. Let me take you to your berth.'

Forlornly enough the old miser moved slowly away with him. But, while descending a stairway, he was seized with such coughing that he was fain to pause.

'That is a very bad cough.'

'Churchyard—ugh, ugh !—churchyard cough.—Ugh ! '

'Have you tried anything for it ? '

'Tired of trying. Nothing does me any good—ugh ! ugh ! Not even the Mammoth Cave.* Ugh ! ugh ! Denned there six months, but coughed so bad the rest of the coughers—ugh ! ugh !—blackballed me out. Ugh, ugh ! Nothing does me good.'

'But have you tried the Omni-Balsamic Reinvigorator, sir ? '

'That 's what that Truman—ugh, ugh !—said I ought to take. Yarb-medicine; you are that yarb-doctor, too ? '

'The same. Suppose you try one of my boxes now. Trust me, from what I know of Mr. Truman, he is not the gentleman to recommend, even in behalf of a friend, anything of whose excellence he is not conscientiously satisfied.'

'Ugh !—how much ? '

'Only two dollars a box.'

'Two dollars ? Why don't you say two millions ? ugh, ugh ! Two dollars, that 's two hundred cents ; that 's eight hundred farthings ; that 's two thousand mills ; and all for one little box of yarb-medicine. My head, my head !—oh, I ought to have a guardeean for my head. Ugh, ugh, ugh, ugh ! '

'Well, if two dollars a box seems too much, take a dozen boxes at twenty dollars, and that will be getting four boxes for nothing ; and you need use none but those four, the rest you can retail out at a premium, and so

cure your cough, and make money by it. Come, you had
better do it. Cash down. Can fill an order in a day
or two. Here now,' producing a box; 'pure herbs.'

At that moment, seized with another spasm, the miser
snatched each interval to fix his half-distrustful, half-
hopeful eye upon the medicine, held alluringly up.
'Sure—ugh! Sure it's all nat'ral? Nothing but yarbs?
If I only thought it was a purely nat'ral medicine now—
all yarbs—ugh, ugh!—oh this cough, this cough—ugh,
ugh!—shatters my whole body. Ugh, ugh, ugh!'

'For heaven's sake, try my medicine, if but a single
box. That it is pure nature you may be confident.
Refer you to Mr. Truman.'

'Don't know his number—ugh, ugh, ugh, ugh! Oh
this cough. He did speak well of this medicine, though;
said solemnly it would cure me—ugh, ugh, ugh, ugh!—
take off a dollar and I'll have a box.'

'Can't, sir, can't.'

'Say a dollar and half. Ugh!'

'Can't. Am pledged to the one-price system, only
honourable one.'

'Take off a shilling—ugh, ugh!'

'Can't.'

'Ugh, ugh, ugh—I'll take it.—There.'

Grudgingly he handed eight silver coins, but while
still in his hand, his cough took him, and they were
shaken upon the deck.

One by one, the herb-doctor picked them up, and,
examining them, said: 'These are not quarters, these
are pistareens; and clipped, and sweated, at that.'

'Oh don't be so miserly—ugh, ugh!—better a beast
than a miser—ugh, ugh!'

'Well, let it go. Anything rather than the idea of
your not being cured of such a cough. And I hope, for
the credit of humanity, you have not made it appear

worse than it is, merely with a view to working upon the weak point of my pity, and so getting my medicine the cheaper. Now, mind, don't take it till night. Just before retiring is the time. There, you can get along now, can't you? I would attend you further, but I land presently, and must go hunt up my luggage.'

CHAPTER XXI

A HARD CASE

'YARBS, yarbs; natur, natur; you foolish old file*you! He diddled you with that hocus-pocus, did he? Yarbs and natur will cure your incurable cough, you think.'

It was a rather eccentric-looking person who spoke; somewhat ursine in aspect; sporting a shaggy spencer* of the cloth called bearskin; a high-peaked cap of raccoon-skin, the long bushy tail switching over behind; raw-hide leggings; grim stubble chin; and to end, a double-barrelled gun in hand—a Missouri bachelor, a Hoosier* gentleman, of Spartan leisure and fortune, and equally Spartan manners and sentiments; and, as the sequel may show, not less acquainted, in a Spartan way of his own, with philosophy and books, than with wood-craft and rifles.

He must have overheard some of the talk between the miser and the herb-doctor; for, just after the withdrawal of the one, he made up to the other—now at the foot of the stairs leaning against the baluster there—with the greeting above.

'Think it will cure me?' coughed the miser in echo; 'why shouldn't it? The medicine is nat'ral yarbs, pure yarbs; yarbs must cure me.'

'Because a thing is nat'ral, as you call it, you think it must be good. But who gave you that cough? Was it, or was it not, nature?'

'Sure, you don't think that natur, Dame Natur, will hurt a body, do you?'

'Natur is good Queen Bess;* but who's responsible for the cholera?'

'But yarbs, yarbs; yarbs are good?'

'What's deadly-nightshade? Yarb, ain't it?'

'Oh, that a Christian man should speak agin natur and yarbs—ugh, ugh, ugh!—ain't sick men sent out into the country; sent out to natur and grass?'

'Ay, and poets send out the sick spirit to green pastures, like lame horses turned out unshod to the turf to renew their hoofs. A sort of yarb-doctors in their way, poets have it that for sore hearts, as for sore lungs, nature is the grand cure. But who froze to death my teamster* on the prairie? And who made an idiot of Peter the Wild Boy?'*

'Then you don't believe in these 'ere yarb-doctors?'

'Yarb-doctors? I remember the lank yarb-doctor I saw once on a hospital-cot in Mobile. One of the faculty passing round and seeing who lay there, said with professional triumph, 'Ah, Dr. Green, your yarbs don't help ye now, Dr. Green. Have to come to us and the mercury now, Dr. Green.—Natur! Y-a-r-b-s!''

'Did I hear something about herbs and herb-doctors?' here said a flute-like voice, advancing.

It was the herb-doctor in person. Carpet-bag in hand, he happened to be strolling back that way.

'Pardon me,' addressing the Missourian, 'but if I caught your words aright, you would seem to have little confidence in nature; which, really, in my way of thinking, looks like carrying the spirit of distrust pretty far.'

'And who of my sublime species may you be?' turning short round upon him, clicking his rifle-lock, with an air which would have seemed half cynic, half wild-cat, were it not for the grotesque excess of the expression, which made its sincerity appear more or less dubious.

'One who has confidence in nature, and confidence in man, with some little modest confidence in himself.'

'That's your Confession of Faith, is it? Confidence in man, eh? Pray, which do you think are most, knaves or fools?'

'Having met with few or none of either, I hardly think I am competent to answer.'

'I will answer for you. Fools are most.'

'Why do you think so?'

'For the same reason that I think oats are numerically more than horses. Don't knaves munch up fools just as horses do oats?'

'A droll, sir; you are a droll. I can appreciate drollery—ha, ha, ha!'

'But I'm in earnest.'

'That's the drollery, to deliver droll extravagance with an earnest air—knaves munching up fools as horses oats.—Faith, very droll, indeed, ha, ha, ha! Yes, I think I understand you now, sir. How silly I was to have taken you seriously, in your droll conceits, too, about having no confidence in nature. In reality you have just as much as I have.'

'*I* have confidence in nature? *I*? I say again there is nothing I am more suspicious of. I once lost ten thousand dollars by nature. Nature embezzled that amount from me; absconded with ten thousand dollars' worth of my property; a plantation on this stream, swept clean away by one of those sudden shiftings of the banks in a freshet; ten thousand dollars' worth of alluvion thrown broad off upon the waters.'

'But have you no confidence that by a reverse shifting that soil will come back after many days?*—ah, here is my venerable friend,' observing the old miser, 'not in your berth yet? Pray, if you *will* keep afoot, don't lean against that baluster; take my arm.'

It was taken ; and the two stood together ; the old miser leaning against the herb-doctor with something of that air of trustful fraternity with which, when standing, the less strong of the Siamese twins* habitually leans against the other.

The Missourian eyed them in silence, which was broken by the herb-doctor.

'You look surprised, sir. Is it because I publicly take under my protection a figure like this ? But I am never ashamed of honesty, whatever his coat.'

'Look you,' said the Missourian, after a scrutinising pause, 'you are a queer sort of chap. Don't know exactly what to make of you. Upon the whole, though, you somewhat remind me of the last boy I had on my place.'

'Good, trustworthy boy, I hope ? '

'Oh, very ! I am now started to get me made some kind of machine to do the sort of work which boys are supposed to be fitted for.'

'Then you have passed a veto upon boys ? '

'And men, too.'

'But, my dear sir, does not that again imply more or less lack of confidence ?—(Stand up a little, just a very little, my venerable friend ; you lean rather hard.)—No confidence in boys, no confidence in men, no confidence in nature. Pray, sir, who or what may you have confidence in ? '

'I have confidence in distrust ; more particularly as applied to you and your herbs.'

'Well,' with a forbearing smile, 'that is frank. But pray, don't forget that when you suspect my herbs you suspect nature.'

'Didn't I say that before ? '

'Very good. For the argument's sake I will suppose you are in earnest. Now, can you, who suspect nature, deny, that this same nature not only kindly brought you into being, but has faithfully nursed you to your present vigorous and independent condition ? Is it not to nature that you are indebted for that robustness of mind which you so unhandsomely use to her scandal ? Pray, is it not to nature that you owe the very eyes by which you criticise her ? '

'No ! for the privilege of vision I am indebted to an oculist, who in my tenth year operated upon me in Philadelphia. Nature made me blind and would have kept me so. My oculist counterplotted her.'

'And yet, sir, by your complexion, I judge you live an out-of-door life ; without knowing it, you are partial to nature ; you fly to nature, the universal mother.'

'Very motherly ! Sir, in the passion-fits of nature, I 've known birds fly from nature to me, rough as I look ; yes, sir, in a tempest, refuge here,' smiting the folds of his bearskin. 'Fact, sir, fact. Come, come, Mr. Palaverer, for all your palavering, did you yourself never shut out nature of a cold, wet night ? Bar her out ? Bolt her out ? Lint her out ? '*

'As to that,' said the herb-doctor calmly, 'much may be said.'

'Say it, then,' ruffling all his hairs. 'You can't, sir, can't.' Then, as in apostrophe : 'Look you, nature ! I don't deny but your clover is sweet, and your dandelions don't roar, but whose hailstones smashed my windows ? '

'Sir,' with unimpaired affability, producing one of his boxes, 'I am pained to meet with one who holds nature a dangerous character. Though your manner is refined your voice is rough ; in short, you seem to have a sore throat. In the calumniated name of nature, I present you with this box ; my venerable friend here has a

similar one ; but to you, a free gift, sir. Through her
regularly authorised agents, of whom I happen to be
one, nature delights in benefiting those who most abuse
her. Pray, take it.'

' Away with it ! Don't hold it so near. Ten to one
there is a torpedo in it. Such things have been. Editors
been killed that way. Take it further off, I say.'

' Good heavens ! my dear sir——'

' I tell you I want none of your boxes,' snapping his
rifle.

' Oh, take it—ugh, ugh ! do take it,' chimed in
the old miser ; ' I wish he would give me one for
nothing.'

' You find it lonely, eh,' turning short round ; ' gulled
yourself, you would have a companion.'

' How can he find it lonely,' returned the herb-doctor,
' or how desire a companion, when here I stand by him ;
I, even I, in whom he has trust. For the gulling, tell me,
is it humane to talk so to this poor old man ? Granting
that his dependence on my medicine is vain, is it kind
to deprive him of what, in mere imagination, if nothing
more, may help eke out, with hope, his disease ? For
you, if you have no confidence, and, thanks to your
native health, can get along without it, so far, at least,
as trusting in my medicine goes ; yet, how cruel an
argument to use, with this afflicted one here. Is it not
for all the world as if some brawny pugilist, aglow in
December, should rush in and put out a hospital-fire,
because, forsooth, he feeling no need of artificial heat,
the shivering patients shall have none ? Put it to your
conscience, sir, and you will admit, that, whatever be the
nature of this afflicted one's trust, you, in opposing it,
evince either an erring head or a heart amiss. Come,
own, are you not pitiless ? '

' Yes, poor soul,' said the Missourian, gravely eyeing

the old man—'yes, it *is* pitiless in one like me to speak
too honestly to one like you. You are a late sitter-up
in this life; past man's usual bed-time; and truth,
though with some it makes a wholesome breakfast,
proves to all a supper too hearty. Hearty food, taken
late, gives bad dreams.'

'What, in wonder's name—ugh, ugh!—is he talking
about?' asked the old miser, looking up to the herb-
doctor.

'Heaven be praised for that!' cried the Missourian.

'Out of his mind, ain't he?' again appealed the old
miser.

'Pray, sir,' said the herb-doctor to the Missourian,
'for what were you giving thanks just now?'

'For this: that, with some minds, truth is, in effect,
not so cruel a thing after all, seeing that, like a loaded
pistol found by poor devils of savages, it raises more
wonder than terror—its peculiar virtue being unguessed,
unless, indeed, by indiscreet handling, it should happen
to go off of itself.'

'I pretend not to divine your meaning there,' said the
herb-doctor, after a pause, during which he eyed the
Missourian with a kind of pinched expression, mixed of
pain and curiosity, as if he grieved at his state of mind,
and, at the same time, wondered what had brought him
to it; 'but this much I know,' he added, 'that the
general cast of your thoughts is, to say the least, unfortunate. There is strength in them, but a strength,
whose source, being physical, must wither. You will
yet recant.'

'Recant?'

'Yes, when, as with this old man, your evil days of
decay come on, when a hoary captive in your chamber,
then will you, something like the dungeoned Italian* we
read of, gladly seek the breast of that confidence begot

in the tender time of your youth, blessed beyond telling
if it return to you in age.'

'Go back to nurse again, eh? Second childhood,
indeed. You are soft.'

'Mercy, mercy!' cried the old miser, 'what is all
this!—ugh, ugh! Do talk sense, my good friends.
Ain't you,' to the Missourian, 'going to buy some of
that medicine?'

'Pray, my venerable friend,' said the herb-doctor,
now trying to straighten himself, 'don't lean *quite* so
hard; my arm grows numb; abate a little, just a very
little.'

'Go,' said the Missourian, 'go lay down in your grave,
old man, if you can't stand of yourself. It's a hard
world for a leaner.'

'As to his grave,' said the herb-doctor, 'that is far
enough off, so he but faithfully take my medicine.'

'Ugh, ugh, ugh!—He says true. No, I ain't—ugh!
a-going to die yet—ugh, ugh, ugh! Many years to live
yet, ugh, ugh, ugh!'

'I approve your confidence,' said the herb-doctor;
'but your coughing distresses me, besides being injurious
to you. Pray, let me conduct you to your berth. You
are best there. Our friend here will wait till my return,
I know.'

With which he led the old miser away, and then,
coming back, the talk with the Missourian was resumed.

'Sir,' said the herb-doctor, with some dignity and
more feeling, 'now that our infirm friend is withdrawn,
allow me, to the full, to express my concern at the
words you allowed to escape you in his hearing. Some
of those words, if I err not, besides being calculated to
beget deplorable distrust in the patient, seemed fitted
to convey unpleasant imputations against me, his
physician.'

' Suppose they did ? ' with a menacing air.

' Why, then—then, indeed,' respectfully retreating, ' I fall back upon my previous theory of your general facetiousness.   I have the fortune to be in company with a humorist—a wag.'

' Fall back you had better, and wag it is,' cried the Missourian, following him up, and wagging his raccoon tail almost into the herb-doctor's face ; ' look you ! '

' At what ? '

' At this coon.   Can you, the fox, catch him ? '

' If you mean,' returned the other, not unself-possessed, ' whether I flatter myself that I can in any way dupe you, or impose upon you, or pass myself off upon you for what I am not, I, as an honest man, answer that I have neither the inclination nor the power to do aught of the kind.'

' Honest man ?   Seems to me you talk more like a craven.'

' You in vain seek to pick a quarrel with me, or put any affront upon me.   The innocence in me heals me.'

' A healing like your own nostrums.   But you are a queer man—a very queer and dubious man ; upon the whole, about the most so I ever met.'

The scrutiny accompanying this seemed unwelcome to the diffidence of the herb-doctor.   As if at once to attest the absence of resentment, as well as to change the subject, he threw a kind of familiar cordiality into his air, and said : ' So you are going to get some machine made to do your work ?   Philanthropic scruples, doubtless, forbid your going as far as New Orleans for slaves ? '

' Slaves ? ' morose again in a twinkling, ' won't have 'em.   Bad enough to see whites ducking and grinning round for a favour, without having those poor devils of niggers congeeing round for their corn. Though, to me, the niggers are the freer of the two. You are an abolitionist, ain't you?' he added, squaring himself with both hands on his rifle, used for a staff, and gazing in the herb-doctor's face with no more reverence than if it were a target. 'You are an abolitionist, ain't you?'*

'As to that, I cannot so readily answer. If by abolitionist you mean a zealot, I am none ; but if you mean a man, who, being a man, feels for all men, slaves included, and by any lawful act, opposed to nobody's interest, and therefore rousing nobody's enmity, would willingly abolish suffering (supposing it, in its degree, to exist) from among mankind, irrespective of colour, then am I what you say.'

'Picked and prudent sentiments. You are the moderate man, the invaluable understrapper of the wicked man. You, the moderate man, may be used for wrong, but are useless for right.'

'From all this,' said the herb-doctor, still forgivingly, 'I infer, that you, a Missourian, though living in a slave-state,* are without slave sentiments.'

'Ay, but are you? Is not that air of yours, so spiritlessly enduring and yielding, the very air of a slave? Who is your master, pray ; or are you owned by a company?'

'*My* master?'

'Ay, for come from Maine or Georgia, you come from a slave-state, and a slave-pen, where the best breeds are to be bought up at any price from a livelihood to the Presidency. Abolitionism, ye gods, but expresses the fellow-feeling of slave for slave.'

'The back-woods would seem to have given you rather eccentric notions,' now with polite superiority smiled the herb-doctor, still with manly intrepidity forbearing each unmanly thrust, 'but to return; since, for your purpose, you will have neither man nor boy, bond nor free, truly, then some sort of machine for you is all there is left. My desires for your success attend you, sir.—Ah!' glancing shoreward, 'here is Cape Giradeau; I must leave you.'

CHAPTER XXII

IN THE POLITE SPIRIT OF THE TUSCULAN DISPUTATIONS*

—'"PHILOSOPHICAL INTELLIGENCE OFFICE"*—novel idea!
But how did you come to dream that I wanted anything
in your absurd line, eh?'

About twenty minutes after leaving Cape Giradeau,
the above was growled out over his shoulder by the
Missourian to a chance stranger who had just accosted
him; a round-backed, baker-kneed*man, in a mean five-
dollar suit, wearing, collar-wise by a chain, a small brass
plate, inscribed P.I.O., and who, with a sort of canine
deprecation, slunk obliquely behind.

'How did you come to dream that I wanted anything
in your line, eh?'

'Oh, respected sir,' whined the other, crouching a
pace nearer, and, in his obsequiousness, seeming to
wag his very coat-tails behind him, shabby though
they were, 'oh, sir, from long experience, one glance
tells me the gentleman who is in need of our humble
services.'

'But suppose I did want a boy—what they jocosely
call a good boy—how could your absurd office help me?—
Philosophical Intelligence Office?'

'Yes, respected sir, an office founded on strictly
philosophical and physio——'

'Look you—come up here—how, by philosophy or
physiology either, make good boys to order? Come up
here. Don't give me a crick in the neck. Come up
here, come, sir, come,' calling as if to his pointer. 'Tell

me, how put the requisite assortment of good qualities into a boy, as the assorted mince into the pie ? '

' Respected sir, our office——'

' You talk much of that office. Where is it ? On board this boat ? '

' Oh no, sir, I just came aboard. Our office——'

' Came aboard at that last landing, eh ? Pray, do you know a herb-doctor there ? Smooth scamp in a snuff-coloured surtout ? '

' Oh, sir, I was but a sojourner at Cape Giradeau. Though, now that you mention a snuff-coloured surtout, I think I met such a man as you speak of stepping ashore as I stepped aboard, and 'pears to me I have seen him somewhere before. Looks like a very mild Christian sort of person, I should say. Do you know him, respected sir ? '

' Not much, but better than you seem to. Proceed with your business.'

With a low shabby bow, as grateful for the permission, the other began : ' Our office——'

' Look you,' broke in the bachelor with ire, ' have you the spinal complaint ? What are you ducking and grovelling about ? Keep still. Where 's your office ? '

' The branch one which I represent, is at Alton, sir, in the free state we now pass '*(pointing somewhat proudly ashore).

' Free, eh ? You a freeman, you flatter yourself ? With those coat-tails and that spinal complaint of servility ? Free ? Just cast up in your private mind who is your master, will you ? '

' Oh, oh, oh ! I don't understand—indeed—indeed. But, respected sir, as before said, our office, founded on principles wholly new——'

' To the devil with your principles ! Bad sign when a man begins to talk of his principles. Hold, come back,

sir; back here, back, sir, back! I tell you no more
boys for me. Nay, I 'm a Mede and Persian.* In my
old home in the woods I 'm pestered enough with squirrels,
weasels, chipmunks, skunks. I want no more wild
vermin to spoil my temper and waste my substance.
Don't talk of boys; enough of your boys; a plague of
your boys; chilblains on your boys! As for Intelligence
Offices, I 've lived in the East, and know 'em. Swindling
concerns kept by low-born cynics, under a fawning
exterior wreaking their cynic malice upon mankind.
You are a fair specimen of 'em.'

'Oh dear, dear, dear!'

'Dear? Yes, a thrice dear purchase one of your
boys would be to me. A rot on your boys!'

'But, respected sir, if you will not have boys, might
we not, in our small way, accommodate you with a
man?'

'Accommodate? Pray, no doubt you could accommodate me with a bosom friend too, couldn't you?
Accommodate! Obliging word accommodate: there 's
accommodation notes now, where one accommodates
another with a loan, and if he don't pay it pretty quickly,
accommodates him with a chain to his foot. Accommodate! God forbid that I should ever be accommodated.
No, no. Look you, as I told that cousin-german of
yours, the herb-doctor, I 'm now on the road to get me
made some sort of machine to do my work. Machines
for me. My cider-mill—does that ever steal my cider?
My mowing-machine—does that ever lay a-bed morn-
ings? My corn-husker—does that ever give me insolence?
No: cider-mill, mowing-machine, corn-husker—all faithfully attend to their business. Disinterested, too; no
board, no wages; yet doing good all their lives long;
shining examples that virtue is its own reward—the only
practical Christians I know.'

'Oh dear, dear, dear, dear!'

'Yes, sir:—boys? Start my soul-bolts, what a difference, in a moral point of view, between a corn-husker
and a boy! Sir, a corn-husker, for its patient continuance in well-doing,* might not unfitly go to heaven.
Do you suppose a boy will?'

'A corn-husker in heaven!' turning up the whites of
his eyes. 'Respected sir, this way of talking as if heaven
were a kind of Washington patent-office museum—oh,
oh, oh!—as if mere machine-work and puppet-work
went to heaven—oh, oh, oh! Things incapable of free
agency, to receive the eternal reward of well-doing—oh,
oh, oh!'

'You Praise-God-Barebones*you, what are you groaning about? Did I say anything of that sort? Seems
to me, though you talk so good, you are mighty quick
at a hint the other way, or else you want to pick a
polemic quarrel with me.'

'It may be so or not, respected sir,' was now the
demure reply; 'but if it be, it is only because as a soldier
out of honour is quick in taking affront, so a Christian
out of religion is quick, sometimes perhaps a little too
much so, in spying heresy.'

'Well,' after an astonished pause, 'for an unaccountable pair, you and the herb-doctor ought to yoke together.'

So saying, the bachelor was eyeing him rather sharply,
when he with the brass plate recalled him to the discussion by a hint, not unflattering, that he (the man with
the brass plate) was all anxiety to hear him further on
the subject of servants.

'About that matter,' exclaimed the impulsive bachelor,
going off at the hint like a rocket, 'all thinking minds
are, nowadays, coming to the conclusion—one derived
from an immense hereditary experience—see what Horace

and others of the ancients say of servants—coming to
the conclusion, I say, that boy or man, the human
animal is, for most work-purposes, a losing animal.
Can't be trusted ; less trustworthy than oxen ; for
conscientiousness a turn-spit dog excels him. Hence
these thousand new inventions—carding machines, horse-
shoe machines, tunnel-boring machines, reaping machines,
apple-paring machines, boot-blacking machines, sewing
machines, shaving machines, run-of-errand machines,
dumb-waiter machines, and the Lord-only-knows-what
machines ; all of which announce the era when that
refractory animal, the working or serving man, shall be
a buried bygone, a superseded fossil. Shortly prior to
which glorious time, I doubt not that a price will be
put upon their peltries as upon the knavish " possums,"
especially the boys. Yes, sir (ringing his rifle down on
the deck), I rejoice to think that the day is at hand,
when, prompted to it by law, I shall shoulder this gun
and go out a-boy-shooting.'

'Oh, now ! Lord, Lord, Lord !—But *our* office, respected
sir, conducted as I ventured to observe——'

'No, sir,' bristlingly settling his stubble chin in his
coon-skins. 'Don't try to oil me ; the herb-doctor tried
that. My experience, carried now through a course—
worse than salivation—a course of five-and-thirty boys,
proves to me that boyhood is a natural state of rascality.'

'Save us, save us ! '

'Yes, sir, yes. My name is Pitch ; I stick to what I
say. I speak from fifteen years' experience ; five-and-
thirty boys ; American, Irish, English, German, African,
Mulatto ; not to speak of that China boy sent me by one
who well knew my perplexities, from California ; and
that Lascar boy from Bombay. Thug ! I found him
sucking the embryo life from my spring eggs. All
rascals, sir, every soul of them ; Caucasian or Mongol.

Amazing the endless variety of rascality in human nature
of the juvenile sort. I remember that, having discharged, one after another, twenty-nine boys—each, too,
for some wholly unforeseen species of viciousness peculiar
to that one peculiar boy—I remember saying to myself :
Now, then, surely, I have got to the end of the list,
wholly exhausted it ; I have only now to get me a boy,
any boy different from those twenty-nine preceding boys,
and he infallibly shall be that virtuous boy I have so
long been seeking. But, bless me ! this thirtieth boy—
by the way, having at the time long forsworn your
intelligence offices, I had him sent to me from the Com-
missioners of Emigration, all the way from New York,
culled out carefully, in fine, at my particular request,
from a standing army of eight hundred boys, the flowers
of all nations, so they wrote me, temporarily in barracks
on an East River island—I say, this thirtieth boy was
in person not ungraceful ; his deceased mother, a lady's-
maid, or something of that sort ; and in manner, why,
in a plebeian way, a perfect Chesterfield ;* very intelligent, too—quick as a flash. But, such suavity ! " Please,
sir ! please, sir ! " always bowing and saying, " Please, sir."
In the strangest way, too, combining a filial affection with
a menial respect. Took such warm, singular interest in
my affairs. Wanted to be considered one of the family—
sort of adopted son of mine, I suppose. Of a morning,
when I would go out to my stable, with what childlike
good-nature he would trot out my nag, " Please, sir, I
think he 's getting fatter and fatter." " But, he don't
look very clean, does he ? " unwilling to be downright
harsh with so affectionate a lad ; " and he seems a little
hollow inside the haunch there, don't he ? or no, perhaps
I don't see plain this morning." " Oh, please, sir, it 's
just there I think he 's gaining so, please." Polite
scamp ! I soon found he never gave that wretched nag

his oats of nights ; didn't bed him either. Was above
that sort of chambermaid work. No end to his wilful
neglects. But the more he abused my service, the more
polite he grew.'

'Oh, sir, some way you mistook him.'

'Not a bit of it. Besides, sir, he was a boy who under
a Chesterfieldian exterior hid strong destructive pro-
pensities. He cut up my horse-blanket for the bits of
leather, for hinges to his chest. Denied it point-blank.
After he was gone, found the shreds under his mattress.
Would slyly break his hoe-handle, too, on purpose to get
rid of hoeing. Then be so gracefully penitent for his
fatal excess of industrious strength. Offer to mend
all by taking a nice stroll to the nighest settlement—
cherry-trees in full bearing all the way—to get the broken
thing cobbled. Very politely stole my pears, odd pennies,
shillings, dollars, and nuts ; regular squirrel at it. But I
could prove nothing. Expressed to him my suspicions.
Said I, moderately enough, " A little less politeness, and
a little more honesty would suit me better." He fired
up ; threatened to sue for libel. I won't say anything
about his afterward, in Ohio, being found in the act
of gracefully putting a bar across a railroad track, for
the reason that a stoker called him the rogue that he
was. But enough : polite boys or saucy boys, white
boys or black boys, smart boys or lazy boys, Caucasian
boys or Mongol boys—all are rascals.'

'Shocking, shocking !' nervously tucking his frayed
cravat-end out of sight. 'Surely, respected sir, you
labour under a deplorable hallucination. Why, pardon
again, you seem to have not the slightest confidence in
boys. I admit, indeed, that boys, some of them at least,
are but too prone to one little foolish foible or other.
But, what then, respected sir, when, by natural laws,
they finally outgrow such things, and wholly ? '

Having until now vented himself mostly in plaintive dissent of canine whines and groans, the man with the brass plate seemed beginning to summon courage to a less timid encounter. But, upon his maiden essay, was not very encouragingly handled, since the dialogue immediately continued as follows :—

'Boys outgrow what is amiss in them ? From bad boys spring good men ? Sir, "the child is father of the man ";* hence, as all boys are rascals, so are all men. But, God bless me, you must know these things better than I ; keeping an intelligence office as you do ; a business which must furnish peculiar facilities for studying mankind. Come, come up here, sir ; confess you know these things pretty well, after all. Do you not know that all men are rascals, and all boys, too ? '

'Sir,' replied the other, spite of his shocked feelings seeming to pluck up some spirit, but not to an indiscreet degree—'Sir, heaven be praised, I am far, very far from knowing what you say. True,' he thoughtfully continued, ' with my associates, I keep an intelligence office, and for ten years, come October, have, one way or other, been concerned in that line ; for no small period in the great city of Cincinnati, too ; and though, as you hint, within that long interval, I must have had more or less favourable opportunity for studying mankind—in a business way, scanning not only the faces, but ransacking the lives of several thousands of human beings, male and female, of various nations, both employers and employed, genteel and ungenteel, educated and uneducated ; yet—of course, I candidly admit, with some random exceptions, I have, so far as my small observation goes, found that mankind thus domestically viewed, confidentially viewed, I may say ; they, upon the whole —making some reasonable allowances for human imperfection—present as pure a moral spectacle as the

purest angel could wish. I say it, respected sir, with
confidence.'

'Gammon !* You don't mean what you say. Else
you are like a landsman at sea : don't know the ropes,
the very things everlastingly pulled before your eyes.
Serpent-like, they glide about, travelling blocks too subtle
for you. In short, the entire ship is a riddle. Why, you
green ones wouldn't know if she were unseaworthy ; but
still, with thumbs stuck back into your arm-holes, pace
the rotten planks, singing like a fool, words put into
your green mouth by the cunning owner, the man who,
heavily insuring it, sends his ship to be wrecked—

"A wet sheet and a flowing sea ! "—*

and, sir, now that it occurs to me, your talk, the whole
of it, is but a wet sheet and a flowing sea, and an idle
wind that follows fast, offering a striking contrast to my
own discourse.'

'Sir,' exclaimed the man with the brass plate, his
patience now more or less tasked, 'permit me with
deference to hint that some of your remarks are injudiciously worded. And thus we say to our patrons,
when they enter our office full of abuse of us because
of some worthy boy we may have sent them—some boy
wholly misjudged for the time. Yes, sir, permit me to
remark that you do not sufficiently consider that, though
a small man, I may have my small share of feelings.'

'Well, well, I didn't mean to wound your feelings at
all. And that they are small, very small, I take your
word for it. Sorry, sorry. But truth is like a threshing-
machine ; tender sensibilities must keep out of the way.
Hope you understand me. Don't want to hurt you.
All I say is, what I said in the first place, only now I
swear it, that all boys are rascals.'

'Sir,' lowly replied the other, still forbearing like an

old lawyer badgered in court, or else like a good-hearted simpleton, the butt of mischievous wags—' Sir, since you come back to the point, will you allow me, in my small, quiet way, to submit to you certain small, quiet views of the subject in hand ? '

' Oh, yes ! ' with insulting indifference, rubbing his chin and looking the other way. ' Oh, yes ; go on.'

' Well, then, respected sir,' continued the other, now assuming as genteel an attitude as the irritating set of his pinched five-dollar suit would permit ; ' well, then, sir, the peculiar principles, the strictly philosophical principles, I may say,' guardedly rising in dignity, as he guardedly rose on his toes, ' upon which our office is founded, has led me and my associates, in our small, quiet way, to a careful analytical study of man, conducted, too, on a quiet theory, and with an unobtrusive aim wholly our own. That theory I will not now at large set forth. But some of the discoveries resulting from it, I will, by your permission, very briefly mention ; such of them, I mean, as refer to the state of boyhood scientifically viewed.'

' Then you have studied the thing ? expressly studied boys ? Why didn't you out with that before ? '

' Sir, in my small business way, I have not conversed with so many masters, gentlemen masters, for nothing. I have been taught that in this world there is a precedence of opinions as well as of persons. You have kindly given me your views. I am now, with modesty, about to give you mine.'

' Stop flunkeying—go on.'

' In the first place, sir, our theory teaches us to proceed by analogy from the physical to the moral. Are we right there, sir ? Now, sir, take a young boy, a young male infant rather, a man-child in short—what, sir, I respectfully ask, do you in the first place remark ? '

' A rascal, sir ! present and prospective, a rascal ! '

' Sir, if passion is to invade, surely science must evacuate. May I proceed ? Well, then, what, in the first place, in a general view, do you remark, respected sir, in that male baby or man-child ? '

The bachelor privily growled, but this time, upon the whole, better governed himself than before, though not, indeed, to the degree of thinking it prudent to risk an articulate response.

' What do you remark ? I respectfully repeat.' But as no answer came, only the low, half-suppressed growl, as of Bruin in a hollow trunk, the questioner continued : ' Well, sir, if you will permit me, in my small way, to speak for you, you remark, respected sir, an incipient creation ; loose sort of sketchy thing ; a little preliminary rag-paper study, or careless cartoon, so to speak, of a man. The idea, you see, respected sir, is there ; but, as yet, wants filling out. In a word, respected sir, the man-child is at present but little, every way ; I don't pretend to deny it ; but, then, he *promises* well, does he not ? Yes, promises very well indeed, I may say. (So, too, we say to our patrons in reference to some noble little youngster objected to for being a *dwarf*.) But, to advance one step further,' extending his threadbare leg, as he drew a pace nearer, ' we must now drop the figure of the rag-paper cartoon, and borrow one—to use presently, when wanted—from the horticultural kingdom. Some bud, lily-bud, if you please. Now, such points as the new-born man-child has—as yet not all that could be desired, I am free to confess—still, such as they are, there they are, and palpable as those of an adult. But we stop not here,' taking another step. ' The man-child not only possesses these present points, small though they are, but, likewise—now our horticultural image comes into play—like the bud of the lily, he

contains concealed rudiments of others ; that is, points
at present invisible, with beauties at present dormant.'

'Come, come, this talk is getting too horticultural
and beautiful altogether. Cut it short, cut it short ! '

'Respected sir,' with a rustily martial sort of gesture,
like a decayed corporal's, 'when deploying into the field
of discourse the vanguard of an important argument
much more in evolving the grand central forces of a new
philosophy of boys, as I may say, surely you will kindly
allow scope adequate to the movement in hand, small
and humble in its way as that movement may be. Is it
worth my while to go on, respected sir ? '

'Yes, stop flunkeying and go on.'

Thus encouraged, again the philosopher with the brass
plate proceeded :—

'Supposing, sir, that worthy gentleman (in such terms,
to an applicant for service, we allude to some patron
we chance to have in our eye), supposing, respected sir,
that worthy gentleman, Adam, to have been dropped
overnight in Eden, as a calf in the pasture ; supposing
that, sir—then how could even the learned serpent
himself have foreknown that such a downy-chinned little
innocent would eventually rival the goat in a beard ?
Sir, wise as the serpent was, that eventuality would
have been entirely hidden from his wisdom.'

'I don't know about that. The Devil is very sagacious.
To judge by the event, he appears to have understood
man better even than the Being who made him.'

'For God's sake, don't say that, sir ! To the point.
Can it now with fairness be denied that, in his beard,
the man-child prospectively possesses an appendix, not
less imposing than patriarchal ; and for this goodly
beard, should we not by generous anticipation give the
man-child, even in his cradle, credit ? Should we not
now, sir ? respectfully I put it.'

'Yes, if like pig-weed he mows it down soon as it shoots,' porcinely rubbing his stubble-chin against his coon-skins.

'I have hinted at the analogy,' continued the other, calmly disregardful of the digression ; 'now to apply it. Suppose a boy evince no noble quality. Then generously give him credit for his prospective one. Don't you see ? So we say to our patrons when they would fain return a boy upon us as unworthy : "Madam, or sir (as the case may be), has this boy a beard ?" "No." "Has he, we respectfully ask, as yet, evinced any noble quality ?" "No, indeed." "Then, madam, or sir, take him back, we humbly beseech ; and keep him till that same noble quality sprouts ; for, have confidence, it, like the beard, is in him."'

'Very fine theory,' scornfully exclaimed the bachelor, yet in secret, perhaps, not entirely undisturbed by these strange new views of the matter ; 'but what trust is to be placed in it ?'

'The trust of perfect confidence, sir. To proceed. Once more, if you please, regard the man-child.'

'Hold !' paw-like thrusting out his bearskin arm, 'don't intrude that man-child upon me too often. He who loves not bread, dotes not on dough. As little of your man-child as your logical arrangements will admit.'

'Anew regard the man-child,' with inspired intrepidity repeated he with the brass plate, 'in the perspective of his developments, I mean. At first the man-child has no teeth, but about the sixth month—am I right, sir ?'

'Don't know anything about it.'

'To proceed then : though at first deficient in teeth, about the sixth month the man-child begins to put forth in that particular. And sweet those tender little puttings-forth are.'

'Very, but blown out of his mouth directly, worthless enough.'

'Admitted. And, therefore, we say to our patrons returning with a boy alleged not only to be deficient in goodness, but redundant in ill: "The lad, madam, or sir, evinces very corrupt qualities, does he ? " " No end to them." " But, have confidence, there will be ; for pray, madam, in this lad's early childhood, were not those frail first teeth, then his, followed by his present sound, even, beautiful and permanent set. And the more objectionable those first teeth became, was not that, madam, we respectfully submit, so much the more reason to look for their speedy substitution by the present sound, even, beautiful and permanent ones." " True, true, can't deny that." " Then, madam, take him back, we respectfully beg, and wait till, in the now swift course of nature, dropping those transient moral blemishes you complain of, he replacingly buds forth in the sound, even, beautiful and permanent virtues." '

'Very philosophical again,' was the contemptuous reply—the outward contempt, perhaps, proportioned to the inward misgiving. ' Vastly philosophical, indeed, but tell me—to continue your analogy—since the second teeth followed—in fact, came from—the first, is there no chance the blemish may be transmitted ? '

'Not at all.' Abating in humility as he gained in the argument. ' The second teeth follow, but do not come from, the first ; successors, not sons. The first teeth are not like the germ blossom of the apple, at once the father of, and incorporated into, the growth it foreruns ; but they are thrust from their place by the independent undergrowth of the succeeding set—an illustration, by the way, which shows more for me than I meant, though not more than I wish.'

'What does it show ? ' Surly-looking as a thunder-

cloud with the inkept unrest of unacknowledged conviction.

'It shows this, respected sir, that in the case of any
boy, especially an ill one, to apply unconditionally the
saying, that the "child is father of the man," is, besides
implying an uncharitable aspersion of the race, affirming
a thing very wide of——'

'—Your analogy,' like a snapping turtle.

'Yes, respected sir.'

'But is analogy argument ?   You are a punster.'

'Punster, respected sir ? ' with a look of being aggrieved.

'Yes, you pun with ideas as another man may with
words.'

'Oh well, sir, whoever talks in that strain, whoever
has no confidence in human reason, whoever despises
human reason, in vain to reason with him.   Still, respected sir,' altering his air, 'permit me to hint that,
had not the force of analogy moved you somewhat, you
would hardly have offered to contemn it.'

'Talk away,' disdainfully ; 'but pray tell me what
has that last analogy of yours to do with your intelligence
office business ? '

'Everything to do with it, respected sir.   From that
analogy we derive the reply made to such a patron as,
shortly after being supplied by us with an adult servant,
proposes to return him upon our hands ; not that, while
with the patron, said adult has given any cause of dis-
satisfaction, but the patron has just chanced to hear
something unfavourable concerning him from some
gentleman who employed said adult long before, while
a boy.   To which too fastidious patron, we, taking said
adult by the hand, and graciously reintroducing him to
the patron, say : "Far be it from you, madam, or sir,
to proceed in your censure against this adult, in anything of the spirit of an *ex-post-facto* law.   Madam, or

sir, would you visit upon the butterfly the sins of the
caterpillar ? In the natural advance of all creatures,
do they not bury themselves over and over again in the
endless resurrection of better and better ? Madam, or
sir, take back this adult ; he may have been a caterpillar, but is now a butterfly.'

'Pun away ; but even accepting your analogical pun,
what does it amount to ? Was the caterpillar one
creature, and is the butterfly another ? The butterfly
is the caterpillar in a gaudy cloak ; stripped of which,
there lies the impostor's long spindle of a body, pretty
much worm-shaped as before.'

'You reject the analogy. To the facts, then. You
deny that a youth of one character can be transformed
into a man of an opposite character. Now then—yes, I
have it. There 's the founder of La Trappe,* and Ignatius
Loyola ;* in boyhood, and some way into manhood, both
devil-may-care bloods, and yet, in the end, the wonders
of the world for anchoritish self-command. These two
examples, by the way, we cite to such patrons as would
hastily return rakish young waiters upon us. " Madam,
or sir—patience ; patience," we say ; " good madam, or
sir, would you discharge forth your cask of good wine,
because, while working, it riles more or less ? Then
discharge not forth this young waiter ; the good in him
is working." " But he is a sad rake." " Therein is his
promise ; the rake being crude material for the saint." '

'Ah, you are a talking man—what I call a wordy man.
You talk, talk.'

'And with submission, sir, what is the greatest judge,
bishop or prophet, but a talking man ? He talks, talks.
It is the peculiar vocation of a teacher to talk. What 's
wisdom itself but table-talk ? The best wisdom in this
world, and the last spoken by its teacher ; did it not
literally and truly come in the form of table-talk ? '

' You, you, you ! ' rattling down his rifle.

' To shift the subject, since we cannot agree. Pray, what is your opinion, respected sir, of St. Augustine ? '

' St. Augustine ? What should I, or you either, know of him ? Seems to me, for one in such a business, to say nothing of such a coat, that though you don't know a great deal, indeed, yet you know a good deal more than you ought to know, or than you have a right to know, or than it is safe or expedient for you to know, or than, in the fair course of life, you could have honestly come to know. I am of opinion you should be served like a Jew in the Middle Ages with his gold ; this knowledge of yours, which you haven't enough knowledge to know how to make a right use of, it should be taken from you. And so I have been thinking all along.'

' You are merry, sir. But you have a little looked into St. Augustine, I suppose.'

' St. Augustine on Original Sin*is my text-book. But you, I ask again, where do you find time or inclination for these out-of-the-way speculations ? In fact, your whole talk, the more I think of it, is altogether un-exampled and extraordinary.'

' Respected sir, have I not already informed you that the quite new method, the strictly philosophical one, on which our office is founded, has led me and my associates to an enlarged study of mankind. It was my fault, if I did not, likewise, hint, that these studies directed always to the scientific procuring of good servants of all sorts, boys included, for the kind gentle-men, our patrons—that these studies, I say, have been conducted equally among all books of all libraries, as among all men of all nations. Then, you rather like St. Augustine, sir ? '

' Excellent genius ! '

' In some points he was ; yet, how comes it that under

his own hand, St. Augustine confesses that, until his
thirtieth year, he was a very sad dog ? '*

'A saint a sad dog ? '

'Not the saint, but the saint's irresponsible little fore-
runner—the boy.'

'All boys are rascals, and so are all men,' again flying
off at his tangent ; 'my name is Pitch ; I stick to what
I say.'

'Ah, sir, permit me—when I behold you on this mild
summer's eve, thus eccentrically clothed in the skins of
wild beasts, I cannot but conclude that the equally grim
and unsuitable habit of your mind is likewise but an
eccentric assumption, having no basis in your genuine
soul, no more than in nature herself.'

'Well, really, now—really,' fidgeted the bachelor, not
unaffected in his conscience by these benign personalities,
'really, really, now, I don't know but that I may have
been a little bit too hard upon those five-and-thirty boys
of mine.'

'Glad to find you a little softening, sir. Who knows
now, but that flexile gracefulness, however questionable
at the time of that thirtieth boy of yours, might have
been the silky husk of the most solid qualities of maturity.
It might have been with him as with the ear of the
Indian corn.'

'Yes, yes, yes,' excitedly cried the bachelor, as the
light of this new illustration broke in, 'yes, yes ; and
now that I think of it, how often I 've sadly watched my
Indian corn in May, wondering whether such sickly,
half-eaten sprouts, could ever thrive up into the stiff,
stately spear of August.'

'A most admirable reflection, sir, and you have only,
according to the analogical theory first started by our
office, to apply it to that thirtieth boy in question, and
see the result. Had you but kept that thirtieth boy—

been patient with his sickly virtues, cultivated them,
hoed round them, why what a glorious guerdon would
have been yours, when at last you should have had a
St. Augustine for an ostler.'

'Really, really—well, I am glad I didn't send him to
jail, as at first I intended.'

'Oh that would have been too bad. Grant he was
vicious. The petty vices of boys are like the innocent
kicks of colts, as yet imperfectly broken. Some boys
know not virtue only for the same reason they know not
French; it was never taught them. Established upon
the basis of parental charity, juvenile asylums exist by
law for the benefit of lads convicted of acts which, in
adults, would have received other requital. Why?
Because, do what they will, society, like our office, at
bottom has a Christian confidence in boys. And all this
we say to our patrons.'

'Your patrons, sir, seem your marines to whom you
may say anything,'*said the other, relapsing. 'Why do
knowing employers shun youths from asylums, though
offered them at the smallest wages? I'll none of your
reformado* boys.'

'Such a boy, respected sir, I would not get for you,
but a boy that never needed reform. Do not smile, for
as whooping-cough and measles are juvenile diseases,
and yet some juveniles never have them, so are there boys
equally free from juvenile vices. True, for the best of
boys, measles may be contagious, and evil communica-
tions corrupt good manners; but a boy with a sound
mind in a sound body—such is the boy I would get you.
If hitherto, sir, you have struck upon a peculiarly bad
vein of boys, so much the more hope now of your hitting
a good one.'

'That sounds a kind of reasonable, as it were—a little
so, really. In fact, though you have said a great many

foolish things, very foolish and absurd things, yet, upon the whole, your conversation has been such as might almost lead one less distrustful than I to repose a certain conditional confidence in you, I had almost added in your office, also. Now, for the humour of it, supposing that even I, I myself, really had this sort of conditional confidence, though but a grain, what sort of a boy, in sober fact, could you send me ? And what would be your fee ? '

' Conducted,' replied the other somewhat loftily, rising now in eloquence as his proselyte, for all his pretences, sunk in conviction, ' conducted upon principles involving care, learning, and labour, exceeding what is usual in kindred institutions, the Philosophical Intelligence Office is forced to charges somewhat higher than customary. Briefly, our fee is three dollars in advance. As for the boy, by a lucky chance, I have a very promising little fellow now in my eye—a very likely little fellow, indeed.'

' Honest ? '

' As the day is long. Might trust him with untold millions. Such, at least, were the marginal observations on the phrenological chart of his head, submitted to me by the mother.'

' How old ? '

' Just fifteen.'

' Tall ? Stout ? '

' Uncommonly so, for his age, his mother remarked.'

' Industrious ? '

' The busy bee.'

The bachelor fell into a troubled revery. At last, with much hesitancy, he spoke :—

' Do you think now, candidly, that—I say candidly—candidly—could I have some small, limited—some faint, conditional degree of confidence in that boy ? Candidly, now ? '

'Candidly, you could.'

'A sound boy?   A good boy?'

'Never knew one more so.'

The bachelor fell into another irresolute revery; then
said: 'Well, now, you have suggested some rather new
views of boys, and men, too. Upon those views in the
concrete I at present decline to determine. Nevertheless, for the sake purely of a scientific experiment, I will
try that boy. I don't think him an angel, mind. No,
no. But I'll try him. There are my three dollars, and
here is my address. Send him along this day two
weeks. Hold, you will be wanting the money for his
passage. There,' handing it somewhat reluctantly.

'Ah, thank you. I had forgotten his passage'; then,
altering in manner, and gravely holding the bills, continued: 'Respected sir, never willingly do I handle
money not with perfect willingness, nay, with a certain
alacrity, paid. Either tell me that you have a perfect
and unquestioning confidence in me (never mind the
boy now) or permit me respectfully to return these bills.'

'Put 'em up, put 'em up!'

'Thank you. Confidence is the indispensable basis of
all sorts of business transactions. Without it, commerce between man and man, as between country and
country, would, like a watch, run down and stop. And
now, supposing that against present expectation the lad
should, after all, evince some little undesirable trait, do
not, respected sir, rashly dismiss him. Have but
patience, have but confidence. Those transient vices
will, ere long, fall out, and be replaced by the sound,
firm, even and permanent virtues. Ah,' glancing shoreward, toward a grotesquely shaped bluff, 'there's the
Devil's Joke, as they call it; the bell for landing will
shortly ring. I must go look up the cook I brought for
the inn-keeper at Cairo.'

CHAPTER XXIII

IN WHICH THE POWERFUL EFFECT OF NATURAL SCENERY
IS EVINCED IN THE CASE OF THE MISSOURIAN, WHO,
IN VIEW OF THE REGION ROUND ABOUT CAIRO, HAS A
RETURN OF HIS CHILLY FIT

At Cairo,* the old-established firm of Fever & Ague is
still settling up its unfinished business ; that Creole grave-
digger, Yellow Jack*—his hand at the mattock and spade
has not lost its cunning ;* while Don Saturninus Typhus*
taking his constitutional with Death, Calvin Edson and
three undertakers, in the morass, snuffs up the mephitic
breeze with zest.

In the dank twilight, fanned with mosquitoes, and
sparkling with fire-flies, the boat now lies before Cairo.
She has landed certain passengers, and tarries for the
coming of expected ones. Leaning over the rail on the
inshore side, the Missourian eyes through the dubious
medium that swampy and squalid domain ; and over it
audibly mumbles his cynical mind to himself, as Apemantus'*dog may have mumbled his bone. He bethinks
him that the man with the brass plate was to land on
this villainous bank, and for that cause, if no other, begins
to suspect him. Like one beginning to rouse himself
from a dose of chloroform treacherously given, he half
divines, too, that he, the philosopher, had unwittingly
been betrayed into being an unphilosophical dupe. To
what vicissitudes of light and shade is man subject ! He

ponders the mystery of human subjectivity in general.
He thinks he perceives with Crossbones,* his favourite
author, that, as one may wake up well in the morning,
very well, indeed, and brisk as a buck, I thank you, but
ere bed-time get under the weather, there is no telling
how—so one may wake up wise, and slow of assent, very
wise and very slow, I assure you, and for all that, before
night, by like trick in the atmosphere, be left in the lurch
a ninny. Health and wisdom equally precious, and
equally little as unfluctuating possessions to be relied on.

But where was slipped in the entering wedge ? Philosophy, knowledge, experience—were those trusty knights
of the castle recreant ? No, but unbeknown to them,
the enemy stole on the castle's south side, its genial one,
where Suspicion, the warder, parleyed. In fine, his too
indulgent, too artless and companionable nature betrayed
him. Admonished by which, he thinks he must be a
little splenetic in his intercourse henceforth.

He revolves the crafty process of sociable chat, by
which, as he fancies, the man with the brass plate wormed
into him, and made such a fool of him as insensibly to
persuade him to waive, in his exceptional case, that
general law of distrust systematically applied to the race.
He revolves, but cannot comprehend, the operation, still
less the operator. Was the man a trickster, it must be
more for the love than the lucre. Two or three dirty
dollars the motive to so many nice wiles ? And yet how
full of mean needs his seeming. Before his mental vision
the person of that threadbare Talleyrand,* that impover-
ished Machiavelli,* that seedy Rosicrucian*—for something
of all these he vaguely deems him—passes now in puzzled
review. Fain, in his disfavour, would he make out a
logical case. The doctrine of analogies recurs. Fallacious
enough doctrine when wielded against one's prejudices,
but in corroboration of cherished suspicions not without

likelihood. Analogically, he couples the slanting cut of the equivocator's coat-tails with the sinister cast in his eye; he weighs slyboot's sleek speech in the light imparted by the oblique import of the smooth slope of his worn boot-heels; the insinuator's undulating flunkeyisms dovetail into those of the flunkey beast that windeth his way on his belly.*

From these uncordial reveries he is roused by a cordial slap on the shoulder, accompanied by a spicy volume of tobacco-smoke, out of which came a voice, sweet as a seraph's:—

'A penny for your thoughts, my fine fellow.'

CHAPTER XXIV

A PHILANTHROPIST UNDERTAKES TO CONVERT A MIS-
ANTHROPE, BUT DOES NOT GET BEYOND CONFUTING
HIM

' HANDS off ! ' cried the bachelor, involuntarily covering
dejection with moroseness.

' Hands off ? that sort of label won't do in our Fair.
Whoever in our Fair* has fine feelings loves to feel the
nap of fine cloth, especially when a fine fellow wears it.'

' And who of my fine-fellow species may you be ?
From the Brazils, ain't you ? Toucan fowl. Fine
feathers on foul meat ! '

This ungentle mention of the toucan was not improbably suggested by the parti-hued, and rather plumagy
aspect of the stranger, no bigot it would seem, but a
liberalist, in dress, and whose wardrobe, almost anywhere
than on the liberal Mississippi, used to all sorts of fantastic
informalities, might, even to observers less critical than
the bachelor, have looked, if anything, a little out of the
common ; but not more so perhaps, than, considering
the bear and raccoon costume, the bachelor's own appearance. In short, the stranger sported a vesture barred
with various hues, that of the cochineal* predominating,
in style participating of a Highland plaid, Emir's robe,
and French blouse ; from its plaited sort of front peeped
glimpses of a flowered regatta-shirt, while, for the rest,
white trowsers of ample duck flowed over maroon-
coloured slippers, and a jaunty smoking-cap of regal
purple crowned him off at top ; king of travelled good-

fellows, evidently. Grotesque as all was, nothing looked
stiff or unused ; all showed signs of easy service, the
least wonted thing setting like a wonted glove. That
genial hand, which had just been laid on the ungenial
shoulder, was now carelessly thrust down before him,
sailor fashion, into a sort of Indian belt, confining the
redundant vesture ; the other held, by its long bright
cherry-stem, a Nuremberg pipe in blast, its great porce-
lain bowl painted in miniature with linked crests and arms
of interlinked nations—a florid show. As by subtle
saturations of its mellowing essence the tobacco had
ripened the bowl, so it looked as if something similar of
the interior spirit came rosily out on the cheek. But
rosy pipe-bowl, or rosy countenance, all was lost on that
unrosy man, the bachelor, who, waiting a moment till
the commotion, caused by the boat's renewed progress,
had a little abated, thus continued :—

'Hark ye,' jeeringly eyeing the cap and belt, 'did you
ever see Signor Marzetti in the African pantomime ? '*

'No ;—good performer ? '

'Excellent ; plays the intelligent ape till he seems it.
With such naturalness can a being endowed with an
immortal spirit enter into that of a monkey. But where 's
your tail ? In the pantomime, Marzetti, no hypocrite
in his monkery, prides himself on that.'

The stranger, now at rest, sideways and genially, on
one hip, his right leg cavalierly crossed before the other,
the toe of his vertical slipper pointed easily down on the
deck, whiffed out a long, leisurely sort of indifferent and
charitable puff, betokening him more or less of the mature
man of the world, a character which, like its opposite,
the sincere Christian's, is not always swift to take offence ;
and then, drawing near, still smoking, again laid his hand,
this time with mild impressiveness, on the ursine shoulder,
and not unamiably said : 'That in your address there is

a sufficiency of the *fortiter in re* few unbiased observers
will question ; but that this is duly attempered with the
suaviter in modo*may admit, I think, of an honest doubt.
My dear fellow,' beaming his eyes full upon him, ' what
injury have I done you, that you should receive my
greeting with a curtailed civility ? '

' Off hands ' ; once more shaking the friendly member
from him. ' Who in the name of the great chimpanzee,
in whose likeness, you, Marzetti, and the other chatterers
are made, who in thunder are you ? '

' A cosmopolitan, a catholic man ; who, being such,
ties himself to no narrow tailor or teacher, but federates,
in heart as in costume, something of the various gallantries
of men under various suns. Oh, one roams not over the
gallant globe in vain. Bred by it, is a fraternal and
fusing feeling. No man is a stranger. You accost anybody. Warm and confiding, you wait not for measured
advances. And though, indeed, mine, in this instance,
have met with no very hilarious encouragement, yet the
principle of a true citizen of the world is still to return
good for ill.—My dear fellow, tell me how I can serve
you.'

' By dispatching yourself, Mr. Popinjay-of-the-world,
into the heart of the Lunar Mountains.* You are another
of them. Out of my sight ! '

' Is the sight of humanity so very disagreeable to you,
then ? Ah, I may be foolish, but for my part, in all its
aspects, I love it. Served up à la Pole, or à la Moor, à
la Ladrone,* or à la Yankee, that good dish, man, still
delights me ; or rather is man a wine I never weary of
comparing and sipping ; wherefore am I a pledged cosmopolitan, a sort of London-Dock-Vault*connoisseur, going
about from Teheran to Natchitoches, a taster of races ;
in all his vintages, smacking my lips over this racy
creature, man, continually. But as there are teetotal

palates which have a distaste even for Amontillado,* so I
suppose there may be teetotal souls which relish not even
the very best brands of humanity. Excuse me, but it
just occurs to me that you, my dear fellow, possibly lead
a solitary life.'

'Solitary?' starting as at a touch of divination.

'Yes: in a solitary life one insensibly contracts
oddities,—talking to one's self now.'

'Been eavesdropping, eh?'

'Why, a soliloquist in a crowd can hardly but be overheard, and without much reproach to the hearer.'

'You are an eavesdropper.'

'Well. Be it so.'

'Confess yourself an eavesdropper?'

'I confess that when you were muttering here I,
passing by, caught a word or two, and, by like chance,
something previous of your chat with the Intelligence-
office man;—a rather sensible fellow, by the way; much
of my style of thinking; would, for his own sake, he were
of my style of dress. Grief to good minds, to see a man
of superior sense forced to hide his light under the bushel
of an inferior coat.—Well, from what little I heard, I
said to myself, Here now is one with the unprofitable
philosophy of disesteem for man. Which disease, in the
main, I have observed—excuse me—to spring from a
certain lowness, if not sourness, of spirits inseparable
from sequestration. Trust me, one had better mix in,
and do like others. Sad business, this holding out against
having a good time. Life is a picnic *en costume*;* one
must take a part, assume a character, stand ready in a
sensible way to play the fool. To come in plain clothes,
with a long face, as a wiseacre, only makes one a dis-
comfort to himself, and a blot upon the scene. Like your
jug of cold water among the wine-flasks, it leaves you
unelated among the elated ones. No, no. This austerity

won't do. Let me tell you too—*en confiance**—that while
revelry may not always merge into ebriety, soberness, in
too deep potations, may become a sort of sottishness.
Which sober sottishness, in my way of thinking, is only
to be cured by beginning at the other end of the horn, to
tipple a little.'

' Pray, what society of vintners and old topers are you
hired to lecture for ? '

' I fear I did not give my meaning clearly. A little
story may help. The story of the worthy old woman of
Goshen,* a very moral old woman, who wouldn't let her
shoats eat fattening apples in fall, for fear the fruit might
ferment upon their brains, and so make them swinish.
Now, during a green Christmas, inauspicious to the old,
this worthy old woman fell into a moping decline, took
to her bed, no appetite, and refused to see her best friends.
In much concern her good man sent for the doctor, who,
after seeing the patient and putting a question or two,
beckoned the husband out, and said : " Deacon, do you
want her cured ? " " Indeed I do." " Go directly, then,
and buy a jug of Santa Cruz."* " Santa Cruz ? my wife
drink Santa Cruz ? " " Either that or die." " But how
much ? " " As much as she can get down." " But
she 'll get drunk ! " " That 's the cure." Wise men,
like doctors, must be obeyed. Much against the grain,
the sober deacon got the unsober medicine, and, equally
against her conscience, the poor old woman took it ;
but, by so doing, ere long recovered health and spirits,
famous appetite, and glad again to see her friends ; and
having by this experience broken the ice of arid absti-
nence, never afterward kept herself a cup too low.'

This story had the effect of surprising the bachelor
into interest, though hardly into approval.

' If I take your parable right,' said he, sinking no little
of his former churlishness, ' the meaning is, that one

cannot enjoy life with gusto unless he renounce the too-sober view of life. But since the too-sober view is, doubtless, nearer true than the too-drunken; I, who rate truth, though cold water, above untruth, though Tokay,* will stick to my earthen jug.'

'I see,' slowly spirting upward a spiral staircase of lazy smoke, 'I see; you go in for the lofty.'

'How?'

'Oh, nothing! but if I wasn't afraid of prosing, I might tell another story about an old boot in a pieman's loft, contracting there between sun and oven an unseemly, dry-seasoned curl and warp. You've seen such leathery old garreteers, haven't you? Very high, sober, solitary, philosophic, grand, old boots, indeed; but I, for my part, would rather be the pieman's trodden slipper on the ground. Talking of piemen, humble-pie before proud-cake for me. This notion of being lone and lofty is a sad mistake. Men I hold in this respect to be like roosters; the one that betakes himself to a lone and lofty perch is the hen-pecked one, or the one that has the pip.'

'You are abusive!' cried the bachelor, evidently touched.

'Who is abused? You, or the race? You won't stand by and see the human race abused? Oh, then, you have some respect for the human race.'

'I have some respect for *myself*,' with a lip not so firm as before.

'And what race may *you* belong to? Now don't you see, my dear fellow, in what inconsistencies one involves himself by affecting disesteem for men. To a charm, my little stratagem succeeded. Come, come, think better of it, and, as a first step to a new mind, give up solitude. I fear, by the way, you have at some time been reading Zimmermann, that old Mr. Megrims* of a Zimmermann, whose book on Solitude is as vain as Hume's on Suicide,* as Bacon's on Knowledge ;* and, like these, will betray him who seeks to steer soul and body by it, like a false religion.   All they, be they what boasted ones you please, who, to the yearning of our kind after a founded rule of content, offer aught not in the spirit of fellowly gladness based on due confidence in what is above, away with them for poor dupes, or still poorer impostors.'

His manner here was so earnest that scarcely any auditor, perhaps, but would have been more or less impressed by it, while, possibly, nervous opponents might have a little quailed under it.   Thinking within himself a moment, the bachelor replied : ' Had you experience, you would know that your tippling theory, take it in what sense you will, is poor as any other.   And Rabelais's pro-wine Koran* no more trustworthy than Mahomet's anti-wine one.'*

' Enough,' for a finality knocking the ashes from his pipe, ' we talk and keep talking, and still stand where we did.   What do you say for a walk ?   My arm, and let 's a turn.   They are to have dancing on the hurricane-deck to-night.   I shall fling them off a Scotch jig, while, to save the pieces, you hold my loose change ; and following that, I propose that you, my dear fellow, stack your gun, and throw your bearskins in a sailor's horn-pipe—I holding your watch.   What do you say ? '

At this proposition the other was himself again, all raccoon.

' Look you,' thumping down his rifle, ' are you Jeremy Diddler No. 3 ? '

' Jeremy Diddler ?   I have heard of Jeremy the prophet and Jeremy Taylor the divine,* but your other Jeremy is a gentleman I am unacquainted with.'

' You are his confidential clerk, ain't you ? '

' Whose, pray ?   Not that I think myself unworthy of being confided in, but I don't understand.'

' You are another of them. Somehow I meet with the
most extraordinary metaphysical scamps to-day. Sort
of visitation of them. And yet that herb-doctor Diddler
somehow takes off the raw edge of the Diddlers that come
after him.'

' Herb-doctor ? who is he ? '

' Like you—another of them.'

' *Who* ? ' Then drawing near, as if for a good long
explanatory chat, his left hand spread, and his pipe-stem
coming crosswise down upon it like a ferule, ' You think
amiss of me. Now to undeceive you, I will just enter
into a little argument and——'

' No, you don't. No more little arguments for me.
Had too many little arguments to-day.'

' But put a case. Can you deny—I dare you to deny—
that the man leading a solitary life is peculiarly exposed
to the sorriest misconceptions touching strangers ? '

' Yes, I *do* deny it,' again, in his impulsiveness, snapping
at the controversial bait, ' and I will confute you there in
a trice. Look, you——'

' Now, now, now, my dear fellow,' thrusting out both
vertical palms for double shields, ' you crowd me too
hard. You don't give one a chance. Say what you will,
to shun a social proposition like mine, to shun society in
any way, evinces a churlish nature—cold, loveless ; as, to
embrace it, shows one warm and friendly, in fact, sunshiny.'

Here the other, all agog again, in his perverse way,
launched forth into the unkindest references to deaf old
worldlings keeping in the deafening world ; and gouty
gluttons limping to their gouty gourmandisings ; and
corseted coquettes clasping their corseted cavaliers in the
waltz, all for disinterested society's sake ; and thousands,
bankrupt through lavishness, ruining themselves out of
pure love of the sweet company of man—no envies,
rivalries, or other unhandsome motive to it.

'Ah, now,' deprecating with his pipe, 'irony is so unjust; never could abide irony; something Satanic about irony. God defend me from Irony, and Satire, his bosom friend.'

'A right knave's prayer, and a right fool's, too,' snapping his rifle-lock.

'Now be frank. Own that was a little gratuitous. But, no, no, you didn't mean it; anyway, I can make allowances. Ah, did you but know it, how much pleasanter to puff at this philanthropic pipe, than still to keep fumbling at that misanthropic rifle. As for your worldling, glutton, and coquette, though, doubtless, being such, they may have their little foibles—as who has not?—yet not one of the three can be reproached with that awful sin of shunning society; awful I call it, for not seldom it presupposes a still darker thing than itself—remorse.'

'Remorse drives man away from man? How came your fellow-creature, Cain, after the first murder, to go and build the first city? And why is it that the modern Cain dreads nothing so much as solitary confinement?'

'My dear fellow, you get excited. Say what you will, I for one must have my fellow-creatures round me. Thick, too—I must have them thick.'

'The pick-pocket, too, loves to have his fellow-creatures round him. Tut, man! no one goes into the crowd but for his end; and the end of too many is the same as the pick-pocket's—a purse.'

'Now, my dear fellow, how can you have the conscience to say that, when it is as much according to natural law that men are social as sheep gregarious. But grant that, in being social, each man has his end, do you, upon the strength of that, do you yourself, I say, mix with man, now, immediately, and be your end a more genial philosophy. Come, let's take a turn.'

Again he offered his fraternal arm; but the bachelor

once more flung it off, and, raising his rifle in energetic invocation, cried : ' Now the high-constable catch and confound all knaves in towns and rats in grain-bins, and if in this boat, which is a human grain-bin for the time, any sly, smooth, philandering rat be dodging now, pin him, thou high rat-catcher, against this rail.'

' A noble burst ! shows you at heart a trump. And when a card 's that, little matters it whether it be spade or diamond. You are good wine that, to be still better, only needs a shaking up. Come, let 's agree that we 'll to New Orleans, and there embark for London—I staying with my friends nigh Primrose Hill, and you putting up at the Piazza, Covent Garden—Piazza, Covent Garden ; for tell me—since you will not be a disciple to the full— tell me, was not that humour, of Diogenes,* which led him to live, a merry-andrew,* in the flower-market, better than that of the less wise Athenian, which made him a skulking scare-crow in pine-barrens ? An injudicious gentleman, Lord Timon.'

' Your hand ! ' seizing it.

' Bless me, how cordial a squeeze. It is agreed we shall be brothers, then ? '

' As much so as a brace of misanthropes can be,' with another and terrific squeeze. ' I had thought that the moderns had degenerated beneath the capacity of mis- anthropy. Rejoiced, though but in one instance, and that disguised, to be undeceived.'

The other stared in blank amaze.

' Won't do. You are Diogenes, Diogenes in disguise. I say—Diogenes masquerading as a cosmopolitan.'

With ruefully altered mien, the stranger still stood mute awhile. At length, in a pained tone, spoke : ' How hard the lot of that pleader who, in his zeal conceding too much, is taken to belong to a side which he but labours, however ineffectually, to convert ! ' Then with another

change of air : ' To you, an Ishmael,*disguising in sportive-
ness my intent, I came ambassador from the human race,
charged with the assurance that for your mislike they
bore no answering grudge, but sought to conciliate accord
between you and them. Yet you take me not for the
honest envoy, but I know not what sort of unheard-of
spy. Sir,' he less lowly added, ' this mistaking of your
man should teach you how you may mistake all men.
For God's sake,' laying both hands upon him, ' get you
confidence. See how distrust has duped you. I, Diogenes ? I he who, going a step beyond misanthropy, was
less a man-hater than a man-hooter ? Better were I
stark and stiff ! '

With which the philanthropist moved away less light-
some than he had come, leaving the discomfited misanthrope to the solitude he held so sapient.

CHAPTER XXV

THE COSMOPOLITAN MAKES AN ACQUAINTANCE

In the act of retiring, the cosmopolitan was met by a passenger, who, with the bluff *abord** of the West, thus addressed him, though a stranger.

' Queer 'coon,* your friend. Had a little scrimmage with him myself. Rather entertaining old 'coon, if he wasn't so deuced analytical. Reminded me somehow of what I 've heard about Colonel John Moredock, of Illinois, only your friend ain't quite so good a fellow at bottom, I should think.'

It was in the semicircular porch of a cabin, opening a recess from the deck, lit by a zoned lamp swung overhead, and sending its light vertically down, like the sun at noon. Beneath the lamp stood the speaker, affording to anyone disposed to it no unfavourable chance for scrutiny ; but the glance now resting on him betrayed no such rudeness.

A man neither tall nor stout, neither short nor gaunt ; but with a body fitted, as by measure, to the service of his mind. For the rest, one less favoured perhaps in his features than his clothes ; and of these the beauty may have been less in the fit than the cut ; to say nothing of the fineness of the nap, seeming out of keeping with something the reverse of fine in the skin ; and the unsuitableness of a violet vest, sending up sunset hues to a countenance betokening a kind of bilious habit.

But, upon the whole, it could not be fairly said that his appearance was unprepossessing ; indeed, to the

congenial, it would have been doubtless not uncongenial ;
while to others, it could not fail to be at least curiously
interesting, from the warm air of florid cordiality, contrasting itself with one knows not what kind of aguish
sallowness of saving discretion lurking behind it. Ungracious critics might have thought that the manner
flushed the man, something in the same fictitious way
that the vest flushed the cheek. And though his teeth
were singularly good, those same ungracious ones might
have hinted that they were too good to be true ; or
rather, were not so good as they might be ; since the best
false teeth are those made with at least two or three
blemishes, the more to look like life. But fortunately
for better constructions, no such critics had the stranger
now in eye ; only the cosmopolitan, who, after, in the
first place, acknowledging his advances with a mute
salute—in which acknowledgment, if there seemed less
of spirit than in his way of accosting the Missourian, it
was probably because of the saddening sequel of that
late interview—thus now replied : ' Colonel John Moredock,' repeating the words abstractedly ; ' that surname
recalls reminiscences. Pray,' with enlivened air, ' was
he any way connected with the Moredocks of Moredock
Hall, Northamptonshire, England ? '

' I know no more of the Moredocks of Moredock Hall
than of the Burdocks of Burdock Hut,' returned the other,
with the air somehow of one whose fortunes had been of
his own making ; ' all I know is, that the late Colonel
John Moredock was a famous one in his time ; eye like
Lochiel's ;* finger like a trigger ; nerve like a catamount's*;
and with but two little oddities—seldom stirred without
his rifle, and hated Indians like snakes.'

' Your Moredock, then, would seem a Moredock of
Misanthrope Hall—the Woods. No very sleek creature,
the colonel, I fancy.'

'Sleek or not, he was no uncombed one, but silky bearded and curly headed, and to all but Indians juicy as a peach. But Indians—how the late Colonel John Moredock, Indian-hater of Illinois, did hate Indians, to be sure!'

'Never heard of such a thing. Hate Indians? Why should he or anybody else hate Indians? *I* admire Indians. Indians I have always heard to be one of the finest of the primitive races, possessed of many heroic virtues. Some noble women, too. When I think of Pocahontas, I am ready to love Indians. Then there's Massasoit, and Philip of Mount Hope,* and Tecumseh, and Red-Jacket, and Logan—all heroes; and there's the Five Nations, and Araucanians—federations and communities of heroes. God bless me; hate Indians? Surely the late Colonel John Moredock must have wandered in his mind.'

'Wandered in the woods considerably, but never wandered elsewhere, that I ever heard.'

'Are you in earnest? Was there ever one who so made it his particular mission to hate Indians that, to designate him, a special word has been coined—Indian-hater?'

'Even so.'

'Dear me, you take it very calmly.—But really, I would like to know something about this Indian-hating. I can hardly believe such a thing to be. Could you favour me with a little history of the extraordinary man you mentioned?'

'With all my heart,' and immediately stepping from the porch, gestured the cosmopolitan to a settee near by, on deck. 'There, sir, sit you there, and I will sit here beside you—you desire to hear of Colonel John Moredock. Well, a day in my boyhood is marked with a white stone —the day I saw the colonel's rifle, powder-horn attached, hanging in a cabin on the west bank of the Wabash

river. I was going westward a long journey through
the wilderness with my father. It was high noon, and
we had stopped at the cabin to unsaddle and bait. The
man at the cabin pointed out the rifle, and told whose
it was, adding that the colonel was that moment sleeping
on wolf-skins in the corn-loft above, so we must not talk
very loud, for the colonel had been out all night hunting
(Indians, mind), and it would be cruel to disturb his
sleep. Curious to see one so famous, we waited two
hours over, in hopes he would come forth ; but he did not.
So, it being necessary to get to the next cabin before
nightfall, we had at last to ride off without the wished-
for satisfaction. Though, to tell the truth, I, for one,
did not go away entirely ungratified, for, while my father
was watering the horses, I slipped back into the cabin,
and stepping a round or two up the ladder, pushed my
head through the trap, and peered about. Not much
light in the loft ; but off, in the further corner, I saw
what I took to be the wolf-skins, and on them a bundle
of something, like a drift of leaves, and at one end, what
seemed a moss-ball ; and over it, deer-antlers branched ;
and close by, a small squirrel sprang out from a maple-
bowl of nuts, brushed the moss-ball with his tail, through
a hole, and vanished, squeaking. That bit of woodland
scene was all I saw. No Colonel Moredock there, unless
that moss-ball was his curly head, seen in the back view.
I would have gone clear up, but the man below had warned
me, that though, from his camping habits, the colonel
could sleep through thunder, he was for the same cause
amazing quick to waken at the sound of footsteps, however soft, and especially if human.'

'Excuse me,' said the other, softly laying his hand on
the narrator's wrist, ' but I fear the colonel was of a distrustful nature—little or no confidence. He *was* a little
suspicious-minded, wasn't he ? '

'Not a bit. Knew too much. Suspected nobody, but was not ignorant of Indians. Well: though, as you may gather, I never fully saw the man, yet, have I, one way and another, heard about as much of him as any other; in particular, have I heard his history again and again from my father's friend, James Hall, the judge,* you know. In every company being called upon to give this history, which none could better do, the judge at last fell into a style so methodic, you would have thought he spoke less to mere auditors than to an invisible amanuensis; seemed talking for the press; very impressive way with him indeed. And I, having an equally impressible memory, think that, upon a pinch, I can render you the judge upon the colonel almost word for word.'

'Do so, by all means,' said the cosmopolitan, well pleased.

'Shall I give you the judge's philosophy, and all?'

'As to that,' rejoined the other gravely, pausing over the pipe-bowl he was filling, 'the desirableness, to a man of a certain mind, of having another man's philosophy given, depends considerably upon what school of philosophy that other man belongs to. Of what school or system was the judge, pray?'

'Why, though he knew how to read and write, the judge never had much schooling. But, I should say he belonged, if anything, to the free-school system. Yes, a true patriot, the judge went in strong for free-schools.'

'In philosophy? The man of a certain mind, then, while respecting the judge's patriotism, and not blind to the judge's capacity for narrative, such as he may prove to have, might, perhaps, with prudence, waive an opinion of the judge's probable philosophy. But I am no rigorist; proceed, I beg; his philosophy or not, as you please.'

'Well, I would mostly skip that part, only, to begin, some reconnoitring of the ground in a philosophical way the judge always deemed indispensable with strangers. For you must know that Indian-hating was no monopoly of Colonel Moredock's ; but a passion, in one form or other, and to a degree, greater or less, largely shared among the class to which he belonged. And Indian-hating still exists ; and, no doubt, will continue to exist, so long as Indians do. Indian-hating, then, shall be my first theme, and Colonel Moredock, the Indian-hater, my next and last.'

With which the stranger, settling himself in his seat, commenced—the hearer paying marked regard, slowly smoking, his glance, meanwhile, steadfastly abstracted towards the deck, but his right ear so disposed toward the speaker that each word came through as little atmospheric intervention as possible. To intensify the sense of hearing, he seemed to sink the sense of sight. No complaisance of mere speech could have been so flattering, or expressed such striking politeness as this mute eloquence of thoroughly digesting attention.

CHAPTER XXVI

CONTAINING THE METAPHYSICS OF INDIAN-HATING, AC-
CORDING TO THE VIEWS OF ONE EVIDENTLY NOT SO
PREPOSSESSED AS ROUSSEAU[*] IN FAVOUR OF SAVAGES

'THE judge always began in these words: "The backwoodsman's hatred of the Indian has been a topic for
some remark. In the earlier times of the frontier the
passion was thought to be readily accounted for. But
Indian rapine having mostly ceased through regions where
it once prevailed, the philanthropist is surprised that
Indian-hating has not in like degree ceased with it. He
wonders why the backwoodsman still regards the red
man in much the same spirit that a jury does a murderer,
or a trapper a wild cat—a creature, in whose behalf
mercy were not wisdom; truce is vain; he must be
executed.

' "A curious point," the judge would continue, "which
perhaps not everybody, even upon explanation, may fully
understand; while, in order for anyone to approach to
an understanding, it is necessary for him to learn, or if
he already know, to bear in mind, what manner of man
the backwoodsman is; as for what manner of man the
Indian is, many know, either from history or experience.

' "The backwoodsman is a lonely man. He is a
thoughtful man. He is a man strong and unsophisti-
cated. Impulsive, he is what some might call unprincipled. At any rate, he is self-willed; being one who
less hearkens to what others may say about things, than
looks for himself, to see what are things themselves. If

in straits, there are few to help ; he must depend upon
himself ; he must continually look to himself. Hence
self-reliance, to the degree of standing by his own judgment, though it stand alone. Not that he deems himself
infallible ; too many mistakes in following trails prove
the contrary ; but he thinks that nature destines such
sagacity as she has given him, as she destines it to the
'possum. To these fellow-beings of the wilds their un-
tutored sagacity is their best dependence. If with either
it prove faulty, if the 'possum's betray it to the trap, or
the backwoodsman's mislead him into ambuscade,* there
are consequences to be undergone, but no self-blame.
As with the 'possum, instincts prevail with the backwoodsman over precepts. Like the 'possum, the backwoodsman presents the spectacle of a creature dwelling
exclusively among the works of God, yet these, truth
must confess, breed little in him of a godly mind. Small
bowing and scraping is his, further than when with bent
knee he points his rifle, or picks its flint. With few
companions, solitude by necessity his lengthened lot,
he stands the trial—no slight one, since, next to dying,
solitude, rightly borne, is perhaps of fortitude the most
rigorous test. But not merely is the backwoodsman
content to be alone, but in no few cases is anxious to be
so. The sight of smoke ten miles off is provocation to
one more remove from man, one step deeper into nature.
Is it that he feels that whatever man may be, man is not
the universe ? that glory, beauty, kindness, are not all
engrossed by him ? that as the presence of man frights
birds away, so, many bird-like thoughts ? Be that how
it will, the backwoodsman is not without some fineness to
his nature. Hairy Orson*as he looks, it may be with him
as with the Shetland seal—beneath the bristles lurks
the fur.

' " Though held in a sort a barbarian, the backwoods-

man would seem to America what Alexander was to Asia
—captain in the vanguard of conquering civilisation.
Whatever the nation's growing opulence or power, does
it not lackey his heels ?   Pathfinder,* provider of security
to those who come after him, for himself he asks nothing
but hardship.   Worthy to be compared with Moses in
the Exodus, or the Emperor Julian in Gaul,* who on foot,
and bare-browed, at the head of covered or mounted
legions, marched so through the elements, day after day.
The tide of emigration, let it roll as it will, never over-
whelms the backwoodsman into itself ;   he rides upon
advance, as the Polynesian upon the comb of the surf.

' " Thus, though he keep moving on through life, he
maintains with respect to nature much the same un-
altered relation throughout ;   with her creatures, too,
including panthers and Indians.   Hence, it is not unlikely
that, accurate as the theory of the Peace Congress* may
be with respect to those two varieties of beings, among
others, yet the backwoodsman might be qualified to throw
out some practical suggestions.

' " As the child born to a backwoodsman must in turn
lead his father's life—a life which, as related to humanity,
is related mainly to Indians—it is thought best not to
mince matters, out of delicacy ;   but to tell the boy pretty
plainly what an Indian is, and what he must expect
from him.   For however charitable it may be to view
Indians as members of the Society of Friends,* yet to
affirm them such to one ignorant of Indians, whose lonely
path lies a long way through their lands, this, in the
event, might prove not only injudicious but cruel.   At
least something of this kind would seem the maxim upon
which backwoods' education is based.   Accordingly, if
in youth the backwoodsman incline to knowledge, as is
generally the case, he hears little from his schoolmasters,
the old chroniclers of the forest, but histories of Indian

lying, Indian theft, Indian double-dealing, Indian fraud
and perfidy, Indian want of conscience, Indian blood-
thirstiness, Indian diabolism—histories which, though of
wild woods, are almost as full of things unangelic as the
Newgate Calendar*or the Annals of Europe.* In these
Indian narratives and traditions the lad is thoroughly
grounded. 'As the twig is bent the tree's inclined.'
The instinct of antipathy against an Indian grows in the
backwoodsman with the sense of good and bad, right and
wrong. In one breath he learns that a brother is to be
loved, and an Indian to be hated.

'"Such are the facts," the judge would say, "upon which,
if one seek to moralise, he must do so with an eye to them.
It is terrible that one creature should so regard another,
should make it conscience to abhor an entire race. It is
terrible ; but is it surprising ? Surprising, that one
should hate a race which he believes to be red from a
cause akin to that which makes some tribes of garden
insects green ? A race whose name is upon the frontier
a *memento mori* ;* painted to him in every evil light ;
now a horse-thief like those in Moyamensing ;* now an
assassin like a New York rowdy ; now a treaty-breaker
like an Austrian ;* now a Palmer*with poisoned arrows ;
now a judicial murderer and Jeffries,* after a fierce farce
of trial condemning his victim to bloody death ; or a
Jew* with hospitable speeches cozening some fainting
stranger into ambuscade, there to burk*him, and account
it a deed grateful to Manitou,* his god.

'"Still, all this is less advanced as truths of the Indians
than as examples of the backwoodsman's impression of
them—in which the charitable may think he does them
some injustice. Certain it is, the Indians themselves
think so ; quite unanimously, too. The Indians, indeed,
protest against the backwoodsman's view of them ; and
some think that one cause of their returning his antipathy

so sincerely as they do, is their moral indignation at being so libelled by him, as they really believe and say. But whether, on this or any point, the Indians should be permitted to testify for themselves, to the exclusion of other testimony, is a question that may be left to the Supreme Court. At any rate, it has been observed that when an Indian becomes a genuine proselyte to Christianity (such cases, however, not being very many ; though, indeed, entire tribes are sometimes nominally brought to the true light), he will not in that case conceal his enlightened conviction, that his race's portion by nature is total depravity ; and, in that way, as much as admits that the backwoodsman's worst idea of it is not very far from true ; while, on the other hand, those red men who are the greatest sticklers for the theory of Indian virtue, and Indian loving-kindness, are sometimes the arrantest horse-thieves and tomahawkers among them. So, at least, avers the backwoodsman. And though, knowing the Indian nature, as he thinks he does, he fancies he is not ignorant that an Indian may in some points deceive himself almost as effectually as in bush-tactics he can another, yet his theory and his practice as above contrasted seem to involve an inconsistency so extreme, that the backwoodsman only accounts for it on the supposition that when a tomahawking red man advances the notion of the benignity of the red race, it is but part and parcel with that subtle strategy which he finds so useful in war, in hunting, and the general conduct of life."

' In further explanation of that deep abhorrence with which the backwoodsman regards the savage, the judge used to think it might perhaps a little help, to consider what kind of stimulus to it is furnished in those forest histories and traditions before spoken of. In which behalf, he would tell the story of the little colony of Wrights and Weavers, originally seven cousins from Virginia, who, after successive removals with their families, at last established themselves near the southern frontier of the Bloody Ground, Kentucky :* " They were strong, brave men ; but, unlike many of the pioneers in those days, theirs was no love of conflict for conflict's sake. Step by step they had been lured to their lonely resting-place by the ever-beckoning seductions of a fertile and virgin land, with a singular exemption, during the march, from Indian molestation. But clearings made and houses built, the bright shield was soon to turn its other side. After repeated persecutions and eventual hostilities, forced on them by a dwindled tribe in their neighbour-hood—persecutions resulting in loss of crops and cattle ; hostilities in which they lost two of their number, illy to be spared, besides others getting painful wounds—the five remaining cousins made, with some serious conces-sions, a kind of treaty with Mocmohoc, the chief, being to this induced by the harryings of the enemy, leaving them no peace. But they were further prompted, indeed, first incited, by the suddenly changed ways of Mocmohoc, who, though hitherto deemed a savage almost perfidious as Cæsar Borgia,* yet now put on a seeming the reverse of this, engaging to bury the hatchet, smoke the pipe, and be friends forever ; not friends in the mere sense of renouncing enmity, but in the sense of kindliness, active and familiar.

' " But what the chief now seemed, did not wholly blind them to what the chief had been ; so that, though in no small degree influenced by his change of bearing, they still distrusted him enough to covenant with him, among other articles on their side, that though friendly visits should be exchanged between the wigwams and the cabins, yet the five cousins should never, on any account, be expected to enter the chief's lodge together. The

intention was, though they reserved it, that if ever, under
the guise of amity, the chief should mean them mischief,
and effect it, it should be but partially ; so that some of
the five might survive, not only for their families' sake,
but also for retribution's. Nevertheless, Mocmohoc did,
upon a time, with such fine art and pleasing carriage win
their confidence, that he brought them all together to a
feast of bear's meat, and there, by stratagem, ended
them. Years after, over their calcined bones and those
of all their families, the chief, reproached for his treachery
by a proud hunter whom he had made captive, jeered
out, ' Treachery ? pale face ! 'Twas they who broke
their covenant first, in coming all together ; they that
broke it first, in trusting Mocmohoc.' "

' At this point the judge would pause, and lifting his
hand, and rolling his eyes, exclaim in a solemn enough
voice, " Circling wiles and bloody lusts. The acuteness
and genius of the chief but make him the more atrocious."

' After another pause, he would begin an imaginary
kind of dialogue between a backwoodsman and a questioner :—

' " But are all Indians like Mocmohoc ?—Not all have
proved such ; but in the least harmful may lie his germ.
There is an Indian nature. ' Indian blood is in me,' is
the half-breed's threat.—But are not some Indians kind ?
—Yes, but kind Indians are mostly lazy, and reputed
simple—at all events, are seldom chiefs ; chiefs among
the red men being taken from the active, and those
accounted wise. Hence, with small promotion, kind
Indians have but proportionate influence. And kind
Indians may be forced to do unkind biddings. So
' beware the Indian, kind or unkind,' said Daniel Boone,*
who lost his sons by them.—But, have all you backwoodsmen been some way victimised by Indians ?—No.
—Well, and in certain cases may not at least some few

of you be favoured by them ?—Yes, but scarce one among us so self-important, or so selfish-minded, as to hold his personal exemption from Indian outrage such a set-off against the contrary experience of so many others, as that he must needs, in a general way, think well of Indians ; or, if he do, an arrow in his flank might suggest a pertinent doubt.

' "In short," according to the judge, "if we at all credit the backwoodsman, his feeling against Indians, to be taken aright, must be considered as being not so much on his own account as on others', or jointly on both accounts. True it is, scarce a family he knows but some member of it, or connection, has been by Indians maimed or scalped. What avails, then, that some one Indian, or some two or three, treat a backwoodsman friendly-like ? He fears me, he thinks. Take my rifle from me, give him motive, and what will come ? Or if not so, how know I what involuntary preparations may be going on in him for things as unbeknown in present time to him as me—a sort of chemical preparation in the soul for malice, as chemical preparation in the body for malady."

' Not that the backwoodsman ever used those words, you see, but the judge found him expression for his mean-ing. And this point he would conclude with saying, that, "what is called a ' friendly Indian ' is a very rare sort of creature ; and well it was so, for no ruthlessness exceeds that of a ' friendly Indian ' turned enemy. A coward friend, he makes a valiant foe.

' "But, thus far the passion in question has been viewed in a general way as that of a community. When to his due share of this the backwoodsman adds his private passion, we have then the stock out of which is formed, if formed at all, the Indian-hater *par excellence*."

' The Indian-hater *par excellence* the judge defined to be one " who, having with his mother's milk drank in

small love for red men, in youth or early manhood, ere
the sensibilities become osseous, receives at their hand
some signal outrage, or, which in effect is much the same,
some of his kin have, or some friend. Now, nature all
around him by her solitudes wooing or bidding him muse
upon this matter, he accordingly does so, till the thought
develops such attraction, that much as straggling vapours
troop from all sides to a storm-cloud, so straggling
thoughts of other outrages troop to the nucleus thought,
assimilate with it, and swell it. At last, taking counsel
with the elements, he comes to his resolution. An
intenser Hannibal, he makes a vow, the hate of which is
a vortex from whose suction scarce the remotest chip of
the guilty race may reasonably feel secure. Next, he
declares himself and settles his temporal affairs. With
the solemnity of a Spaniard turned monk, he takes leave
of his kin ; or rather, these leave-takings have something
of the still more impressive finality of death-bed adieus.
Last, he commits himself to the forest primeval ; there,
so long as life shall be his, to act upon a calm, cloistered
scheme of strategical, implacable, and lonesome vengeance. Ever on the noiseless trail ; cool, collected,
patient ; less seen than felt ; snuffing, smelling—a Leather-
stocking Nemesis.* In the settlements he will not be
seen again ; in eyes of old companions tears may start
at some chance thing that speaks of him ; but they never
look for him, nor call ; they know he will not come.
Suns and seasons fleet ; the tiger-lily blows and falls ;
babes are born and leap in their mothers' arms ; but,
the Indian-hater is good as gone to his long home,* and
' Terror ' is his epitaph.''

'Here the judge, not unaffected, would pause again,
but presently resume : "How evident that in strict
speech there can be no biography of an Indian-hater *par
excellence*, any more than one of a sword-fish, or other

deep-sea denizen ; or, which is still less imaginable, one of a dead man. The career of the Indian-hater *par excellence* has the impenetrability of the fate of a lost steamer. Doubtless, events, terrible ones, have happened, must have happened ; but the powers that be in nature have taken order that they shall never become news.

' " But, luckily for the curious, there is a species of diluted Indian-hater, one whose heart proves not so steely as his brain. Soft enticements of domestic life too often draw him from the ascetic trail ; a monk who apostatises to the world at times. Like a mariner, too, though much abroad, he may have a wife and family in some green harbour which he does not forget. It is with him as with the Papist converts in Senegal ; fasting and mortification prove hard to bear."

' The judge, with his usual judgment, always thought that the intense solitude to which the Indian-hater consigns himself, has, by its overawing influence, no little to do with relaxing his vow. He would relate instances where, after some months' lonely scoutings, the Indian-hater is suddenly seized with a sort of calenture*; hurries openly toward the first smoke, though he knows it is an Indian's, announces himself as a lost hunter, gives the savage his rifle, throws himself upon his charity, embraces him with much affection, imploring the privilege of living a while in his sweet companionship. What is too often the sequel of so distempered a procedure may be best known by those who best know the Indian. Upon the whole, the judge, by two-and-thirty good and sufficient reasons, would maintain that there was no known vocation whose consistent following calls for such self-containings as that of the Indian-hater *par excellence*. In the highest view, he considered such a soul one peeping out but once an age.

'For the diluted Indian-hater, although the vacations he permits himself impair the keeping of the character, yet, it should not be overlooked that this is the man who, by his very infirmity, enables us to form surmises, however inadequate, of what Indian-hating in its perfection is.'

'One moment,' gently interrupted the cosmopolitan here, ' and let me refill my calumet.'*

Which being done, the other proceeded :—

CHAPTER XXVII

SOME ACCOUNT OF A MAN OF QUESTIONABLE MORALITY, BUT WHO, NEVERTHELESS, WOULD SEEM ENTITLED TO THE ESTEEM OF THAT EMINENT ENGLISH MORALIST* WHO SAID HE LIKED A GOOD HATER

' COMING to mention the man to whose story all thus far said was but the introduction, the judge, who, like you, was a great smoker, would insist upon all the company taking cigars, and then lighting a fresh one himself, rise in his place, and, with the solemnest voice, say—" Gentlemen, let us smoke to the memory of Colonel John Moredock "; when, after several whiffs taken standing in deep silence and deeper revery, he would resume his seat and his discourse, something in these words :—

' " Though Colonel John Moredock was not an Indian-hater *par excellence*, he yet cherished a kind of sentiment toward the red man, and in that degree, and so acted out his sentiment as sufficiently to merit the tribute just rendered to his memory.

' " John Moredock was the son of a woman married thrice, and thrice widowed by a tomahawk. The three successive husbands of this woman had been pioneers, and with them she had wandered from wilderness to wilderness, always on the frontier. With nine children, she at last found herself at a little clearing, afterwards Vincennes. There she joined a company about to remove to the new country of Illinois. On the eastern side of Illinois there were then no settlements ; but on the west

side, the shore of the Mississippi, there were, near the
mouth of the Kaskaskia, some old hamlets of French.
To the vicinity of those hamlets, very innocent and
pleasant places, a new Arcadia,*Mrs. Moredock's party was
destined ; for thereabouts, among the vines, they meant
to settle.   They embarked upon the Wabash in boats,
proposing descending that stream into the Ohio, and the
Ohio into the Mississippi, and so, northwards, toward
the point to be reached.   All went well till they made
the rock of the Grand Tower on the Mississippi, where
they had to land and drag their boats round a point
swept by a strong current.   Here a party of Indians,
lying in wait, rushed out and murdered nearly all of
them.   The widow was among the victims with her
children, John excepted, who, some fifty miles distant,
was following with a second party.

' " He was just entering upon manhood, when thus left
in nature sole survivor of his race.   Other youngsters might
have turned mourners ; he turned avenger.   His nerves
were electric wires—sensitive, but steel.   He was one who,
from self-possession, could be made neither to flush nor
pale.   It is said that when the tidings were brought him,
he was ashore sitting beneath a hemlock eating his dinner
of venison—and as the tidings were told him, after the
first start he kept on eating, but slowly and deliberately,
chewing the wild news with the wild meat, as if both
together, turned to chyle, together should sinew him to
his intent.   From that meal he rose an Indian-hater.
He rose ; got his arms, prevailed upon some comrades
to join him, and without delay started to discover who
were the actual transgressors.   They proved to belong
to a band of twenty renegades from various tribes, out-
laws even among Indians, and who had formed themselves
into a marauding crew.   No opportunity for action
being at the time presented, he dismissed his friends ;

told them to go on, thanking them, and saying he would
ask their aid at some future day. For upwards of a
year, alone in the wilds, he watched the crew. Once,
what he thought a favourable chance having occurred—
it being midwinter, and the savages encamped, apparently
to remain so—he anew mustered his friends, and marched
against them ; but getting wind of his coming, the enemy
fled, and in such panic that everything was left behind
but their weapons. During the winter, much the same
thing happened upon two subsequent occasions. The
next year he sought them at the head of a party pledged
to serve him for forty days. At last the hour came.
It was on the shore of the Mississippi. From their covert,
Moredock and his men dimly descried the gang of Cains*
in the red dusk of evening, paddling over to a jungled
island in mid-stream, there the more securely to lodge ;
for Moredock's retributive spirit in the wilderness spoke
ever to their trepidations now, like the voice calling
through the garden.* Waiting until dead of night, the
whites swam the river, towing after them a raft laden
with their arms. On landing, Moredock cut the fasten-
ings of the enemy's canoes, and turned them, with his
own raft, adrift ; resolved that there should be neither
escape for the Indians, nor safety, except in victory, for
the whites. Victorious the whites were ; but three of
the Indians saved themselves by taking to the stream.
Moredock's band lost not a man.

' "Three of the murderers survived. He knew their
names and persons. In the course of three years each
successively fell by his own hand. All were now dead.
But this did not suffice. He made no avowal, but to
kill Indians had become his passion. As an athlete, he
had few equals ; as a shot, none ; in single combat, not
to be beaten. Master of that woodland cunning enabling
the adept to subsist where the tyro would perish, and

expert in all those arts by which an enemy is pursued
for weeks, perhaps months, without once suspecting it,
he kept to the forest. The solitary Indian that met
him, died. When a number* was descried, he would either
secretly pursue their track for some chance to strike at
least one blow ; or if, while thus engaged, he himself was
discovered, he would elude them by superior skill.

'"Many years he spent thus ; and though after a
time he was, in a degree, restored to the ordinary life of
the region and period, yet it is believed that John Moredock never let pass an opportunity of quenching an
Indian. Sins of commission in that kind may have been
his, but none of omission.

'"It were to err to suppose," the judge would say,
"that this gentleman was naturally ferocious, or peculiarly possessed of those qualities, which, unhelped by
provocation of events, tend to withdraw man from social
life. On the contrary, Moredock was an example of
something apparently self-contradicting, certainly curious,
but, at the same time, undeniable ; namely, that nearly
all Indian-haters have at bottom loving hearts ; at any
rate, hearts, if anything, more generous than the average.
Certain it is, that, to the degree in which he mingled in
the life of the settlements, Moredock showed himself not
without humane feelings. No cold husband or colder
father, he ; and, though often and long away from his
household, bore its needs in mind, and provided for them.
He could be very convivial ; told a good story (though
never of his more private exploits), and sung a capital
song. Hospitable, not backward to help a neighbour ;
by report, benevolent, as retributive, in secret ; while,
in a general manner, though sometimes grave—as is not
unusual with men of his complexion, a sultry and tragical
brown—yet with nobody, Indians excepted, otherwise
than courteous in a manly fashion ; a moccasined gentle-

man, admired and loved.   In fact, no one more popular,
as an incident to follow may prove.

‘ “ His bravery, whether in Indian fight, or any other,
was unquestionable.   An officer in the ranging service
during the war of 1812, he acquitted himself with more
than credit.   Of his soldierly character, this anecdote
is told : Not long after Hull’s dubious surrender at
Detroit,* Moredock with some of his rangers rode up at
night to a log-house, there to rest till morning.   The
horses being attended to, supper over, and sleeping-
places assigned the troop, the host showed the colonel
his best bed, not on the ground like the rest, but a bed
that stood on legs.   But out of delicacy, the guest
declined to monopolise it, or indeed, to occupy it at all ;
when, to increase the inducement, as the host thought,
he was told that a general officer had once slept in that
bed.   ‘ Who,   pray ? ’   asked   the   colonel.   ‘ General
Hull.’   ‘ Then   you   must   not   take   offence,’   said   the
colonel, buttoning up his coat, ‘ but, really, no coward’s
bed for me, however comfortable.’   Accordingly he took
up with valour’s bed—a cold one on the ground.

‘ “ At one time the colonel was a member of the terri-
torial council of Illinois, and at the formation of the
state government, was pressed to become a candidate
for governor, but begged to be excused.   And, though
he declined to give his reasons for declining, yet by those
who best knew him the cause was not wholly unsurmised.
In his official capacity he might be called upon to enter
into friendly treaties with Indian tribes, a thing not to
be thought of.   And even did no such contingency arise,
yet he felt there would be an impropriety in the Governor
of Illinois stealing out now and then, during a recess of
the legislative bodies, for a few days’ shooting at human
beings, within the limits of his paternal chief-magistracy.
If the governorship offered large honours, from Moredock

it demanded larger sacrifices. These were incompatibles. In short, he was not unaware that to be a consistent Indian-hater involves the renunciation of ambition, with its objects—the pomps and glories of the world; and since religion, pronouncing such things vanities, accounts it merit to renounce them, therefore, so far as this goes, Indian-hating, whatever may be thought of it in other respects, may be regarded as not wholly without the efficacy of a devout sentiment." '

Here the narrator paused. Then, after his long and irksome sitting, started to his feet, and regulating his disordered shirt-frill, and at the same time adjustingly shaking his legs down in his rumpled pantaloons, concluded : 'There, I have done; having given you, not my story, mind, or my thoughts, but another's. And now, for your friend Coonskins, I doubt not, that, if the judge were here, he would pronounce him a sort of comprehensive Colonel Moredock, who, too much spreading his passion, shallows it.'

CHAPTER XXVIII

MOOT POINTS TOUCHING THE LATE COLONEL
JOHN MOREDOCK

'CHARITY, charity !' exclaimed the cosmopolitan, ' never a sound judgment without charity. When man judges man, charity is less a bounty from our mercy than just allowance for the insensible lee-way of human fallibility. God forbid that my eccentric friend should be what you hint. You do not know him, or but imperfectly. His outside deceived you ; at first it came near deceiving even me. But I seized a chance, when, owing to indignation against some wrong, he laid himself a little open ; I seized that lucky chance, I say, to inspect his heart, and found it an inviting oyster in a forbidding shell. His outside is but put on. Ashamed of his own goodness, he treats mankind as those strange old uncles in romances do their nephews—snapping at them all the time and yet loving them as the apple of their eye.'

'Well, my words with him were few. Perhaps he is not what I took him for. Yes, for aught I know, you may be right.'

'Glad to hear it. Charity, like poetry, should be cultivated, if only for its being graceful. And now, since you have renounced your notion, I should be happy would you, so to speak, renounce your story, too. That story strikes me with even more incredulity than wonder. To me some parts don't hang together. If the man of hate, how could John Moredock be also the man of love ? Either his lone campaigns are fabulous as Hercules' ;

or else, those being true, what was thrown in about his geniality is but garnish. In short, if ever there was such a man as Moredock, he, in my way of thinking, was either misanthrope or nothing ; and his misanthropy the more intense from being focused on one race of men. Though, like suicide, man-hatred would seem peculiarly a Roman and a Grecian passion—that is, pagan ; yet, the annals of neither Rome nor Greece can produce the equal in man-hatred of Colonel Moredock, as the judge and you have painted him. As for this Indian-hating in general, I can only say of it what Dr. Johnson said of the alleged Lisbon earthquake*: " Sir, I don't believe it." '

' Didn't believe it ? Why not ? Clashed with any little prejudice of his ? '

' Dr. Johnson had no prejudice ; but, like a certain other person,' with an ingenuous smile, ' he had sensibilities, and those were pained.'

' Dr. Johnson was a good Christian, wasn't he ? '

' He was.'

' Suppose he had been something else.'

' Then small incredulity as to the alleged earthquake.'

' Suppose he had been also a misanthrope ? '

' Then small incredulity as to the robberies and murders alleged to have been perpetrated under the pall of smoke and ashes. The infidels of the time were quick to credit those reports and worse. So true is it that, while religion, contrary to the common notion, implies, in certain cases, a spirit of slow reserve as to assent, infidelity, which claims to despise credulity, is sometimes swift to it.'

' You rather jumble together misanthropy and infidelity.'

' I do not jumble them ; they are co-ordinates. For misanthropy, springing from the same root with disbelief of religion, is twin with that. It springs from the same root, I say ; for, set aside materialism, and what is an

atheist, but one who does not, or will not, see in the
universe a ruling principle of love ; and what a misanthrope, but one who does not, or will not, see in man a
ruling principle of kindness ? Don't you see ? In either
case the vice consists in a want of confidence.'

'What sort of a sensation is misanthropy ? '

'Might as well ask me what sort of sensation is hydro-
phobia. Don't know ; never had it. But I have often
wondered what it can be like. Can a misanthrope feel
warm, I ask myself ; take ease ? be companionable with
himself ? Can a misanthrope smoke a cigar and muse ?
How fares he in solitude ? Has the misanthrope such a
thing as an appetite ? Shall a peach refresh him ? The
effervescence of champagne, with what eye does he behold
it ? Is summer good to him ? Of long winters how
much can he sleep ? What are his dreams ? How feels
he, and what does he, when suddenly awakened, alone,
at dead of night, by fusillades of thunder ? '

'Like you,' said the stranger, ' I can't understand the
misanthrope. So far as my experience goes, either mankind is worthy one's best love, or else I have been lucky.
Never has it been my lot to have been wronged, though
but in the smallest degree. Cheating, backbiting, super-
ciliousness, disdain, hard-heartedness, and all that brood,
I know but by report. Cold regards tossed over the
sinister shoulder of a former friend, ingratitude in a
beneficiary, treachery in a confidant—such things may
be ; but I must take somebody's word for it. Now
the bridge that has carried me so well over, shall I not
praise it ? '

'Ingratitude to the worthy bridge not to do so. Man
is a noble fellow, and in an age of satirists, I am not displeased to find one who has confidence in him, and
bravely stands up for him.'

'Yes, I always speak a good word for man ; and

what is more, am always ready to do a good deed for him.'

'You are a man after my own heart,' responded the cosmopolitan, with a candour which lost nothing by its calmness. 'Indeed,' he added, 'our sentiments agree so, that were they written in a book, whose was whose, few but the nicest critics might determine.'

'Since we are thus joined in mind,' said the stranger, 'why not be joined in hand?'

'My hand is always at the service of virtue,' frankly extending it to him as to virtue personified.

'And now,' said the stranger, cordially retaining his hand, 'you know our fashion here at the West. It may be a little low, but it is kind. Briefly, we being newly made friends must drink together. What say you?'

'Thank you; but indeed, you must excuse me.'

'Why?'

'Because, to tell the truth, I have to-day met so many old friends, all free-hearted, convivial gentlemen, that really, really, though for the present I succeed in mastering it, I am at bottom almost in the condition of a sailor who, stepping ashore after a long voyage, ere night reels with loving welcomes, his head of less capacity than his heart.'

At the allusion to old friends, the stranger's countenance a little fell, as a jealous lover's might at hearing from his sweetheart of former ones. But rallying, he said : 'No doubt they treated you to something strong; but wine—surely, that gentle creature, wine; come, let us have a little gentle wine at one of these little tables here. Come, come.' Then essaying to roll about like a full pipe in the sea, sang in a voice which had had more of good-fellowship, had there been less of a latent squeak to it :—

> ' Let us drink of the wine of the vine benign,
> That sparkles warm in Zansovine.'*

The cosmopolitan, with longing eye upon him, stood as sorely tempted and wavering a moment; then, abruptly stepping toward him, with a look of dissolved surrender, said: 'When mermaid songs move figure-heads, then may glory, gold, and women try their blandishments on me. But a good fellow, singing a good song, he woos forth my every spike, so that my whole hull, like a ship's, sailing by a magnetic rock, caves in with acquiescence. Enough: when one has a heart of a certain sort, it is in vain trying to be resolute.'

CHAPTER XXIX

THE BOON COMPANIONS

The wine, port, being called for, and the two seated at the little table, a natural pause of convivial expectancy ensued; the stranger's eye turned toward the bar near by, watching the red-cheeked, white-aproned man there, blithely dusting the bottle, and invitingly arranging the salver and glasses; when, with a sudden impulse turning round his head toward his companion, he said, ' Ours is friendship at first sight, ain't it ? '

' It is,' was the placidly pleased reply; ' and the same may be said of friendship at first sight as of love at first sight : it is the only true one, the only noble one. It bespeaks confidence. Who would go sounding his way into love or friendship, like a strange ship by night, into an enemy's harbour ? '

' Right. Boldly in before the wind. Agreeable, how we always agree. By the way, though but a formality, friends should know each other's names. What is yours, pray ? '

' Francis Goodman. But those who love me, call me Frank. And yours ? '

' Charles Arnold Noble.* But do you call me Charlie.'

' I will, Charlie ; nothing like preserving in manhood the fraternal familiarities of youth. It proves the heart a rosy boy to the last.'

' My sentiments again. Ah ! '

It was a smiling waiter, with the smiling bottle, the cork drawn ; a common quart bottle, but for the occasion

fitted at bottom into a little bark basket, braided with
porcupine quills, gaily tinted in the Indian fashion.
This being set before the entertainer, he regarded it with
affectionate interest, but seemed not to understand, or
else to pretend not to, a handsome red label pasted on
the bottle, bearing the capital letters, P.W.

' P.W.,' said he at last, perplexedly eyeing the pleasing
poser, ' now what does P.W. mean ? '

' Shouldn't wonder,' said the cosmopolitan gravely,
' if it stood for port wine. You called for port wine,
didn't you ? '

' Why so it is, so it is ! '

' I find some little mysteries not very hard to clear
up,' said the other, quietly crossing his legs.

This commonplace seemed to escape the stranger's
hearing, for, full of his bottle, he now rubbed his somewhat sallow hands over it, and with a strange kind of
cackle, meant to be a chirrup, cried : ' Good wine, good
wine ; is it not the peculiar bond of good feeling ? '
Then brimming both glasses, pushed one over, saying,
with what seemed intended for an air of fine disdain :
' Ill betide those gloomy sceptics who maintain that
nowadays pure wine is unpurchasable ; that almost
every variety on sale is less the vintage of vineyards
than laboratories ; that most bar-keepers are but a set
of male Brinvillierses,* with complaisant arts practising
against the lives of their best friends, their customers.'

A shade passed over the cosmopolitan. After a few
minutes' downcast musing, he lifted his eyes and said :
' I have long thought, my dear Charlie, that the spirit
in which wine is regarded by too many in these days is
one of the most painful examples of want of confidence.
Look at these glasses. He who could mistrust poison
in this wine would mistrust consumption in Hebe's cheek.
While, as for suspicions against the dealers in wine and

sellers of it, those who cherish such suspicions can have
but limited trust in the human heart. · Each human heart
they must think to be much like each bottle of port, not
such port as this, but such port as they hold to.   Strange
traducers, who see good faith in nothing, however sacred.
Not medicines, not the wine in sacraments, has escaped
them.   The doctor with his phial, and the priest with
his chalice, they deem equally the unconscious dispensers
of bogus cordials to the dying.'

' Dreadful ! '

' Dreadful indeed,' said the cosmopolitan solemnly.
' These distrusters stab at the very soul of confidence.
If this wine,' impressively holding up his full glass, ' if
this wine with its bright promise be not true, how shall
man be, whose promise can be no brighter ?   But if wine
be false, while men are true, whither shall fly convivial
geniality ?   To think of sincerely genial souls drinking
each other's health at unawares in perfidious and murder-
ous drugs ! '

' Horrible ! '

' Much too much so to be true, Charlie.   Let us forget
it.   Come, you are my entertainer on this occasion, and
yet you don't pledge me.   I have been waiting for it.'

' Pardon, pardon,' half confusedly and half osten-
tatiously lifting his glass.   ' I pledge you, Frank, with
my whole heart, believe me,' taking a draught too decorous to be large, but which, small though it was, was
followed by a slight involuntary wryness to the mouth.

' And I return you the pledge, Charlie, heart-warm as
it came to me, and honest as this wine I drink it in,'
reciprocated the cosmopolitan with princely kindliness
in his gesture, taking a generous swallow, concluding in
a smack, which, though audible, was not so much so as
to be unpleasing.

' Talking of alleged spuriousness of wines,' said he,

tranquilly setting down his glass, and then sloping back
his head and with friendly fixedness eyeing the wine,
' perhaps the strangest part of those allegings is, that
there is, as claimed, a kind of man who, while convinced
that on this continent most wines are shams, yet still
drinks away at them ; accounting wine so fine a thing,
that even the sham article is better than none at all.
And if the temperance people urge that, by this course,
he will sooner or later be undermined in health, he answers,
" And do you think I don't know that ? But health
without cheer I hold a bore ; and cheer, even of the
spurious sort, has its price, which I am willing to pay." '

' Such a man, Frank,' must have a disposition ungovernably bacchanalian.'

' Yes, if such a man there be, which I don't credit.
It is a fable, but a fable from which I once heard a person
of less genius than grotesqueness draw a moral even
more extravagant than the fable itself. He said that it
illustrated, as in a parable, how that a man of a disposition ungovernably good-natured might still familiarly
associate with men, though, at the same time, he
believed the greater part of men false-hearted—accounting society so sweet a thing that even the spurious sort
was better than none at all. And if the Rochefoucaultites*urge that, by this course, he will sooner or later
be undermined in security, he answers, " And do you
think I don't know that ? But security without society
I hold a bore ; and society, even of the spurious sort,
has its price, which I am willing to pay." '

' A most singular theory,' said the stranger with a
slight fidget, eyeing his companion with some inquisi-
tiveness, ' indeed, Frank, a most slanderous thought,'
he exclaimed in sudden heat and with an involuntary
look almost of being personally aggrieved.

' In one sense it merits all you say, and more,' rejoined

the other with wonted mildness, 'but, for a kind of
drollery in it, charity might, perhaps, overlook something
of the wickedness. Humour is, in fact, so blessed a thing,
that even in the least virtuous product of the human
mind, if there can be found but nine good jokes, some
philosophers are clement enough to affirm that those nine
good jokes should redeem all the wicked thoughts, though
plenty as the populace of Sodom.* At any rate, this same
humour has something, there is no telling what, of
beneficence in it, it is such a catholicon and charm—
nearly all men agreeing in relishing it, though they may
agree in little else—and in its way it undeniably does
such a deal of familiar good in the world, that no wonder
it is almost a proverb, that a man of humour, a man
capable of a good loud laugh—seem how he may in other
things—can hardly be a heartless scamp.'

'Ha, ha, ha!' laughed the other, pointing to the
figure of a pale pauper-boy on the deck below, whose
pitiableness was touched, as it were, with ludicrousness
by a pair of monstrous boots, apparently some mason's
discarded ones, cracked with drouth, half eaten by lime,
and curled up about the toe like a bassoon. 'Look—
ha, ha, ha!'

'I see,' said the other, with what seemed quiet appreciation, but of a kind expressing an eye to the grotesque,
without blindness to what in this case accompanied it,
'I see; and the way in which it moves you, Charlie,
comes in very à propos to point the proverb I was speaking of. Indeed, had you intended this effect, it could
not have been more so. For who that heard that laugh,
but would as naturally argue from it a sound heart as
sound lungs? True, it is said that a man may smile,
and smile, and smile, and be a villain*; but it is not said
that a man may laugh, and laugh, and laugh, and be one,
is it, Charlie?'

' Ha, ha, ha !—no no, no no.'

' Why, Charlie, your explosions illustrate my remarks almost as aptly as the chemist's imitation volcano did his lectures. But even if experience did not sanction the proverb, that a good laugher cannot be a bad man, I should yet feel bound in confidence to believe it, since it is a saying current among the people, and I doubt not originated among them, and hence *must* be true ; for the voice of the people* is the voice of truth. Don't you think so ? '

' Of course I do. If Truth don't speak through the people, it never speaks at all ; so I heard one say.'

' A true saying. But we stray. The popular notion of humour, considered as index to the heart, would seem curiously confirmed by Aristotle*—I think, in his *Politics* (a work, by the by, which, however it may be viewed upon the whole, yet, from the tenor of certain sections, should not, without precaution, be placed in the hands of youth)—who remarks that the least lovable men in history seem to have had for humour not only a disrelish, but a hatred ; and this, in some cases, along with an extraordinary dry taste for practical punning. I remember it is related of Phalaris,* the capricious tyrant of Sicily, that he once caused a poor fellow to be beheaded on a horse-block, for no other cause than having a horse-laugh.'

' Funny Phalaris ! '

' Cruel Phalaris ! '

As after fire-crackers, there was a pause, both looking downward on the table as if mutually struck by the contrast of exclamations, and pondering upon its significance, if any. So, at least, it seemed ; but on one side it might have been otherwise : for presently glancing up, the cosmopolitan said : ' In the instance of the moral, drolly cynic, drawn from the queer bacchanalian fellow we were speaking of, who had his reasons for still drinking spurious wine, though knowing it to be such—there, I say, we have an example of what is certainly a wicked thought, but conceived in humour. I will now give you one of a wicked thought conceived in wickedness. You shall compare the two, and answer, whether in the one case the sting is not neutralised by the humour, and whether in the other the absence of humour does not leave the sting free play. I once heard a wit, a mere wit, mind, an irreligious Parisian wit, say, with regard to the temperance movement, that none, to their personal benefit, joined it sooner than niggards and knaves; because, as he affirmed, the one by it saved money and the other made money, as in ship-owners cutting off the spirit ration without giving its equivalent, and gamblers and all sorts of subtle tricksters sticking to cold water, the better to keep a cool head for business.'

'A wicked thought, indeed!' cried the stranger, feelingly.

'Yes,' leaning over the table on his elbow and genially gesturing at him with his forefinger: 'yes, and, as I said, you don't remark the sting of it?'

'I do, indeed. Most calumnious thought, Frank!'

'No humour in it?'

'Not a bit!'

'Well now, Charlie,' eyeing him with moist regard, 'let us drink. It appears to me you don't drink freely.'

'Oh, oh—indeed, indeed—I am not backward there. I protest, a freer drinker than friend Charlie you will find nowhere,' with feverish zeal snatching his glass, but only in the sequel to dally with it. 'By the way, Frank,' said he, perhaps, or perhaps not, to draw attention from himself, 'by the way, I saw a good thing the other day; capital thing; a panegyric on the press. It pleased me so, I got it by heart at two readings. It is a kind of poetry,

but in a form which stands in something the same relation
to blank verse which that does to rhyme. A sort of free-
and-easy chant with refrains to it. Shall I recite it ? '

'Anything in praise of the press I shall be happy to
hear,' rejoined the cosmopolitan, ' the more so,' he gravely
proceeded, ' as of late I have observed in some quarters a
disposition to disparage the press.'

' Disparage the press ? '

' Even so ; some gloomy souls affirming that it is
proving with that great invention as with brandy or
eau-de-vie, which, upon its first discovery, was believed
by the doctors to be, as its French name implies, a pana-
cea—a notion which experience, it may be thought, has
not fully verified.'

' You surprise me, Frank. Are there really those who
so decry the press ? Tell me more. Their reasons.'

' Reasons they have none, but affirmations they have
many ; among other things affirming that, while under
dynastic despotisms, the press is to the people little but
an improvisatore,* under popular ones it is too apt to be
their Jack Cade.* In fine, these sour sages regard the
press in the light of a Colt's revolver,* pledged to no cause
but his in whose chance hands it may be ; deeming the
one invention an improvement upon the pen, much akin
to what the other is upon the pistol ; involving, along
with the multiplication of the barrel, no consecration of
the aim. The term " freedom of the press " they consider on a par with *freedom of Colt's revolver*. Hence, for
truth and the right, they hold, to indulge hopes from the
one is little more sensible than for Kossuth and Mazzini*
to indulge hopes from the other. Heart-breaking views
enough, you think ; but their refutation is in every true
reformer's contempt. Is it not so ? '

' Without doubt. But go on, go on. I like to hear
you,' flatteringly brimming up his glass for him.

'For one,' continued the cosmopolitan, grandly swelling his chest, 'I hold the press to be neither the people's improvisatore, nor Jack Cade; neither their paid fool, nor conceited drudge. I think interest never prevails with it over duty. The press still speaks for truth though impaled, in the teeth of lies though intrenched. Disdaining for it the poor name of cheap diffuser of news, I claim for it the independent apostleship of Advancer of Knowledge :—the iron Paul! Paul, I say; for not only does the press advance knowledge, but righteousness. In the press, as in the sun, resides, my dear Charlie, a dedicated principle of beneficent force and light. For the Satanic press, by its co-appearance with the apostolic, it is no more an aspersion to that, than to the true sun is the co-appearance of the mock one. For all the baleful-looking parhelion,* god Apollo dispenses the day. In a word, Charlie, what the sovereign of England is titularly, I hold the press to be actually—Defender of the Faith !—defender of the faith in the final triumph of truth over error, metaphysics over superstition, theory over falsehood, machinery over nature, and the good man over the bad. Such are my views, which, if stated at some length, you, Charlie, must pardon, for it is a theme upon which I cannot speak with cold brevity. And now I am impatient for your panegyric, which, I doubt not, will put mine to the blush.'

'It is rather in the blush-giving vein,' smiled the other; 'but such as it is, Frank, you shall have it.'

'Tell me when you are about to begin,' said the cosmopolitan, 'for, when at public dinners the press is toasted, I always drink the toast standing, and shall stand while you pronounce the panegyric.'

'Very good, Frank; you may stand up now.'

He accordingly did so, when the stranger likewise rose, and uplifting the ruby wine-flask, began.

CHAPTER XXX

' " PRAISE be unto the press,* not Faust's, but Noah's ;
let us extol and magnify the press, the true press of
Noah, from which breaketh the true morning. Praise
be unto the press, not the black press but the red ; let
us extol and magnify the press, the red press of Noah,
from which cometh inspiration. Ye pressmen of the
Rhineland and the Rhine, join in with all ye who tread
out the glad tidings on isle Madeira or Mitylene.*—Who
giveth redness of eyes by making men long to tarry at
the fine print ?—Praise be unto the press, the rosy press
of Noah, which giveth rosiness of hearts, by making men
long to tarry at the rosy wine.—Who hath babblings and
contentions ? Who, without cause, inflicteth wounds ?
Praise be unto the press, the kindly press of Noah, which
knitteth friends, which fuseth foes.—Who may be bribed ?
—Who may be bound ?—Praise be unto the press, the
free press of Noah, which will not lie for tyrants, but
make tyrants speak the truth.—Then praise be unto the
press, the frank old press of Noah ; then let us extol and
magnify the press, the brave old press of Noah ; then let
us with roses garland and enwreath the press, the grand
old press of Noah, from which flow streams of knowledge
which give man a bliss no more unreal than his pain." '

' You deceived me,' smiled the cosmopolitan, as both
now resumed their seats ; ' you roguishly took advantage
of my simplicity ; you archly played upon my enthusiasm.

But never mind ; the offence, if any, was so charming, I almost wish you would offend again. As for certain poetic left-handers in your panegyric, those I cheerfully concede to the indefinite privileges of the poet. Upon the whole, it was quite in the lyric style—a style I always admire on account of that spirit of Sibyllic confidence*and assurance which is, perhaps, its prime ingredient. But come,' glancing at his companion's glass, ' for a lyrist, you let the bottle stay with you too long.'

' The lyre and the vine forever ! ' cried the other in his rapture, or what seemed such, heedless of the hint ; ' the vine, the vine ! is it not the most graceful and bounteous of all growths ? And, by its being such, is not something meant—divinely meant ? As I live, a vine, a Catawba vine,* shall be planted on my grave ! '

' A genial thought ; but your glass there.'

' Oh, oh,' taking a moderate sip, ' but you, why don't you drink ? '

' You have forgotten, my dear Charlie, what I told you of my previous convivialities to-day.'

' Oh,' cried the other, now in manner quite abandoned to the lyric mood, not without contrast to the easy sociability of his companion. ' Oh, one can't drink too much of good old wine—the genuine, mellow old port. Pooh, pooh ! drink away.'

' Then keep me company.'

' Of course,' with a flourish, taking another sip—' suppose we have cigars. Never mind your pipe there ; a pipe is best when alone. I say, waiter, bring some cigars —your best.'

They were brought in a pretty little bit of western pottery, representing some kind of Indian utensil, mummy coloured, set down in a mass of tobacco leaves, whose long, green fans, fancifully grouped, formed with peeps of red the sides of the receptacle.

Accompanying it were two accessories, also bits of pottery, but smaller, both globes ; one in guise of an apple flushed with red and gold to the life ; and, through a cleft at top, you saw it was hollow. This was for the ashes.* The other, gray, with wrinkled surface, in the likeness of a wasp's nest, was the match-box.

'There,' said the stranger, pushing over the cigar-stand, ' help yourself, and I will touch you off,' taking a match. ' Nothing like tobacco,' he added, when the fumes of the cigar began to wreathe, glancing from the smoker to the pottery. ' I will have a Virginia tobacco-plant set over my grave beside the Catawba vine.'

' Improvement upon your first idea, which by itself was good—but you don't smoke.'

' Presently, presently—let me fill your glass again. You don't drink.'

' Thank you ; but no more just now. Fill *your* glass.'

' Presently, presently ; do you drink on. Never mind me. Now that it strikes me, let me say, that he who, out of superfine gentility or fanatic morality, denies himself tobacco, suffers a more serious abatement in the cheap pleasures of life than the dandy in his iron boot, or the celibate on his iron cot. While for him who would fain revel in tobacco, but cannot, it is a thing at which philanthropists must weep, to see such an one, again and again, madly returning to the cigar, which, for his in-competent stomach, he cannot enjoy, while still, after each shameful repulse, the sweet dream of the impossible good goads him on to his fierce misery once more—poor eunuch ! '

' I agree with you,' said the cosmopolitan, still gravely social, ' but you don't smoke.'

' Presently, presently, do you smoke on. As I was saying about——'

' But *why* don't you smoke—come. You don't think

that tobacco, when in league with wine, too much en-
hances the latter's vinous quality—in short, with certain
constitutions tends to impair self-possession, do you ? '

'To think that, were treason. to good fellowship,' was
the warm disclaimer. ' No, no. But the fact is, there
is an unpropitious flavour in my mouth just now. Ate
of a diabolical ragout at dinner, so I shan't smoke till I
have washed away the lingering memento of it with wine.
But smoke away, you, and pray, don't forget to drink.
By the way, while we sit here so companionably, giving
loose to any companionable nothing, your uncompanion-
able friend, Coonskins, is, by pure contrast, brought to
recollection. If he were but here now, he would see how
much of real heart-joy he denies himself by not hob-a-
nobbing with his kind.'

'Why,' with loitering emphasis, slowly withdrawing
his cigar, ' I thought I had undeceived you there. I
thought you had come to a better understanding of my
eccentric friend.'

'Well, I thought so, too ; but first impressions will
return, you know. In truth, now that I think of it, I
am led to conjecture from chance things which dropped
from Coonskins, during the little interview I had with him,
that he is not a Missourian by birth, but years ago came
West here, a young misanthrope from the other side of
the Alleghanies, less to make his fortune, than to flee
man. Now, since they say trifles sometimes effect great
results, I shouldn't wonder, if his history were probed,
it would be found that what first indirectly gave his sad
bias to Coonskins was his disgust at reading in boyhood
the advice of Polonius to Laertes*—advice which, in the
selfishness it inculcates, is almost on a par with a sort of
ballad upon the economies of money-making, to be occasionally seen pasted against the desk of small retail
traders in New England.'

'I do hope now, my dear fellow,' said the cosmopolitan with an air of bland protest, 'that, in my presence at least, you will throw out nothing to the prejudice of the sons of the Puritans.'

'Hey-day and high times indeed,' exclaimed the other, nettled, 'sons of the Puritans forsooth! And who be Puritans, that I, an Alabamaian, must do them reverence? A set of sourly conceited old Malvolios* whom Shakespeare laughs his fill at in his comedies.'

'Pray, what were you about to suggest with regard to Polonius,' observed the cosmopolitan with quiet forbearance, expressive of the patience of a superior mind at the petulance of an inferior one; 'how do you characterise his advice to Laertes?'

'As false, fatal, and calumnious,' exclaimed the other, with a degree of ardour befitting one resenting a stigma upon the family escutcheon, 'and for a father to give his son—monstrous. The case you see is this: The son is going abroad, and for the first. What does the father? Invoke God's blessing upon him? Put the blessed Bible in his trunk? No. Crams him with maxims smacking of my Lord Chesterfield, with maxims of France, with maxims of Italy.'

'No, no, be charitable, not that. Why, does he not among other things say :—

"The friends thou hast, and their adoption tried,
    Grapple them to thy soul with hooks of steel"?

Is that compatible with maxims of Italy?'

'Yes, it is, Frank. Don't you see? Laertes is to take the best of care of his friends—his proved friends, on the same principle that a wine-corker takes the best of care of his proved bottles. When a bottle gets a sharp knock and don't break, he says, "Ah, I'll keep that bottle." Why? Because he loves it? No, he has particular use for it.'

' Dear, dear ! ' appealingly turning in distress, ' that—
that kind of criticism—is—is—in fact—it won't do.'

' Won't truth do, Frank ?   You are so charitable with
everybody, do but consider the tone of the speech.   Now
I put it to you, Frank ; is there anything in it hortatory
to high, heroic, disinterested effort ?   Anything like
" sell all thou hast and give to the poor " ?* And, in other
points, what desire seems most in the father's mind, that
his son should cherish nobleness for himself, or be on his
guard against the contrary thing in others ?   An irreligious warner, Frank—no devout counsellor, is Polonius.
I hate him.   Nor can I bear to hear your veterans of the
world affirm, that he who steers through life by the advice
of old Polonius will not steer among the breakers.'

' No, no—I hope nobody affirms that,' rejoined the
cosmopolitan, with tranquil abandonment ; sideways
reposing his arm at full length upon the table.   ' I hope
nobody affirms that ; because, if Polonius' advice be
taken in your sense, then the recommendation of it by
men of experience would appear to involve more or less
of an unhandsome sort of reflection upon human nature.
And yet,' with a perplexed air, ' your suggestions have
put things in such a strange light to me as in fact a little
to disturb my previous notions of Polonius and what he
says.   To be frank, by your ingenuity you have unsettled
me there, to that degree that were it not for our coincidence of opinion in general, I should almost think I was
now at length beginning to feel the ill effect of an imma-
ture mind, too much consorting with a mature one,
except on the ground of first principles in common.'

' Really and truly,' cried the other with a kind of
tickled modesty and pleased concern, ' mine is an understanding too weak to throw out grapnels and hug another
to it.   I have indeed heard of some great scholars in these
days, whose boast is less that they have made disciples

than victims.   But for me, had I the power to do such things, I have not the heart to desire.'

'I believe you, my dear Charlie.   And yet, I repeat, by your commentaries on Polonius you have, I know not how, unsettled me ; so that now I don't exactly see how Shakespeare meant the words he puts in Polonius' mouth.'

'Some say that he meant them to open people's eyes ; but I don't think so.'

'Open their eyes ? ' echoed the cosmopolitan, slowly expanding his ; 'what is there in this world for one to open his eyes to ?   I mean in the sort of invidious sense you cite ? '

'Well, others say he meant to corrupt people's morals ; and still others, that he had no express intention at all, but in effect opens their eyes and corrupts their morals in one operation.   All of which I reject.'

'Of course you reject so crude an hypothesis ; and yet, to confess, in reading Shakespeare in my closet, struck by some passage, I have laid down the volume, and said : "This Shakespeare is a queer man."   At times seeming irresponsible, he does not always seem reliable.   There appears to be a certain—what shall I call it ?—hidden sun, say, about him, at once enlightening and mystifying.   Now, I should be afraid to say what I have sometimes thought that hidden sun might be.'

'Do you think it was the true light ? ' with clandestine geniality again filling the other's glass.

'I would prefer to decline answering a categorical question there.   Shakespeare has got to be a kind of deity.   Prudent minds, having certain latent thoughts concerning him, will reserve them in a condition of lasting probation.   Still, as touching avowable speculations, we are permitted a tether.   Shakespeare himself is to be adored, not arraigned ; but, so we do it with humility,

we may a little canvass his characters. There's his
Autolycus* now, a fellow that always puzzled me. How
is one to take Autolycus ? A rogue so happy, so lucky,
so triumphant, of so almost captivatingly vicious a career
that a virtuous man reduced to the poor-house (were such
a contingency conceivable), might almost long to change
sides with him. And yet, see the words put into his
mouth : " Oh," cries Autolycus, as he comes galloping,
gay as a buck, upon the stage, " oh," he laughs, " oh
what a fool is Honesty, and Trust, his sworn brother, a
very simple gentleman." Think of that. Trust, that is,
confidence — that is, the thing in this universe the
sacredest—is rattlingly pronounced just the simplest.
And the scenes in which the rogue figures seem purposely
devised for verification of his principles. Mind, Charlie,
I do not say it *is* so, far from it ; but I *do* say it seems
so. Yes, Autolycus would seem a needy varlet acting
upon the persuasion that less is to be got by invoking
pockets than picking them, more to be made by an expert
knave than a bungling beggar ; and for this reason, as he
thinks, that the soft heads outnumber the soft hearts.
The devil's drilled recruit, Autolycus is joyous as if he
wore the livery of heaven. When disturbed by the
character and career of one thus wicked and thus happy,
my sole consolation is in the fact that no such creature
ever existed, except in the powerful imagination which
evoked him. And yet, a creature, a living creature, he
is, though only a poet was his maker. It may be, that
in that paper-and-ink investiture of his, Autolycus acts
more effectively upon mankind than he would in a flesh-
and-blood one. Can his influence be salutary ? True,
in Autolycus there is humour ; but though, according
to my principle, humour is in general to be held a saving
quality, yet the case of Autolycus is an exception ; because it is his humour which, so to speak, oils his mis-

chievousness. The bravadoing mischievousness of Autolycus is slid into the world on humour, as a pirate schooner,
with colours flying, is launched into the sea on greased
ways.'

'I approve of Autolycus as little as you,' said the
stranger, who, during his companion's commonplaces,
had seemed less attentive to them than to maturing
within his own mind the original conceptions destined
to eclipse them. 'But I cannot believe that Autolycus,
mischievous as he must prove upon the stage, can be
near so much so as such a character as Polonius.'

'I don't know about that,' bluntly, and yet not im-
politely, returned the cosmopolitan ; ' to be sure, accepting your view of the old courtier, then if between him
and Autolycus you raise the question of unprepossessing-
ness, I grant you the latter comes off best. For a moist
rogue may tickle the midriff, while a dry worldling may
but wrinkle the spleen.'

'But Polonius is not dry,' said the other excitedly ;
' he drules.* One sees the fly-blown old fop drule and
look wise. His vile wisdom is made the viler by his
vile rheuminess. The bowing and cringing, time-serving
old sinner—is such an one to give manly precepts to
youth ? The discreet, decorous, old dotard-of-state ;
senile prudence ; fatuous soullessness ! The ribanded
old dog is paralytic all down one side, and that the side
of nobleness. His soul is gone out. Only nature's
automatonism keeps him on his legs. As with some old
trees, the bark survives the pith, and will still stand
stiffly up, though but to rim round punk,* so the body
of old Polonius has outlived his soul.'

'Come, come,' said the cosmopolitan with serious air,
almost displeased ; 'though I yield to none in admiration of earnestness, yet, I think, even earnestness may
have limits. To human minds, strong language is always

more or less distressing. Besides, Polonius is an old man—as I remember him upon the stage—with snowy locks. Now charity requires that such a figure—think of it how you will—should at least be treated with civility. Moreover, old age is ripeness, and I once heard say, " Better ripe than raw." '

' But not better rotten than raw ! ' bringing down his hand with energy on the table.

' Why, bless me,' in mild surprise contemplating his heated comrade, ' how you fly out against this unfortunate Polonius—a being that never was, nor will be. And yet, viewed in a Christian light,' he added pensively, ' I don't know that anger against this man of straw is a whit less wise than anger against a man of flesh. Madness, to be mad with anything.'

' That may be, or may not be,' returned the other, a little testily, perhaps ; ' but I stick to what I said, that it is better to be raw than rotten. And what is to be feared on that head, may be known from this : that it is with the best of hearts as with the best of pears—a dangerous experiment to linger too long upon the scene. This did Polonius. Thank fortune, Frank, I am young, every tooth sound in my head, and if good wine can keep me where I am, long shall I remain so.'

' True,' with a smile. ' But wine, to do good, must be drunk. You have talked much and well, Charlie ; but drunk little and indifferently—fill up.'

' Presently, presently,' with a hasty and preoccupied air. ' If I remember right, Polonius hints as much as that one should, under no circumstances, commit the indiscretion of aiding in a pecuniary way an unfortunate friend. He drules out some stale stuff about " loan losing both itself and friend," don't he ? But our bottle ; is it glued fast ? Keep it moving, my dear Frank. Good wine, and upon my soul, I begin to feel it, and

through me old Polonius—yes, this wine, I fear, is what
excites me so against that detestable old dog without a
tooth.'

Upon this, the cosmopolitan, cigar in mouth, slowly
raised the bottle, and brought it slowly to the light,
looking at it steadfastly, as one might at a thermometer
in August, to see not how low it was, but how high.
Then whiffing out a puff, set it down, and said : ' Well,
Charlie, if what wine you have drunk came out of this
bottle, in that case I should say that if—supposing a
case—that if one fellow had an object in getting another
fellow fuddled, and this fellow to be fuddled was of your
capacity, the operation would be comparatively inex-
pensive. What do you think, Charlie ? '

' Why, I think I don't much admire the supposition,'
said Charlie, with a look of resentment ; ' it ain't safe,
depend upon it, Frank, to venture upon too jocose
suppositions with one's friends.'

' Why, bless you, Charlie,* my supposition wasn't
personal, but general. You mustn't be so touchy.'

' If I am touchy it is the wine. Sometimes, when I
freely drink it, it has a touchy effect on me, I have
observed.'

' Freely drink ? you haven't drunk the perfect measure
of one glass yet. While for me, this must be my fourth
or fifth, thanks to your importunity ; not to speak of all
I drank this morning, for old acquaintance' sake. Drink,
drink ; you must drink.'

' Oh, I drink while you are talking,' laughed the other ;
' you have not noticed it, but I have drunk my share.
Have a queer way I learned from a sedate old uncle, who
used to tip off his glass unperceived. Do you fill up,
and my glass, too. There ! Now away with that stump,
and have a new cigar. Good fellowship forever ! ' again
in the lyric mood. ' Say, Frank, are we not men ? I

say, are we not human ? Tell me, were they not human
who engendered us, as before heaven I believe they shall
be whom we shall engender ? Fill up, up, up, my friend.
Let the ruby tide aspire, and all ruby aspirations with
it ! Up, fill up ! Be we convivial. And conviviality,
what is it ? The word, I mean ; what expresses it ?
A living together. But bats live together, and did you
ever hear of convivial bats ? '

'If I ever did,' observed the cosmopolitan, ' it has
quite slipped my recollection.'

'But *why* did you never hear of convivial bats, nor
anybody else ? Because bats, though they live together,
live not together genially. Bats are not genial souls.
But men are ; and how delightful to think that the word
which among men signifies the highest pitch of geniality,
implies, as indispensable auxiliary, the cheery benediction
of the bottle. Yes, Frank, to live together in the finest
sense, we must drink together. And so, what wonder
that he who loves not wine, that sober wretch has a lean
heart—a heart like a wrung-out old blueing-bag,* and
loves not his kind ? Out upon him, to the rag-house
with him, hang him—the ungenial soul ! '

'Oh, now, now, can't you be convivial without being
censorious ? I like easy, unexcited conviviality. For
the sober man, really, though for my part I naturally love
a cheerful glass, I will not prescribe my nature as the law
to other natures. So don't abuse the sober man. Conviviality is one good thing, and sobriety is another good
thing. So don't be one-sided.'

'Well, if I am one-sided, it is the wine. Indeed,
indeed, I have indulged too genially. My excitement
upon slight provocation shows it. But yours is a stronger
head ; drink you. By the way, talking of geniality, it
is much on the increase in these days, ain't it ? '

'It is, and I hail the fact. Nothing better attests the

advance of the humanitarian spirit. In former and less humanitarian ages—the ages of amphitheatres and gladiators—geniality was mostly confined to the fireside and table. But in our age—the age of joint-stock companies and free-and-easies*—it is with this precious quality as with precious gold in old Peru, which Pizarro* found making up the scullion's sauce-pot as the Inca's crown. Yes, we golden boys, the moderns, have geniality everywhere—a bounty broadcast like noonlight.'

'True, true ; my sentiments again. Geniality has invaded each department and profession. We have genial senators, genial authors, genial lecturers, genial doctors, genial clergymen, genial surgeons, and the next thing we shall have genial hangmen.'

'As to the last-named sort of person,' said the cosmopolitan, 'I trust that the advancing spirit of geniality will at last enable us to dispense with him. No murderers—no hangmen. And surely, when the whole world shall have been genialised, it will be as out of place to talk of murderers, as in a Christianised world to talk of sinners.'

'To pursue the thought,' said the other, 'every blessing is attended with some evil, and——'

'Stay,' said the cosmopolitan, 'that may be better let pass for a loose saying, than for hopeful doctrine.'

'Well, assuming the saying's truth, it would apply to the future supremacy of the genial spirit, since then it will fare with the hangman as it did with the weaver when the spinning-jenny whizzed into the ascendant. Thrown out of employment, what could Jack Ketch turn his hand to ? Butchering ? '

'That he could turn his hand to it seems probable ; but that, under the circumstances, it would be appropriate might in some minds admit of a question. For one, I am inclined to think—and I trust it will not be held fastidiousness—that it would hardly be suitable to the

dignity of our nature, that an individual, once employed
in attending the last hours of human unfortunates,
should, that office being extinct, transfer himself to the
business of attending the last hours of unfortunate
cattle. I would suggest that the individual turn valet—
a vocation to which he would, perhaps, appear not
wholly unadapted by his familiar dexterity about the
person. In particular, for giving a finishing tie to a
gentleman's cravat, I know few who would, in all likelihood, be, from previous occupation, better fitted than
the professional person in question.'

'Are you in earnest ? ' regarding the serene speaker
with unaffected curiosity ; ' are you really in earnest ? '

' I trust I am never otherwise,' was the mildly earnest
reply ; ' but talking of the advance of geniality, I am
not without hopes that it will eventually exert its influence even upon so difficult a subject as the misanthrope.'

' A genial misanthrope ! I thought I had stretched
the rope pretty hard in talking of genial hangmen. A
genial misanthrope is no more conceivable than a surly
philanthropist.'

' True,' lightly depositing in an unbroken little cylinder
the ashes of his cigar, ' true, the two you name are well
opposed.'

' Why, you talk as if there was such a being as a surly
philanthropist.'

' I do. My eccentric friend, whom you call Coonskins,
is an example. Does he not, as I explained to you, hide
under a surly air a philanthropic heart ? Now, the genial
misanthrope, when, in the process of eras, he shall turn
up, will be the converse of this ; under an affable air,
he will hide a misanthropical heart. In short, the genial
misanthrope will be a new kind of monster, but still no
small improvement upon the original one, since, instead
of making faces and throwing stones at people, like that

poor old crazy man, Timon, he will take steps, fiddle in hand, and set the tickled world a-dancing. In a word, as the progress of Christianisation mellows those in manner whom it cannot mend in mind, much the same will it prove with the progress of genialisation. And so, thanks to geniality, the misanthrope, reclaimed from his boorish address, will take on refinement and softness— to so genial a degree, indeed, that it may possibly fall out that the misanthrope of the coming century will be almost as popular as, I am sincerely sorry to say, some philanthropists of the present time would seem not to be, as witness my eccentric friend named before.'

'Well,' cried the other, a little weary, perhaps, of a speculation so abstract, ' well, however it may be with the century to come, certainly in the century which is, whatever else one may be, he must be genial or he is nothing. So fill up, fill up, and be genial ! '

'I am trying my best,' said the cosmopolitan, still calmly companionable. ' A moment since, we talked of Pizarro, gold, and Peru ; no doubt, now, you remember that when the Spaniard first entered Atahualpa's treasure chamber, and saw such profusion of plate stacked up, right and left, with the wantonness of old barrels in a brewer's yard, the needy fellow felt a twinge of misgiving, of want of confidence, as to the genuineness of an opulence so profuse. He went about rapping the shining vases with his knuckles. But it was all gold, pure gold, good gold, sterling gold, which how cheerfully would have been stamped such at Goldsmiths' Hall. And just so those needy minds, which, through their own insincerity, having no confidence in mankind, doubt lest the liberal geniality of this age be spurious. They are small Pizarros in their way—by the very princeliness of men's geniality stunned into distrust of it.'

'Far be such distrust from you and me, my genial friend,' cried the other fervently ; 'fill up, fill up !'

'Well, this all along seems a division of labour,' smiled the cosmopolitan. 'I do about all the drinking, and you do about all—the genial. But yours is a nature competent to do that to a large population. And now, my friend,' with a peculiarly grave air, evidently foreshadowing something not unimportant, and very likely of close personal interest ; 'wine, you know, opens the heart, and——'

'Opens it !' with exultation, 'it thaws it right out. Every heart is ice-bound till wine melt it, and reveal the tender grass and sweet herbage budding below, with every dear secret, hidden before like a dropped jewel in a snow-bank, lying there unsuspected through winter till spring.'

'And just in that way, my dear Charlie, is one of my little secrets now to be shown forth.'

'Ah !' eagerly moving round his chair, 'what is it ?'

'Be not so impetuous, my dear Charlie. Let me explain. You see, naturally, I am a man not overgifted with assurance ; in general, I am, if anything, diffidently reserved ; so, if I shall presently seem otherwise, the reason is, that you, by the geniality you have evinced in all your talk, and especially the noble way in which, while affirming your good opinion of men, you intimated that you never could prove false to any man, but most by your indignation at a particularly illiberal passage in Polonius' advice—in short, in short,' with extreme embarrassment, 'how shall I express what I mean, unless I add that by your whole character you impel me to throw myself upon your nobleness ; in one word, put confidence in you, a generous confidence ?'

'I see, I see,' with heightened interest, 'something of

moment you wish to confide.   Now, what is it, Frank ?
Love affair ? '

'No, not that.'

'What, then, my *dear* Frank ?   Speak—depend upon
me to the last.   Out with it.'

'Out it shall come, then,' said the cosmopolitan.   'I
am in want, urgent want, of money.'

CHAPTER XXXI

A METAMORPHOSIS MORE SURPRISING THAN ANY
IN OVID[*]

'IN want of money!' pushing back his chair as from a suddenly disclosed man-trap or crater.

'Yes,' naïvely assented the cosmopolitan, 'and you are going to loan me fifty dollars. I could almost wish I was in need of more, only for your sake. Yes, my dear Charlie, for your sake; that you might the better prove your noble kindliness, my dear Charlie.'

'None of your dear Charlies,' cried the other, springing to his feet, and buttoning up his coat, as if hastily to depart upon a long journey.

'Why, why, why?' painfully looking up.

'None of your why, why, whys!' tossing out a foot, 'go to the devil, sir! Beggar, impostor!—never so deceived in a man in my life.'

CHAPTER XXXII

SHOWING THAT THE AGE OF MAGIC AND MAGICIANS
IS NOT YET OVER

WHILE speaking or rather hissing those words, the boon companion underwent much such a change as one reads of in fairy-books. Out of old material sprang a new creature. Cadmus glided into the snake.*

The cosmopolitan rose, the traces of previous feeling vanished ; looked steadfastly at his transformed friend a moment, then, taking ten half-eagles from his pocket, stooped down, and laid them, one by one, in a circle round him ; and, retiring a pace, waved his long tasselled pipe with the air of a necromancer, an air heightened by his costume, accompanying each wave with a solemn murmur of cabalistical words.

Meantime, he within the magic ring stood suddenly rapt, exhibiting every symptom of a successful charm— a turned cheek, a fixed attitude, a frozen eye ; spellbound, not more by the waving wand than by the ten invincible talismans on the floor.

' Reappear, reappear, reappear, oh, my former friend ! Replace this hideous apparition with thy blest shape, and be the token of thy return the words, " My dear Frank." '

' My dear Frank,' now cried the restored friend, cordially stepping out of the ring, with regained self-possession regaining lost identity, ' My dear Frank, what a funny man you are ; full of fun as an egg of meat. How could you tell me that absurd story of your being in need ?

But I relish a good joke too well to spoil it by letting on. Of course, I humoured the thing; and, on my side, put on all the cruel airs you would have me. Come, this little episode of fictitious estrangement will but enhance the delightful reality. Let us sit down again, and finish our bottle.'

'With all my heart,' said the cosmopolitan, dropping the necromancer with the same facility with which he had assumed it. 'Yes,' he added, soberly picking up the gold pieces, and returning them with a chink to his pocket, 'yes, I am something of a funny man now and then; while for you, Charlie,' eyeing him in tenderness, 'what you say about your humouring the thing is true enough; never did man second a joke better than you did just now. You played your part better than I did mine; you played it, Charlie, to the life.'

'You see, I once belonged to an amateur play company; that accounts for it. But come, fill up, and let's talk of something else.'

'Well,' acquiesced the cosmopolitan, seating himself, and quietly brimming his glass, 'what shall we talk about?'

'Oh, anything you please,' a sort of nervously accommodating.

'Well, suppose we talk about Charlemont?'

'Charlemont? What's Charlemont? Who's Charlemont?'

'You shall hear, my dear Charlie,' answered the cosmopolitan. 'I will tell you the story of Charlemont, the gentleman-madman.'

CHAPTER XXXIII

WHICH MAY PASS FOR WHATEVER IT MAY PROVE
TO BE WORTH

BUT ere be given the rather grave story of Charlemont, a reply must in civility be made to a certain voice which methinks I hear, that, in view of past chapters, and more particularly the last, where certain antics appear, exclaims: How unreal all this is ! Who did ever dress or act like your cosmopolitan ? And who, it might be returned, did ever dress or act like harlequin ?

Strange, that in a work of amusement, this severe fidelity to real life should be exacted by anyone, who, by taking up such a work, sufficiently shows that he is not unwilling to drop real life, and turn, for a time, to something different. Yes, it is, indeed, strange that anyone should clamour for the thing he is weary of ; that anyone, who, for any cause, finds real life dull, should yet demand of him who is to divert his attention from it, that he should be true to that dullness.

There is another class, and with this class we side, who sit down to a work of amusement tolerantly as they sit at a play, and with much the same expectations and feelings. They look that fancy shall evoke scenes different from those of the same old crowd round the custom-house counter, and same old dishes on the boarding-house table, with characters unlike those of the same old acquaintances they meet in the same old way every day in the same old street. And as, in real life, the proprieties will not allow people to act out themselves with that unreserve permitted to the stage ; so, in books of fiction, they look not only for more entertainment, but, at bottom, even for more reality, than real life itself can show. Thus, though they want novelty, they want nature, too ; but nature unfettered, exhilarated, in effect transformed. In this way of thinking, the people in a fiction, like the people in a play, must dress as nobody exactly dresses, talk as nobody exactly talks, act as nobody exactly acts. It is with fiction as with religion : it should present another world, and yet one to which we feel the tie.

If, then, something is to be pardoned to well-meant endeavour, surely a little is to be allowed to that writer who, in all his scenes, does but seek to minister to what, as he understands it, is the implied wish of the more indulgent lovers of entertainment, before whom harlequin can never appear in a coat too parti-coloured, or cut capers too fantastic.

One word more. Though everyone knows how bootless it is to be in all cases vindicating one's self, never mind how convinced one may be that he is never in the wrong ; yet, so precious to man is the approbation of his kind, that to rest, though but under an imaginary censure applied to but a work of imagination, is no easy thing. The mention of this weakness will explain why all such readers as may think they perceive something inharmonious between the boisterous hilarity of the cosmopolitan with the bristling cynic, and his restrained good-nature with the boon companion, are now referred to that chapter where some similar apparent inconsistency in another character is, on general principles, modestly endeavoured to be apologised for.

CHAPTER XXXIV

IN WHICH THE COSMOPOLITAN TELLS THE STORY OF
THE GENTLEMAN-MADMAN

'CHARLEMONT was a young merchant of French descent,
living in St. Louis—a man not deficient in mind, and
possessed of that sterling and captivating kindliness,
seldom in perfection seen but in youthful bachelors,
united at times to a remarkable sort of gracefully devil-
may-care and witty good-humour. Of course, he was
admired by everybody, and loved, as only mankind can
love, by not a few. But in his twenty-ninth year a change
came over him. Like one whose hair turns gray in a
night, so in a day Charlemont turned from affable to
morose. His acquaintances were passed without greeting; while, as for his confidential friends, them he
pointedly, unscrupulously, and with a kind of fierceness,
cut dead.

'One, provoked by such conduct, would fain have
resented it with words as disdainful; while another,
shocked by the change, and, in concern for a friend,
magnanimously overlooking affronts, implored to know
what sudden, secret grief had distempered him. But
from resentment and from tenderness Charlemont alike
turned away.

'Ere long, to the general surprise, the merchant
Charlemont was gazetted,* and the same day it was reported that he had withdrawn from town, but not
before placing his entire property in the hands of responsible assignees for the benefit of creditors.

'Whither he had vanished, none could guess. At length, nothing being heard, it was surmised that he must have made away with himself—a surmise, doubtless, originating in the remembrance of the change some months previous to his bankruptcy—a change of a sort only to be ascribed to a mind suddenly thrown from its balance.

'Years passed. It was spring-time, and lo, one bright morning, Charlemont lounged into the St. Louis coffee-houses—gay, polite, humane, companionable, and dressed in the height of costly elegance. Not only was he alive, but he was himself again. Upon meeting with old acquaintances, he made the first advances, and in such a manner that it was impossible not to meet him half-way. Upon other old friends, whom he did not chance casually to meet, he either personally called, or left his card and compliments for them; and to several, sent presents of game or hampers of wine.

'They say the world is sometimes harshly unforgiving, but it was not so to Charlemont. The world feels a return of love for one who returns to it as he did. Expressive of its renewed interest was a whisper, an inquiring whisper, how now, exactly, so long after his bankruptcy, it fared with Charlemont's purse. Rumour, seldom at a loss for answers, replied that he had spent nine years in Marseilles in France, and there acquiring a second fortune, had returned with it, a man devoted henceforth to genial friendships.

'Added years went by, and the restored wanderer still the same; or rather, by his noble qualities, grew up like golden maize in the encouraging sun of good opinions. But still the latent wonder was, what had caused that change in him at a period when, pretty much as now, he was, to all appearance, in the possession of the same fortune, the same friends, the same popularity. But

nobody thought it would be the thing to question him
here.

' At last, at a dinner at his house, when all the guests
but one had successively departed ; this remaining guest,
an old acquaintance, being just enough under the influence of wine to set aside the fear of touching upon a
delicate point, ventured, in a way which perhaps spoke
more favourably for his heart than his tact, to beg of
his host to explain the one enigma of his life. Deep
melancholy overspread the before cheery face of Charlemont ; he sat for some moments tremulously silent ;
then pushing a full decanter toward the guest, in a choked
voice, said : " No, no ! when by art, and care, and time,
flowers are made to bloom over a grave, who would seek
to dig all up again only to know the mystery ?—The wine."
When both glasses were filled, Charlemont took his, and
lifting it, added lowly : " If ever, in days to come, you
shall see ruin at hand, and, thinking you understand
mankind, shall tremble for your friendships, and tremble
for your pride ; and, partly through love for the one and
fear for the other, shall resolve to be beforehand with
the world, and save it from a sin by prospectively taking
that sin to yourself, then will you do as one I now dream
of once did, and like him will you suffer ; but how fortunate and how grateful should you be, if like him, after
all that had happened, you could be a little happy again."

' When the guest went away, it was with the persuasion,
that though outwardly restored in mind as in fortune,
yet some taint of Charlemont's old malady survived,
and that it was not well for friends to touch one dangerous
string.'

CHAPTER XXXV

IN WHICH THE COSMOPOLITAN STRIKINGLY EVINCES
THE ARTLESSNESS OF HIS NATURE

'WELL, what do you think of the story of Charlemont?' mildly asked he who had told it.

'A very strange one,' answered the auditor, who had been such not with perfect ease, 'but is it true?'

'Of course not; it is a story which I told with the purpose of every story-teller—to amuse. Hence, if it seem strange to you, that strangeness is the romance; it is what contrasts it with real life; it is the invention, in brief, the fiction as opposed to the fact. For do but ask yourself, my dear Charlie,' lovingly leaning over toward him; 'I rest it with your own heart now, whether such a fore-reaching motive as Charlemont hinted he had acted on in his change—whether such a motive, I say, were a sort of one at all justified by the nature of human society? Would you, for one, turn the cold shoulder to a friend—a convivial one, say, whose pennilessness should be suddenly revealed to you?'

'How can you ask me, my dear Frank? You know I would scorn such meanness.' But rising somewhat disconcerted—'really, early as it is, I think I must retire; my head,' putting up his hand to it, 'feels unpleasantly; this confounded elixir of logwood, little as I drank of it, has played the deuce with me.'

'Little as you drank of this elixir of logwood? Why,

Charlie, you are losing your mind. To talk so of the genuine, mellow old port. Yes, I think that by all means you had better away, and sleep it off. There— don't apologise—don't explain—go, go—I understand you exactly. I will see you to-morrow.'

CHAPTER XXXVI

IN WHICH THE COSMOPOLITAN IS ACCOSTED BY A MYSTIC,
WHEREUPON ENSUES PRETTY MUCH SUCH TALK AS
MIGHT BE EXPECTED

As, not without some haste, the boon companion withdrew, a stranger* advanced, and touching the cosmopolitan, said : ' I think I heard you say you would see
that man again. Be warned ; don't you do so.'

He turned, surveying the speaker ; a blue-eyed man,
sandy-haired, and Saxon-looking ; perhaps five-and-
forty ; tall, and, but for a certain angularity, well made ;
little touch of the drawing-room about him, but a look
of plain propriety of a Puritan sort, with a kind of farmer
dignity. His age seemed betokened more by his brow,
placidly thoughtful, than by his general aspect, which
had that look of youthfulness in maturity, peculiar sometimes to habitual health of body, the original gift of
nature, or in part the effect or reward of steady temperance of the passions, kept so, perhaps, by constitu-
tion as much as morality. A neat, comely, almost ruddy
cheek, coolly fresh, like a red clover-blossom at coolish
dawn—the colour of warmth preserved by the virtue of
chill. Toning the whole man, was one-knows-not-what
of shrewdness and mythiness, strangely jumbled ; in
that way, he seemed a kind of cross between a Yankee
peddler and a Tartar priest, though it seemed as if, at a
pinch, the first would not in all probability play second
fiddle to the last.

' Sir,' said the cosmopolitan, rising and bowing with

slow dignity, 'if I cannot with unmixed satisfaction hail
a hint pointed at one who has just been clinking the
social glass with me, on the other hand, I am not disposed to underrate the motive which, in the present case,
could alone have prompted such an intimation. My
friend, whose seat is still warm, has retired for the night,
leaving more or less in his bottle here. Pray, sit down
in his seat, and partake with me ; and then, if you choose
to hint aught further unfavourable to the man, the genial
warmth of whose person in part passes into yours, and
whose genial hospitality meanders through you—be it so.'

'Quite beautiful conceits,' said the stranger, now
scholastically and artistically eyeing the picturesque
speaker, as if he were a statue in the Pitti Palace ;* ' very
beautiful ' : then with the gravest interest, ' yours, sir,
if I mistake not, must be a beautiful soul—one full of all
love and truth ; for where beauty is, there must those be.'

'A pleasing belief,' rejoined the cosmopolitan, beginning with an even air, ' and to confess, long ago it pleased
me. Yes, with you and Schiller,* I am pleased to believe
that beauty is at bottom incompatible with ill, and
therefore am so eccentric as to have confidence in the
latent benignity of that beautiful creature, the rattle-
snake, whose lithe neck and burnished maze of tawny
gold, as he sleekly curls aloft in the sun, who on the
prairie can behold without wonder ? '

As he breathed these words, he seemed so to enter into
their spirit—as some earnest descriptive speakers will—
as unconsciously to wreathe his form and sidelong crest
his head, till he all but seemed the creature described.
Meantime, the stranger regarded him with little surprise,
apparently, though with much contemplativeness of a
mystical sort, and presently said : ' When charmed by
the beauty of that viper, did it never occur to you to
change personalities with him ? to feel what it was to

a snake ? to glide unsuspected in grass ? to sting, to kill at a touch ; your whole beautiful body one iridescent scabbard of death ? In short, did the wish never occur to you to feel yourself exempt from knowledge, and conscience, and revel for a while in the care-free, joyous life of a perfectly instinctive, unscrupulous, and irresponsible creature ? '

' Such a wish,' replied the other, not perceptibly disturbed, ' I must confess, never consciously was mine. Such a wish, indeed, could hardly occur to ordinary imaginations, and mine I cannot think much above the average.'

' But now that the idea is suggested,' said the stranger, with infantile intellectuality, ' does it not raise the desire ? '

' Hardly. For though I do not think I have any uncharitable prejudice against the rattle-snake, still I should not like to be one. If I were a rattle-snake now, there would be no such thing as being genial with men— men would be afraid of me, and then I should be a very lonesome and miserable rattle-snake.'

' True, men would be afraid of you. And why ? Because of your rattle, your hollow rattle—a sound, as I have been told, like the shaking together of small, dry skulls in a tune of the Waltz of Death.* And here we have another beautiful truth. When any creature is by its make inimical to other creatures, nature in effect labels that creature, much as an apothecary does a poison. So that whoever is destroyed by a rattle-snake, or other harmful agent, it is his own fault. He should have respected the label. Hence that significant passage in Scripture, " Who will pity the charmer that is bitten with a serpent ? " '*

' *I* would pity him,' said the cosmopolitan, a little bluntly, perhaps.

'But don't you think,' rejoined the other, still main-taining his passionless air, ' don't you think, that for a man to pity where nature is pitiless, is a little presuming ? '

'Let casuists decide the casuistry, but the compassion the heart decides for itself. But, sir,' deepening in seri-ousness, ' as I now for the first realise, you but a moment since introduced the word irresponsible in a way I am not used to. Now, sir, though, out of a tolerant spirit, as I hope, I try my best never to be frightened at any speculation, so long as it is pursued in honesty, yet, for once, I must acknowledge that you do really, in the point cited, cause me uneasiness ; because a proper view of the universe, that view which is suited to breed a proper confidence, teaches, if I err not, that since all things are justly presided over, not very many living agents but must be some way accountable.'

'Is a rattle-snake accountable ? ' asked the stranger, with such a preternaturally cold, gemmy glance out of his pellucid blue eye, that he seemed more a metaphysical merman than a feeling man ; ' is a rattle-snake account-able ? '

'If I will not affirm that it is,' returned the other, with the caution of no inexperienced thinker, ' neither will I deny it. But if we suppose it so, I need not say that such accountability is neither to you, nor me, nor the Court of Common Pleas,* but to something superior.'

He was proceeding, when the stranger would have interrupted him ; but as reading his argument in his eye, the cosmopolitan, without waiting for it to be put into words, at once spoke to it : ' You object to my supposi-tion, for but such it is, that the rattle-snake's accounta-bility is not by nature manifest ; but might not much the same thing be urged against man's ? A *reductio ad absurdum*,* proving the objection vain. But if now,' he continued, ' you consider what capacity for mischief

there is in a rattle-snake (observe, I do not charge it with
being mischievous, I but say it has the capacity), could
you well avoid admitting that that would be no sym-
metrical view of the universe which should maintain
that, while to man it is forbidden to kill, without judicial
cause, his fellow, yet the rattle-snake has an implied
permit of unaccountability to murder any creature it
takes capricious umbrage at—man included?—But,'
with a wearied air, 'this is no genial talk; at least it is
not so to me. Zeal at unawares embarked me in it. I
regret it. Pray, sit down, and take some of this wine.'

'Your suggestions are new to me,' said the other, with
a kind of condescending appreciativeness, as of one who,
out of devotion to knowledge, disdains not to appropriate
the least crumb of it, even from a pauper's board; 'and,
as I am a very Athenian in hailing a new thought, I
cannot consent to let it drop so abruptly. Now, the
rattle-snake——'

'Nothing more about rattle-snakes, I beseech,' in distress; 'I must positively decline to re-enter upon that
subject. Sit down, sir, I beg, and take some of this
wine.'

'To invite me to sit down with you is hospitable,'
collectedly acquiescing now in the change of topics;
'and hospitality being fabled to be of oriental origin,
and forming, as it does, the subject of a pleasing Arabian
romance, as well as being a very romantic thing in itself—
hence I always hear the expressions of hospitality with
pleasure. But, as for the wine, my regard for that
beverage is so extreme, and I am so fearful of letting it
sate me, that I keep my love for it in the lasting condition of an untried abstraction. Briefly, I quaff immense
draughts of wine from the page of Hafiz,* but wine from
a cup I seldom as much as sip.'

The cosmopolitan turned a mild glance upon the speaker,

who, now occupying the chair opposite him, sat there purely and coldly radiant as a prism. It seemed as if one could almost hear him vitreously chime and ring. That moment a waiter passed, whom, arresting with a sign, the cosmopolitan bid go bring a goblet of ice-water. 'Ice it well, waiter,' said he; 'and now,' turning to the stranger, 'will you, if you please, give me your reason for the warning words you first addressed to me ? '

'I hope they were not such warnings as most warnings are,' said the stranger; 'warnings which do not forewarn, but in mockery come after the fact. And yet something in you bids me think now, that whatever latent design your impostor friend might have had upon you, it as yet remains unaccomplished. You read his label.'

'And what did it say ? "This is a genial soul." So you see you must either give up your doctrine of labels, or else your prejudice against my friend. But tell me,' with renewed earnestness, 'what do you take him for ? What is he ? '

'What are you ? What am I ? Nobody knows who anybody is. The data which life furnishes, toward forming a true estimate of any being, are as insufficient to that end as in geometry one side given would be to determine the triangle.'

'But is not this doctrine of triangles some way inconsistent with your doctrine of labels ? '

'Yes; but what of that ? I seldom care to be consistent.* In a philosophical view, consistency is a certain level at all times, maintained in all the thoughts of one's mind. But, since nature is nearly all hill and dale, how can one keep naturally advancing in knowledge without submitting to the natural inequalities in the progress ? Advance into knowledge is just like advance upon the grand Erie canal, where, from the character of the country, change of level is inevitable; you are locked up and locked down with perpetual inconsistencies, and yet all the time you get on; while the dullest part of the whole route is what the boatmen call the "long level"—a consistently flat surface of sixty miles through stagnant swamps.'

'In one particular,' rejoined the cosmopolitan,' your simile is, perhaps, unfortunate. For, after all these weary lockings-up and lockings-down, upon how much of a higher plain do you finally stand? Enough to make it an object? Having from youth been taught reverence for knowledge, you must pardon me if, on but this one account, I reject your analogy. But really you some way bewitch me with your tempting discourse, so that I keep straying from my point unawares. You tell me you cannot certainly know who or what my friend is; pray, what do you conjecture him to be?'

'I conjecture him to be what, among the ancient Egyptians, was called a ——' using some unknown word.

'A ——! And what is that?'

'A —— is what Proclus,* in a little note to his third book on the theology of Plato, defines as —— ——' coming out with a sentence of Greek.

Holding up his glass, and steadily looking through its transparency, the cosmopolitan rejoined: 'That, in so defining the thing, Proclus set it to modern understandings in the most crystal light it was susceptible of, I will not rashly deny; still, if you could put the definition in words suited to perceptions like mine, I should take it for a favour.'

'A favour!' slightly lifting his cool eyebrows; 'a bridal favour I understand, a knot of white ribands, a very beautiful type of the purity of true marriage; but of other favours I am yet to learn; and still, in a vague way, the word, as you employ it, strikes me as un-pleasingly significant in general of some poor, unheroic submission to being done good to.'

Here the goblet of iced-water was brought, and, in compliance with a sign from the cosmopolitan, was placed before the stranger, who, not before expressing acknowledgments, took a draught, apparently refreshing—its very coldness, as with some is the case, proving not entirely uncongenial.

At last, setting down the goblet, and gently wiping from his lips the beads of water freshly clinging there as to the valve of a coral-shell upon a reef, he turned upon the cosmopolitan, and, in a manner the most cool, self-possessed, and matter-of-fact possible, said : 'I hold to the metempsychosis ; and whoever I may be now, I feel that I was once the stoic Arrian,* and have inklings of having been equally puzzled by a word in the current language of that former time, very probably answering to your word *favour*.'

'Would you favour me by explaining ? ' said the cosmopolitan, blandly.

'Sir,' responded the stranger, with a very slight degree of severity, 'I like lucidity, of all things, and am afraid I shall hardly be able to converse satisfactorily with you, unless you bear it in mind.'

'The cosmopolitan ruminatingly eyed him awhile, then said : 'The best way, as I have heard, to get out of a labyrinth, is to retrace one's steps. I will accordingly retrace mine, and beg you will accompany me. In short, once again to return to the point : for what reason did you warn me against my friend ? '

'Briefly, then, and clearly, because, as before said, I conjecture him to be what, among the ancient Egyptians——'

'Pray, now,' earnestly deprecated the cosmopolitan, 'pray, now, why disturb the repose of those ancient

Egyptians? What to us are their words or their thoughts?
Are we pauper Arabs, without a house of our own, that,
with the mummies, we must turn squatters among the
dust of the Catacombs?'

'Pharaoh's poorest brick-maker lies proudlier in his
rags than the Emperor of all the Russias in his hollands,*'
oracularly said the stranger; 'for death, though in a
worm, is majestic; while life, though in a king, is con-
temptible. So talk not against mummies. It is a part
of my mission to teach mankind a due reverence for
mummies.'

Fortunately, to arrest these incoherencies, or rather,
to vary them, a haggard, inspired-looking man* now
approached—a crazy beggar, asking alms under the form
of peddling a rhapsodical tract, composed by himself,
and setting forth his claims to some rhapsodical apostleship. Though ragged and dirty, there was about him no
touch of vulgarity; for, by nature, his manner was not
unrefined, his frame slender, and appeared the more so
from the broad, untanned frontlet of his brow, tangled
over with a dishevelled mass of raven curls, throwing a
still deeper tinge upon a complexion like that of a shrivelled
berry. Nothing could exceed his look of picturesque
Italian ruin and dethronement, heightened by what
seemed just one glimmering peep of reason, insufficient
to do him any lasting good, but enough, perhaps, to
suggest a torment of latent doubts at times, whether his
addled dream of glory were true.

Accepting the tract offered him, the cosmopolitan
glanced over it, and, seeming to see just what it was,
closed it, put it in his pocket, eyed the man a moment,
then, leaning over and presenting him with a shilling,
said to him, in tones kind and considerate: 'I am
sorry, my friend, that I happen to be engaged just
now; but, having purchased your work, I promise

myself much satisfaction in its perusal at my earliest
leisure.'

In his tattered, single-breasted frock-coat, buttoned
meagrely up to his chin, the shatter-brain made him a
bow, which, for courtesy, would not have misbecome a
viscount, then turned with silent appeal to the stranger.
But the stranger sat more like a cold prism than ever,
while an expression of keen Yankee cuteness, now replacing
his former mystical one, lent added icicles to his aspect.
His whole air said : ' Nothing from me.' The repulsed
petitioner threw a look full of resentful pride and cracked
disdain upon him, and went his way.

' Come, now,' said the cosmopolitan, a little reproachfully, ' you ought to have sympathised with that man ;
tell me, did you feel no fellow-feeling ? Look at his
tract here, quite in the transcendental vein.'

' Excuse me,' said the stranger, declining the tract,
' I never patronise scoundrels.'

' Scoundrels ? '

' I detected in him, sir, a damning peep of sense—
damning, I say ; for sense in a seeming madman is
scoundrelism. I take him for a cunning vagabond, who
picks up a vagabond living by adroitly playing the madman. Did you not remark how he flinched under my
eye ? '

' Really,' drawing a long, astonished breath, ' I could
hardly have divined in you a temper so subtlely distrustful. Flinched ? to be sure he did, poor fellow ;
you received him with so lame a welcome. As for his
adroitly playing the madman, invidious critics might
object the same to some one or two strolling magi of
these days. But that is a matter I know nothing about.
But, once more, and for the last time, to return to the
point : why, sir, did you warn me against my friend ?
I shall rejoice, if, as I think it will prove, your want of

confidence in my friend rests upon a basis equally slender with your distrust of the lunatic. Come, why did you warn me? Put it, I beseech, in few words, and those English.'

'I warned you against him because he is suspected for what on these boats is known—so they tell me—as a Mississippi operator.'

'An operator, ah? he operates, does he? My friend, then, is something like what the Indians call a Great Medicine, is he? He operates, he purges, he drains off the repletions.'

'I perceive, sir,' said the stranger, constitutionally obtuse to the pleasant drollery, 'that your notion, of what is called a Great Medicine, needs correction. The Great Medicine among the Indians is less a bolus*than a man in grave esteem for his politic sagacity.'

'And is not my friend politic? Is not my friend sagacious? By your own definition, is not my friend a Great Medicine?'

'No, he is an operator, a Mississippi operator; an equivocal character. That he is such, I little doubt, having had him pointed out to me as such by one desirous of initiating me into any little novelty of this western region, where I never before travelled. And, sir, if I am not mistaken, you also are a stranger here (but, indeed, where in this strange universe is not one a stranger?), and that is a reason why I felt moved to warn you against a companion who could not be otherwise than perilous to one of a free and trustful disposition. But I repeat the hope, that, thus far at least, he has not succeeded with you, and trust that, for the future, he will not.'

'Thank you for your concern; but hardly can I equally thank you for so steadily maintaining the hypothesis of my friend's objectionableness. True, I but made his

acquaintance for the first to-day, and know little of his
antecedents; but that would seem no just reason why a
nature like his should not of itself inspire confidence.
And since your own knowledge of the gentleman is not,
by your account, so exact as it might be, you will pardon
me if I decline to welcome any further suggestions unflattering to him. Indeed, sir,' with friendly decision,
' let us change the subject.'

CHAPTER XXXVII

THE MYSTICAL MASTER INTRODUCES THE PRACTICAL DISCIPLE

' BOTH, the subject and the interlocutor,' replied the stranger rising, and waiting the return toward him of a promenader, that moment turning at the further end of his walk.

' Egbert ! ' said he, calling.

Egbert, a well-dressed, commercial-looking gentleman of about thirty, responded in a way strikingly deferential, and in a moment stood near, in the attitude less of an equal companion apparently than a confidential follower.*

' This,' said the stranger, taking Egbert by the hand and leading him to the cosmopolitan, ' this is Egbert, a disciple. I wish you to know Egbert. Egbert was the first among mankind to reduce to practice the principles of Mark Winsome—principles previously accounted as less adapted to life than the closet. Egbert,' turning to the disciple, who, with seeming modesty, a little shrank under these compliments, ' Egbert, this,' with a salute toward the cosmopolitan, ' is, like all of us, a stranger. I wish you, Egbert, to know this brother stranger ; be communicative with him. Particularly if, by anything hitherto dropped, his curiosity has been roused as to the precise nature of my philosophy, I trust you will not leave such curiosity ungratified. You, Egbert, by simply setting forth your practice, can do more to en-lighten one as to my theory, than I myself can by mere speech. Indeed, it is by you that I myself best understand myself. For to every philosophy are certain rear parts, very important parts, and these, like the rear of one's head, are best seen by reflection. Now, as in a glass, you, Egbert, in your life, reflect to me the more important part of my system. He, who approves you, approves the philosophy of Mark Winsome.'

Though portions of this harangue may, perhaps, in the phraseology seem self-complaisant, yet no trace of self-complacency was perceptible in the speaker's manner, which throughout was plain, unassuming, dignified, and manly; the teacher and prophet seemed to lurk more in the idea, so to speak, than in the mere bearing of him who was the vehicle of it.

'Sir,' said the cosmopolitan, who seemed not a little interested in this new aspect of matters, 'you speak of a certain philosophy, and a more or less occult one it may be, and hint of its bearing upon practical life; pray, tell me, if the study of this philosophy tends to the same formation of character with the experiences of the world ? '

'It does; and that is the test of its truth; for any philosophy that, being in operation contradictory to the ways of the world, tends to produce a character at odds with it, such a philosophy must necessarily be but a cheat and a dream.'

'You a little surprise me,' answered the cosmopolitan; 'for, from an occasional profundity in you, and also from your allusions to a profound work on the theology of Plato, it would seem but natural to surmise that, if you are the originator of any philosophy, it must needs so partake of the abstruse, as to exalt it above the comparatively vile uses of life.'

'No uncommon mistake with regard to me,' rejoined the other. Then meekly standing like a Raphael :* 'If still in golden accents old Memnon* murmurs his riddle, none the less does the balance-sheet of every man's ledger

unriddle the profit or loss of life. Sir,' with calm energy,
' man came into this world, not to sit down and muse,
not to befog himself with vain subtleties, but to gird up
his loins and to work. Mystery is in the morning, and
mystery in the night, and the beauty of mystery is everywhere ; but still the plain truth remains, that mouth
and purse must be filled. If, hitherto, you have supposed
me a visionary, be undeceived. I am no one-ideaed one,
either ; no more than the seers before me. Was not
Seneca a usurer ? Bacon a courtier ? and Swedenborg,*
though with one eye on the invisible, did he not keep the
other on the main chance ? Along with whatever else it
may be given me to be, I am a man of serviceable knowledge, and a man of the world. Know me for such.
And as for my disciple here,' turning toward him, ' if
you look to find any soft Utopianisms and last year's
sunsets in him, I smile to think how he will set you right.
The doctrines I have taught him will, I trust, lead him
neither to the mad-house nor the poor-house, as so many
other doctrines have served credulous sticklers. Furthermore,' glancing upon him paternally, ' Egbert is both my
disciple and my poet. For poetry is not a thing of ink
and rhyme, but of thought and act, and, in the latter
way, is by anyone to be found anywhere, when in useful
action sought. In a word, my disciple here is a thriving
young merchant, a practical poet in the West India trade.
There,' presenting Egbert's hand to the cosmopolitan,
' I join you, and leave you.' With which words, and
without bowing, the master withdrew.

CHAPTER XXXVIII

THE DISCIPLE UNBENDS, AND CONSENTS TO ACT
A SOCIAL PART

In the master's presence the disciple had stood as one
not ignorant of his place; modesty was in his expression,
with a sort of reverential depression. But the presence
of the superior withdrawn, he seemed lithely to shoot up
erect from beneath it, like one of those wire men from a
toy snuff-box.

He was, as before said, a young man of about thirty.
His countenance of that neuter sort, which, in repose,
is neither prepossessing nor disagreeable; so that it
seemed quite uncertain how he would turn out. His
dress was neat, with just enough of the mode to save it
from the reproach of originality; in which general
respect, though with a readjustment of details, his costume seemed modelled upon his master's. But, upon the
whole, he was, to all appearances, the last person in the
world that one would take for the disciple of any transcendental philosophy; though, indeed, something about
his sharp nose and shaved chin seemed to hint that if
mysticism, as a lesson, ever came in his way, he might,
with the characteristic knack of a true New-Englander,
turn even so profitless a thing to some profitable account.

'Well,' said he, now familiarly seating himself in the
vacated chair, 'what do you think of Mark? Sublime
fellow, ain't he?'

'That each member of the human guild is worthy

respect, my friend,' rejoined the cosmopolitan, 'is a fact
which no admirer of that guild will question ; but that,
in view of higher natures, the word sublime, so frequently
applied to them, can, without confusion, be also applied
to man, is a point which man will decide for himself ;
though, indeed, if he decide it in the affirmative, it is not
for me to object. But I am curious to know more of
that philosophy of which, at present, I have but inklings.
You, its first disciple among men, it seems, are peculiarly
qualified to expound it. Have you any objections to
begin now ? '

'None at all,' squaring himself to the table. 'Where
shall I begin ? At first principles ? '

'You remember that it was in a practical way that you
were represented as being fitted for the clear exposition.
Now, what you call first principles, I have, in some things,
found to be more or less vague. Permit me, then, in a
plain way, to suppose some common case in real life, and
that done, I would like you to tell me how you, the practical disciple of the philosophy I wish to know about,
would, in that case, conduct.'

'A business-like view. Propose the case.'

'Not only the case, but the persons. The case is this :
There are two friends, friends from childhood, bosom
friends ; one of whom, for the first time, being in need,
for the first time seeks a loan from the other, who, so far
as fortune goes, is more than competent to grant it. And
the persons are to be you and I : you, the friend from whom
the loan is sought—I, the friend who seeks it ; you, the
disciple of the philosophy in question—I, a common
man, with no more philosophy than to know that when
I am comfortably warm I don't feel cold, and when I
have the ague I shake. Mind, now, you must work up
your imagination, and, as much as possible, talk and
behave just as if the case supposed were a fact.   For

brevity, you shall call me Frank, and I will call you Charlie. Are you agreed ? '

' Perfectly. You begin.'

The cosmopolitan paused a moment, then, assuming a serious and care-worn air, suitable to the part to be enacted, addressed his hypothesised friend.

CHAPTER XXXIX

THE HYPOTHETICAL FRIENDS

' CHARLIE, I am going to put confidence in you.'

' You always have, and with reason. What is it,
Frank ? '

' Charlie, I am in want—urgent want of money.'

' That 's not well.'

' But it *will* be well, Charlie, if you loan me a hundred
dollars. I would not ask this of you, only my need is
sore, and you and I have so long shared hearts and minds
together, however unequally on my side, that nothing
remains to prove our friendship than, with the same
inequality on my side, to share purses. You will do
me the favour, won't you ? '

' Favour ? What do you mean by asking me to do
you a favour ? '

' Why, Charlie, you never used to talk so.'

' Because, Frank, you on your side, never used to
talk so.'

' But won't you loan me the money ? '

' No, Frank.'

' Why ? '

' Because my rule forbids. I give away money, but
never loan it ; and of course the man who calls himself
my friend is above receiving alms.* The negotiation of a
loan is a business transaction. And I will transact no
business with a friend. What a friend is, he is socially
and intellectually ; and I rate social and intellectual
friendship too high to degrade it on either side into a

pecuniary make-shift. To be sure there are, and I have, what is called business friends; that is, commercial acquaintances, very convenient persons. But I draw a red-ink line between them and my friends in the true sense—my friends social and intellectual. In brief, a true friend has nothing to do with loans; he should have a soul above loans. Loans are such unfriendly accommodations as are to be had from the soulless corporation of a bank, by giving the regular security and paying the regular discount.'

'An *unfriendly* accommodation? Do those words go together handsomely?'

'Like the poor farmer's team, of an old man and a cow—not handsomely, but to the purpose. Look, Frank, a loan of money on interest is a sale of money on credit. To sell a thing on credit may be an accommodation, but where is the friendliness? Few men in their senses, except operators, borrow money on interest, except upon a necessity akin to starvation. Well, now, where is the friendliness of my letting a starving man have, say, the money's worth of a barrel of flour upon the condition that, on a given day, he shall let me have the money's worth of a barrel and a half of flour; especially if I add this further proviso, that if he fail so to do, I shall then, to secure to myself the money's worth of my barrel and his half-barrel, put his heart up at public auction, and, as it is cruel to part families, throw in his wife's and children's?'

'I understand,' with a pathetic shudder; 'but even did it come to that, such a step on the creditor's part, let us, for the honour of human nature, hope, were less the intention than the contingency.'

'But, Frank, a contingency not unprovided for in the taking beforehand of due securities.'

'Still, Charlie, was not the loan in the first place a friend's act?'

'And the auction in the last place an enemy's act. Don't you see ? The enmity lies couched in the friendship, just as the ruin in the relief.'

'I must be very stupid to-day, Charlie, but really, I can't understand this. Excuse me, my dear friend, but it strikes me that in going into the philosophy of the subject, you go somewhat out of your depth.'

'So said the incautious wader-out to the ocean ; but the ocean replied : "It is just the other way, my wet friend," and drowned him.'

'That, Charlie, is a fable about as unjust to the ocean, as some of Æsop's are to the animals. The ocean is a magnanimous element, and would scorn to assassinate a poor fellow, let alone taunting him in the act. But I don't understand what you say about enmity couched in friendship, and ruin in relief.'

'I will illustrate, Frank. The needy man is a train slipped off the rail. He who loans him money on interest is the one who, by way of accommodation, helps get the train back where it belongs ; but then, by way of making all square, and a little more, telegraphs to an agent, thirty miles ahead by a precipice, to throw just there, on his account, a beam across the track. Your needy man's principle-and-interest friend is, I say again, a friend with an enmity in reserve. No, no, my dear friend, no interest for me. I scorn interest.'

'Well, Charlie, none need you charge. Loan me without interest.'

'That would be alms again.'

'Alms, if the sum borrowed is returned ? '

'Yes ; an alms, not of the principle, but the interest.'

'Well, I am in sore need, so I will not decline the alms. Seeing that it is you, Charlie, gratefully will I accept the alms of the interest. No humiliation between friends.'

'Now, how in the refined view of friendship can you

suffer yourself to talk so, my dear Frank. It pains me.
For though I am not of the sour mind of Solomon, that,
in the hour of need, a stranger is better than a brother*;
yet, I entirely agree with my sublime master, who, in his
Essay on Friendship,* says so nobly, that if he want a
terrestrial convenience, not to his friend celestial (or
friend social and intellectual) would he go; no: for his
terrestrial convenience, to his friend terrestrial (or humbler
business friend) he goes. Very lucidly he adds the
reason : Because, for the superior nature, which on no
account can ever descend to do good, to be annoyed with
requests to do it, when the inferior one, which by no
instruction can ever rise above that capacity, stands
always inclined to it—this is unsuitable.'

'Then I will not consider you as my friend celestial,
but as the other.'

'It racks me to come to that ; but, to oblige you, I 'll
do it. We are business friends ; business is business.
You want to negotiate a loan. Very good. On what
paper ? Will you pay three per cent. a month ? Where
is your security ? '

'Surely, you will not exact those formalities from your
old schoolmate—him with whom you have so often
sauntered down the groves of Academe, discoursing of
the beauty of virtue, and the grace that is in kindliness—
and all for so paltry a sum. Security ? Our being
fellow-academics, and friends from childhood up, is
security.'

'Pardon me, my dear Frank, our being fellow-academics is the worst of securities ; while, our having been
friends from childhood up is just no security at all. You
forget we are now business friends.'

'And you, on your side, forget, Charlie, that as your
business friend I can give you no security ; my need
being so sore that I cannot get an indorser.'

' No indorser, then, no business loan.'

' Since then, Charlie, neither as the one nor the other sort of friend you have defined, can I prevail with you ; how if, combining the two, I sue as both ? '

' Are you a centaur ? '

' When all is said, then, what good have I of your friendship, regarded in what light you will ? '

' The good which is in the philosophy of Mark Winsome, as reduced to practice by a practical disciple.'

' And why don't you add, much good may the philosophy of Mark Winsome do me ? Ah,' turning invokingly, ' what is friendship, if it be not the helping hand and the feeling heart, the good Samaritan pouring out at need the purse as the vial ! '

' Now, my dear Frank, don't be childish. Through tears never did man see his way in the dark. I should hold you unworthy that sincere friendship I bear you, could I think that friendship in the ideal is too lofty for you to conceive. And let me tell you, my dear Frank, that you would seriously shake the foundations of our love, if ever again you should repeat the present scene. The philosophy, which is mine in the strongest way, teaches plain-dealing. Let me, then, now, as at the most suitable time, candidly disclose certain circumstances you seem in ignorance of. Though our friendship began in boyhood, think not that, on my side at least, it began injudiciously. Boys are little men, it is said. You, I juvenilely picked out for my friend, for your favourable points at the time ; not the least of which were your good manners, handsome dress, and your parents' rank and repute of wealth. In short, like any grown man, boy though I was, I went into the market and chose me my mutton, not for its leanness, but its fatness. In other words, there seemed in you, the schoolboy who always had silver in his pocket, a reasonable probability that

you would never stand in lean need of fat succour ; and
if my early impression has not been verified by the event,
it is only because of the caprice of fortune producing a
fallibility of human expectations, however discreet.'

' Oh, that I should listen to this cold-blooded disclosure ! '

' A little cold blood in your ardent veins, my dear
Frank, wouldn't do you any harm, let me tell you.
Cold-blooded ? You say that, because my disclosure
seems to involve a vile prudence on my side. But not
so. My reason for choosing you in part for the points
I have mentioned, was solely with a view of preserving
inviolate the delicacy of the connection. For—do but
think of it—what more distressing to delicate friendship,
formed early, than your friend's eventually, in manhood,
dropping in of a rainy night for his little loan of five
dollars or so ? Can delicate friendship stand that ?
And, on the other side, would delicate friendship, so long
as it retained its delicacy, do that ? Would you not
instinctively say of your dripping friend in the entry,
" I have been deceived, fraudulently deceived, in this
man ; he is no true friend that, in platonic love to demand
love-rites " ? '

' And rites, doubly rights, they are, cruel Charlie ! '

' Take it how you will, heed well how, by too im-
portunately claiming those rights, as you call them, you
shake those foundations I hinted of. For though, as it
turns out, I, in my early friendship, built me a fair house
on a poor site ; yet such pains and cost have I lavished
on that house, that, after all, it is dear to me. No, I
would not lose the sweet boon of your friendship, Frank.
But beware.'

' And of what ? Of being in need ? Oh, Charlie !
you talk not to a god, a being who in himself holds his
own estate, but to a man who, being a man, is the sport

of fate's wind and wave, and who mounts toward heaven
or sinks toward hell, as the billows roll him in trough or
on crest.'

'Tut ! Frank. Man is no such poor devil as that comes
to—no poor drifting sea-weed of the universe. Man
has a soul ; which, if he will, puts him beyond fortune's
finger and the future's spite. Don't whine like fortune's
whipped dog, Frank, or by the heart of a true friend, I
will cut ye.'

'Cut me you have already, cruel Charlie, and to the
quick. Call to mind the days we went nutting, the
times we walked in the woods, arms wreathed about each
other, showing trunks invined like the trees :—oh,
Charlie ! '

'Pish ! we were boys.'

'Then lucky the fate of the first-born of Egypt,* cold
in the grave ere maturity struck them with a sharper
frost.—Charlie ? '

'Fie ! You 're a girl.'

'Help, help, Charlie, I want help ! '

'Help ? to say nothing of the friend, there is something wrong about the man who wants help. There is
somewhere a defect, a want, in brief, a need, a crying
need, somewhere about that man.'

'So there is, Charlie.—Help, help ! '

'How foolish a cry, when to implore help, is itself the
proof of undesert of it.'

'Oh, this, all along, is not you, Charlie, but some
ventriloquist who usurps your larynx. It is Mark
Winsome that speaks, not Charlie.'

'If so, thank heaven, the voice of Mark Winsome is
not alien but congenial to my larynx. If the philosophy
of that illustrious teacher find little response among
mankind at large, it is less that they do not possess
teachable tempers, than because they are so unfortunate

as not to have natures predisposed to accord with him.'

'Welcome, that compliment to humanity,' exclaimed Frank with energy, ' the truer because unintended. And long in this respect may humanity remain what you affirm it. And long it will; since humanity, inwardly feeling how subject it is to straits, and hence how precious is help, will, for selfishness' sake, if no other, long post-pone ratifying a philosophy that banishes help from the world. But Charlie, Charlie! speak as you used to; tell me you will help me. Were the case reversed, not less freely would I loan you the money than you would ask me to loan it.'

'*I* ask? *I* ask a loan? Frank, by this hand, under no circumstances would I accept a loan, though without asking pressed on me. The experience of China Aster might warn me.'

'And what was that?'

'Not very unlike the experience of the man that built himself a palace of moon-beams, and when the moon set was surprised that his palace vanished with it. I will tell you about China Aster. I wish I could do so in my own words, but unhappily, the original story-teller here has so tyrannised over me, that it is quite impossible for me to repeat his incidents without sliding into his style. I forewarn you of this, that you may not think me so maudlin as, in some parts, the story would seem to make its narrator. It is too bad that any intellect, especially in so small a matter, should have such power to impose itself upon another, against its best exerted will, too. However, it is satisfaction to know that the main moral, to which all tends, I fully approve. But, to begin.'

CHAPTER XL

IN WHICH THE STORY OF CHINA ASTER IS AT SECOND-HAND TOLD BY ONE WHO, WHILE NOT DISAPPROVING THE MORAL, DISCLAIMS THE SPIRIT OF THE STYLE

' CHINA ASTER* was a young candle-maker of Marietta,* at the mouth of the Muskingum—one whose trade would seem a kind of subordinate branch of that parent craft and mystery of the hosts of heaven, to be the means, effectively or otherwise, of shedding some light through the darkness of a planet benighted. But he made little money by the business. Much ado had poor China Aster and his family to live ; he could, if he chose, light up from his stores a whole street, but not so easily could he light up with prosperity the hearts of his household.

' Now, China Aster, it so happened, had a friend, Orchis, a shoemaker ; one whose calling it is to defend the understandings of men from naked contact with the substance of things ; a very useful vocation, and which, spite of all the wiseacres may prophesy, will hardly go out of fashion so long as rocks are hard and flints will gall. All at once, by a capital prize in a lottery, this useful shoemaker was raised from a bench to a sofa. A small nabob was the shoemaker now, and the understandings of men, let them shift for themselves. Not that Orchis was, by prosperity, elated into heartlessness. Not at all. Because, in his fine apparel, strolling one morning into the candlery, and gaily switching about at the candle-boxes with his gold-headed cane, while poor China Aster, with his greasy paper cap and leather

apron, was selling one candle for one penny to a poor
orange-woman, who, with the patronising coolness of a
liberal customer, required it to be carefully rolled up and
tied in a half-sheet of paper—lively Orchis, the woman
being gone, discontinued his gay switchings and said :
" This is poor business for you, friend China Aster ; your
capital is too small. You must drop this vile tallow and
hold up pure spermaceti to the world. I tell you what
it is, you shall have one thousand dollars to extend with.
In fact, you must make money, China Aster. I don't
like to see your little boy paddling about without shoes,
as he does."

' " Heaven bless your goodness, friend Orchis," replied
the candle-maker, " but don't take it illy if I call to mind
the word of my uncle, the blacksmith, who, when a loan
was offered him, declined it, saying : ' To ply my own
hammer, light though it be, I think best, rather than
piece it out heavier by welding to it a bit off a neighbour's hammer, though that may have some weight to
spare ; otherwise, were the borrowed bit suddenly wanted
again, it might not split off at the welding, but too much
to one side or the other.' "

' " Nonsense, friend China Aster, don't be so honest ;
your boy is barefoot. Besides, a rich man lose by a
poor man ? Or a friend be the worse by a friend ?
China Aster, I am afraid that, in leaning over into your
vats here, this morning, you have spilled out your wisdom.
Hush ! I won't hear any more. Where's your desk ?
Oh, here." With that, Orchis dashed off a cheque on his
bank, and off-handedly presenting it, said : " There,
friend China Aster, is your one thousand dollars ; when
you make it ten thousand, as you soon enough will (for
experience, the only true knowledge, teaches me that,
for everyone, good luck is in store), then, China Aster,
why, then you can return me the money or not, just as

you please. But, in any event, give yourself no concern, for I shall never demand payment."

'Now, as kind heaven will so have it that to a hungry man bread is a great temptation, and, therefore, he is not too harshly to be blamed, if, when freely offered, he take it, even though it be uncertain whether he shall ever be able to reciprocate ; so, to a poor man, proffered money is equally enticing, and the worst that can be said of him, if he accept it, is just what can be said in the other case of the hungry man. In short, the poor candle-maker's scrupulous morality succumbed to his unscrupulous necessity, as is now and then apt to be the case. He took the cheque, and was about carefully putting it away for the present, when Orchis, switching about again with his gold-headed cane, said : "By the way, China Aster, it don't mean anything, but suppose you make a little memorandum of this ; won't do any harm, you know." So China Aster gave Orchis his note for one thousand dollars on demand. Orchis took it, and looked at it a moment, "Pooh, I told you, friend China Aster, I wasn't going ever to make any *demand*." Then tearing up the note, and switching away again at the candle-boxes, said, carelessly ; "Put it at four years." So China Aster gave Orchis his note for one thousand dollars at four years. "You see I 'll never trouble you about this," said Orchis, slipping it in his pocket-book, "give yourself no further thought, friend China Aster, than how best to invest your money. And don't forget my hint about spermaceti. Go into that, and I 'll buy all my light of you," with which encouraging words, he, with wonted, rattling kindness, took leave.

'China Aster remained standing just where Orchis had left him ; when, suddenly, two elderly friends, having nothing better to do, dropped in for a chat. The chat over, China Aster, in greasy cap and apron, ran after

Orchis, and said : " Friend Orchis, heaven will reward
you for your good intentions, but here is your cheque,
and now give me my note."

' " Your honesty is a bore, China Aster," said Orchis,
not without displeasure. " I won't take the cheque from
you."

' " Then you must take it from the pavement, Orchis,"
said China Aster ; and, picking up a stone, he placed the
cheque under it on the walk.

' " China Aster," said Orchis, inquisitively eyeing him,
" after my leaving the candlery just now, what asses
dropped in there to advise with you, that now you hurry
after me, and act so like a fool ?   Shouldn't wonder if
it was those two old asses that the boys nickname Old
Plain Talk and Old Prudence."

' " Yes, it was those two, Orchis, but don't call them
names."

' " A brace of spavined old croakers.   Old Plain Talk
had a shrew for a wife, and that 's made him shrewish ;
and Old Prudence, when a boy, broke down in an apple-
stall, and that discouraged him for life.   No better sport
for a knowing spark like me than to hear Old Plain Talk
wheeze out his sour old saws, while Old Prudence stands
by, leaning on his staff, wagging his frosty old pow, and
chiming in at every clause."

' " How can you speak so, friend Orchis, of those who
were my father's friends ? "

' " Save me from my friends, if those old croakers
were Old Honesty's friends.   I call your father so, for
everyone used to.   Why did they let him go in his old
age on the town ?   Why, China Aster, I 've often heard
from my mother, the chronicler, that those two old
fellows, with Old Conscience—as the boys called the
crabbed old quaker, that 's dead now—they three used
to go to the poorhouse when your father was there, and

get round his bed, and talk to him for all the world as
Eliphaz, Bildad, and Zophar did to poor old pauper Job.*
Yes, Job's comforters were Old Plain Talk, and Old
Prudence, and Old Conscience, to your poor old father.
Friends ? I should like to know who you call foes ?
With their everlasting croaking and reproaching they
tormented poor Old Honesty, your father, to death."

‘At these words, recalling the sad end of his worthy
parent, China Aster could not restrain some tears. Upon
which Orchis said : "Why, China Aster, you are the
dolefullest creature. Why don't you, China Aster, take
a bright view of life ? You will never get on in your
business or anything else, if you don't take the bright
view of life. It's the ruination of a man to take the
dismal one." Then, gaily poking at him with his gold-
headed cane, "Why don't you, then ? Why don't you
be bright and hopeful, like me ? Why don't you have
confidence, China Aster ?"

‘ "I 'm sure I don't know, friend Orchis," soberly
replied China Aster, "but maybe my not having drawn
a lottery prize, like you, may make some difference."

‘ "Nonsense ! before I knew anything about the prize
I was gay as a lark, just as gay as I am now. In fact,
it has always been a principle with me to hold to the
bright view."

‘Upon this, China Aster looked a little hard at Orchis,
because the truth was, that until the lucky prize came
to him, Orchis had gone under the nickname of Doleful
Dumps, he having been beforetimes of a hypochondriac
turn, so much so as to save up and put by a few dollars
of his scanty earnings against that rainy day he used
to groan so much about.

‘ "I tell you what it is, now, friend China Aster," said
Orchis, pointing down to the cheque under the stone, and
then slapping his pocket, "the cheque shall lie there if

you say so, but your note shan't keep it company. In fact, China Aster, I am too sincerely your friend to take advantage of a passing fit of the blues in you. You *shall* reap the benefit of my friendship." With which, buttoning up his coat in a jiffy, away he ran, leaving the cheque behind.

' At first, China Aster was going to tear it up, but thinking that this ought not to be done except in the presence of the drawer of the cheque, he mused a while, and picking it up, trudged back to the candlery, fully resolved to call upon Orchis soon as his day's work was over, and destroy the cheque before his eyes. But it so happened that when China Aster called, Orchis was out, and, having waited for him a weary time in vain, China Aster went home, still with the cheque, but still resolved not to keep it another day. Bright and early next morning he would a second time go after Orchis, and would, no doubt, make a sure thing of it, by finding him in his bed ; for since the lottery prize came to him, Orchis, besides becoming more cheery, had also grown a little lazy. But as destiny would have it, that same night China Aster had a dream, in which a being in the guise of a smiling angel, and holding a kind of cornucopia in her hand, hovered over him, pouring down showers of small gold dollars, thick as kernels of corn. " I am Bright Future, friend China Aster," said the angel, " and if you do what friend Orchis would have you do, just see what will come of it." With which Bright Future, with another swing of her cornucopia, poured such another shower of small gold dollars upon him, that it seemed to bank him up all round, and he waded about in it like a maltster in malt.

' Now, dreams are wonderful things, as everybody knows—so wonderful, indeed, that some people stop not short of ascribing them directly to heaven ; and China

Aster, who was of a proper turn of mind in everything, thought that in consideration of the dream, it would be but well to wait a little, ere seeking Orchis again. During the day, China Aster's mind dwelling continually upon the dream, he was so full of it, that when Old Plain Talk dropped in to see him, just before dinner-time, as he often did, out of the interest he took in Old Honesty's son, China Aster told all about his vision, adding that he could not think that so radiant an angel could deceive ; and, indeed, talked at such a rate that one would have thought he believed the angel some beautiful human philanthropist. Something in this sort Old Plain Talk understood him, and, accordingly, in his plain way, said : " China Aster, you tell me that an angel appeared to you in a dream. Now, what does that amount to but this, that you dreamed an angel appeared to you ? Go right away, China Aster, and return the cheque, as I advised you before. If friend Prudence were here, he would say just the same thing." With which words Old Plain Talk went off to find friend Prudence, but not succeeding, was returning to the candlery himself, when, at distance mistaking him for a dun who had long annoyed him, China Aster in a panic barred all his doors, and ran to the back part of the candlery, where no knock could be heard.

' By this sad mistake, being left with no friend to argue the other side of the question, China Aster was so worked upon at last, by musing over his dream, that nothing would do but he must get the cheque cashed, and lay out the money the very same day in buying a good lot of spermaceti to make into candles, by which opera· tion he counted upon turning a better penny than he ever had before in his life ; in fact, this he believed would prove the foundation of that famous fortune which the angel had promised him.

'Now, in using the money, China Aster was resolved
punctually to pay the interest every six months till the
principal should be returned, howbeit not a word about
such a thing had been breathed by Orchis; though,
indeed, according to custom, as well as law, in such
matters, interest would legitimately accrue on the loan,
nothing to the contrary having been put in the bond.
Whether Orchis at the time had this in mind or not,
there is no sure telling; but, to all appearance, he never so
much as cared to think about the matter, one way or other.

'Though the spermaceti venture rather disappointed
China Aster's sanguine expectations, yet he made out
to pay the first six months' interest, and though his next
venture turned out still less prosperously, yet by pinch-
ing his family in the matter of fresh meat, and, what
pained him still more, his boys' schooling, he contrived
to pay the second six months' interest, sincerely grieved
that integrity, as well as its opposite, though not in an
equal degree, costs something, sometimes.

'Meanwhile, Orchis had gone on a trip to Europe by
advice of a physician; it so happening that, since the
lottery prize came to him, it had been discovered to
Orchis that his health was not very firm, though he had
never complained of anything before but a slight ailing
of the spleen, scarce worth talking about at the time.
So Orchis, being abroad, could not help China Aster's
paying his interest as he did, however much he might
have been opposed to it; for China Aster paid it to Orchis'
agent, who was of too business-like a turn to decline
interest regularly paid in on a loan.

'But overmuch to trouble the agent on that score
was not again to be the fate of China Aster; for, not
being of that sceptical spirit which refuses to trust
customers, his third venture resulted, through bad debts,
in almost a total loss—a bad blow for the candle-maker.

Neither did Old Plain Talk and Old Prudence neglect
the opportunity to read him an uncheerful enough lesson
upon the consequences of his disregarding their advice
in the matter of having nothing to do with borrowed
money. " It 's all just as I predicted," said Old Plain
Talk, blowing his old nose with his old bandana. " Yea,
indeed it is," chimed in Old Prudence, rapping his staff
on the floor, and then leaning upon it, looking with solemn
forebodings upon China Aster. Low-spirited enough
felt the poor candle-maker ; till all at once who should
come with a bright face to him but his bright friend,
the angel, in another dream. Again the cornucopia
poured out its treasure, and promised still more. Revived by the vision, he resolved not to be down-hearted,
but up and at it once more—contrary to the advice of
Old Plain Talk, backed as usual by his crony, which was
to the effect, that, under present circumstances, the best
thing China Aster could do, would be to wind up his
business, settle, if he could, all his liabilities, and then go
to work as a journeyman, by which he could earn good
wages, and give up, from that time henceforth, all thoughts
of rising above being a paid subordinate to men more
able than himself, for China Aster's career thus far
plainly proved him the legitimate son of Old Honesty,
who, as everyone knew, had never shown much business
talent, so little, in fact, that many said of him that he
had no business to be in business. And just this plain
saying Plain Talk now plainly applied to China Aster,
and Old Prudence never disagreed with him. But the
angel in the dream did, and, maugre Plain Talk, put quite
other notions into the candle-maker.

' He considered what he should do toward re-estab-
lishing himself. Doubtless, had Orchis been in the
country, he would have aided him in this strait. As it
was, he applied to others ; and as in the world, much as

some may hint to the contrary, an honest man in misfortune still can find friends to stay by him and help him, even so it proved with China Aster, who at last succeeded in borrowing from a rich old farmer the sum of six hundred dollars, at the usual interest of money-lenders, upon the security of a secret bond signed by China Aster's wife and himself, to the effect that all such right and title to any property that should be left her by a well-to-do childless uncle, an invalid tanner, such property should, in the event of China Aster's failing to return the borrowed sum on the given day, be the lawful possession of the money-lender. True, it was just as much as China Aster could possibly do to induce his wife, a careful woman, to sign this bond ; because she had always regarded her promised share in her uncle's estate as an anchor well to windward of the hard times in which China Aster had always been more or less involved, and from which, in her bosom, she never had seen much chance of his freeing himself. Some notion may be had of China Aster's standing in the heart and head of his wife, by a short sentence commonly used in reply to such persons as happened to sound her on the point. " China Aster," she would say, " is a good husband, but a bad business man ! " Indeed, she was a connection on the maternal side of Old Plain Talk's. But had not China Aster taken good care not to let Old Plain Talk and Old Prudence hear of his dealings with the old farmer, ten to one they would, in some way, have interfered with his success in that quarter.

' It has been hinted that the honesty of China Aster was what mainly induced the money-lender to befriend him in his misfortune, and this must be apparent ; for, had China Aster been a different man, the money-lender might have dreaded lest, in the event of his failing to meet his note, he might some way prove slippery—more especially as, in the hour of distress, worked upon by remorse for so jeopardising his wife's money, his heart might prove a traitor to his bond, not to hint that it was more than doubtful how such a secret security and claim, as in the last resort would be the old farmer's, would stand in a court of law. But though one inference from all this may be, that had China Aster been something else than what he was, he would not have been trusted, and, therefore, he would have been effectually shut out from running his own and wife's head into the usurer's noose; yet those who, when everything at last came out, maintained that, in this view and to this extent, the honesty of the candle-maker was no advantage to him; in so saying, such persons said what every good heart must deplore, and no prudent tongue will admit.

'It may be mentioned, that the old farmer made China Aster take part of his loan in three old dried-up cows and one lame horse, not improved by the glanders. These were thrown in at a pretty high figure, the old money-lender having a singular prejudice in regard to the high value of any sort of stock raised on his farm. With a great deal of difficulty, and at more loss, China Aster disposed of his cattle at public auction, no private purchaser being found who could be prevailed upon to invest. And now, raking and scraping in every way, and working early and late, China Aster at last started afresh, nor without again largely and confidently extending himself. However, he did not try his hand at the spermaceti again, but, admonished by experience, returned to tallow. But, having bought a good lot of it, by the time he got it into candles, tallow fell so low, and candles with it, that his candles per pound barely sold for what he had paid for the tallow. Meantime, a year's unpaid interest had accrued on Orchis' loan, but China Aster gave himself not so much concern about that as about the interest now due to the old farmer. But he was glad that the principal there had yet some time to run. However, the skinny old fellow gave him some trouble by coming after him every day or two on a scraggy old white horse, furnished with a musty old saddle, and goaded into his shambling old paces with a withered old raw hide. All the neighbours said that surely Death himself on the pale horse* was after poor China Aster now. And something so it proved ; for, ere long, China Aster found himself involved in troubles mortal enough.

At this juncture Orchis was heard of. Orchis, it seemed, had returned from his travels, and clandestinely married, and, in a kind of queer way, was living in Pennsylvania among his wife's relations, who, among other things, had induced him to join a church, or rather semi-religious school, of Come-Outers ;* and what was still more, Orchis, without coming to the spot himself, had sent word to his agent to dispose of some of his property in Marietta, and remit him the proceeds. Within a year after, China Aster received a letter from Orchis, commending him for his punctuality in paying the first year's interest, and regretting the necessity that he (Orchis) was now under of using all his dividends ; so he relied upon China Aster's paying the next six months' interest, and of course with the back interest. Not more surprised than alarmed, China Aster thought of taking steamboat to go and see Orchis, but he was saved that expense by the unexpected arrival in Marietta of Orchis in person, suddenly called there by that strange kind of capriciousness lately characterising him.

No sooner did China Aster hear of his old friend's arrival than he hurried to call upon him. He found him curiously rusty in dress, sallow in cheek, and decidedly less gay and cordial in manner, which the more surprised

China Aster, because, in former days, he had more than
once heard Orchis, in his light rattling way, declare that
all he (Orchis) wanted to make him a perfectly happy,
hilarious, and benignant man, was a voyage to Europe
and a wife, with a free development of his inmost nature.

'Upon China Aster's stating his case, his rusted
friend was silent for a time ; then, in an odd way, said
that he would not crowd China Aster, but still his (Orchis')
necessities were urgent. Could not China Aster mortgage the candlery ? He was honest, and must have
moneyed friends ; and could he not press his sales of
candles ? Could not the market be forced a little in
that particular ? The profits on candles must be very
great. Seeing, now, that Orchis had the notion that the
candle-making business was a very profitable one, and
knowing sorely enough what an error was here, China
Aster tried to undeceive him. But he could not drive
the truth into Orchis—Orchis being very obtuse here,
and, at the same time, strange to say, very melancholy.
Finally, Orchis glanced off from so unpleasing a subject
into the most unexpected reflections, taken from a
religious point of view, upon the unstableness and deceit-
fulness of the human heart. But having, as he thought,
experienced something of that sort of thing, China Aster
did not take exception to his friend's observations, but
still refrained from so doing, almost as much for the
sake of sympathetic sociality as anything else. Presently,
Orchis, without much ceremony, rose, and saying he must
write a letter to his wife, bade his friend good-bye, but
without warmly shaking him by the hand as of old.

'In much concern at the change, China Aster made
earnest inquiries in suitable quarters, as to what things,
as yet unheard of, had befallen Orchis, to bring about
such a revolution ; and learned at last that, besides
travelling, and getting married, and joining the sect of

Come-Outers, Orchis had somehow got a bad dyspepsia, and lost considerable property through a breach of trust on the part of a factor in New York. Telling these things to Old Plain Talk, that man of some knowledge of the world shook his old head, and told China Aster that, though he hoped it might prove otherwise, yet it seemed to him that all he had communicated about Orchis worked together for bad omens as to his future forbearance—especially, he added with a grim sort of smile, in view of his joining the sect of Come-Outers ; for, if some men knew what was their inmost natures, instead of coming out with it, they would try their best to keep it in, which, indeed, was the way with the prudent sort. In all which sour notions Old Prudence, as usual, chimed in.

' When interest-day came again, China Aster, by the utmost exertions, could only pay Orchis' agent a small part of what was due, and a part of that was made up by his children's gift money (bright tenpenny pieces and new quarters, kept in their little money-boxes), and pawning his best clothes, with those of his wife and children, so that all were subjected to the hardship of staying away from church. And the old usurer, too, now beginning to be obstreperous, China Aster paid him his interest and some other pressing debts with money got by, at last, mortgaging the candlery.

' When next interest-day came round for Orchis, not a penny could be raised. With much grief of heart, China Aster so informed Orchis' agent. Meantime, the note to the old usurer fell due, and nothing from China Aster was ready to meet it ; yet, as heaven sends its rain on the just and unjust alike, by a coincidence not unfavourable to the old farmer, the well-to-do uncle, the tanner, having died, the usurer entered upon possession of such part of his property left by will to the wife of China Aster. When still the next interest-day for

Orchis came round, it found China Aster worse off than
ever; for, besides his other troubles, he was now weak
with sickness. Feebly dragging himself to Orchis'
agent, he met him in the street, told him just how it was;
upon which the agent, with a grave enough face, said
that he had instructions from his employer not to crowd
him about the interest at present, but to say to him that
about the time the note would mature, Orchis would have
heavy liabilities to meet, and therefore the note must
at that time be certainly paid, and, of course, the back
interest with it; and not only so, but, as Orchis had had
to allow the interest for good part of the time, he hoped
that, for the back interest, China Aster would, in recipro-
cation, have no objections to allowing interest on the
interest annually. To be sure, this was not the law;
but, between friends who accommodate each other, it
was the custom.

'Just then, Old Plain Talk with Old Prudence turned
the corner, coming plump upon China Aster as the agent
left him; and whether it was a sunstroke, or whether
they accidentally ran against him, or whether it was
his being so weak, or whether it was everything together,
or how it was exactly, there is no telling, but poor China
Aster fell to the earth, and, striking his head sharply,
was picked up senseless. It was a day in July; such a
light and heat as only the midsummer banks of the inland
Ohio know. China Aster was taken home on a door;
lingered a few days with a wandering mind, and kept
wandering on, till at last, at dead of night, when nobody
was aware, his spirit wandered away into the other world.

'Old Plain Talk and Old Prudence, neither of whom
ever omitted attending any funeral, which, indeed, was
their chief exercise—these two were among the sincerest
mourners who followed the remains of the son of their
ancient friend to the grave,

' It is needless to tell of the executions that followed ;
how that the candlery was sold by the mortgagee ; how
Orchis never got a penny for his loan ; and how, in the
case of the poor widow, chastisement was tempered with
mercy ; for, though she was left penniless, she was not
left childless. Yet, unmindful of the alleviation, a spirit
of complaint, at what she impatiently called the bitterness of her lot and the hardness of the world, so preyed
upon her, as ere long to hurry her from the obscurity of
indigence to the deeper shades of the tomb.

' But though the straits in which China Aster had
left his family had, besides apparently dimming the
world's regard, likewise seemed to dim its sense of the
probity of its deceased head, and though this, as some
thought, did not speak well for the world, yet it happened
in this case, as in others, that, though the world may
for a time seem insensible to that merit which lies under
a cloud, yet, sooner or later, it always renders honour
where honour is due ; for, upon the death of the widow,
the freemen of Marietta, as a tribute of respect for China
Aster, and an expression of their conviction of his high
moral worth, passed a resolution, that, until they at-
tained maturity, his children should be considered the
town's guests. No mere verbal compliment, like those
of some public bodies ; for, on the same day, the orphans
were officially installed in that hospitable edifice where
their worthy grandfather, the town's guest before them,
had breathed his last breath.

' But sometimes honour may be paid to the memory
of an honest man, and still his mound remain without
a monument. Not so, however, with the candle-maker.
At an early day, Plain Talk had procured a plain stone,
and was digesting in his mind what pithy word or two
to place upon it, when there was discovered, in China
Aster's otherwise empty wallet, an epitaph, written,

probably, in one of those disconsolate hours, attended
with more or less mental aberration, perhaps, so frequent
with him for some months prior to his end. A memorandum on the back expressed the wish that it might
be placed over his grave. Though with the sentiment of
the epitaph Plain Talk did not disagree, he himself being
at times of a hypochondriac turn—at least, so many
said—yet the language struck him as too much drawn
out ; so, after consultation with Old Prudence, he decided
upon making use of the epitaph, yet not without verbal
retrenchments. And though, when these were made,
the thing still appeared wordy to him, nevertheless,
thinking that, since a dead man was to be spoken about,
it was but just to let him speak for himself, especially
when he spoke sincerely, and when, by so doing, the more
salutary lesson would be given, he had the retrenched
inscription chiselled as follows upon the stone :—

"HERE LIE
THE REMAINS OF
CHINA ASTER THE CANDLE-MAKER,
WHOSE CAREER
WAS AN EXAMPLE OF THE TRUTH OF SCRIPTURE, AS FOUND
IN THE
SOBER PHILOSOPHY
OF
SOLOMON THE WISE;
FOR HE WAS RUINED BY ALLOWING HIMSELF TO BE PERSUADED,
AGAINST HIS BETTER SENSE,
INTO THE FREE INDULGENCE OF CONFIDENCE,
AND
AN ARDENTLY BRIGHT VIEW OF LIFE
TO THE EXCLUSION
OF
THAT COUNSEL WHICH COMES BY HEEDING
THE
OPPOSITE VIEW."

'This inscription raised some talk in the town, and was rather severely criticised by the capitalist—one of a very cheerful turn—who had secured his loan to China Aster by the mortgage ; and though it also proved obnoxious to the man who, in town-meeting, had first moved for the compliment to China Aster's memory, and, indeed, was deemed by him a sort of slur upon the candle-maker, to that degree that he refused to believe that the candle-maker himself had composed it, charging Old Plain Talk with the authorship, alleging that the internal evidence showed that none but that veteran old croaker could have penned such a jeremiad—yet, for all this, the stone stood. In everything, of course, Old Plain Talk was seconded by Old Prudence ; who, one day going to the graveyard, in great-coat and over-shoes— for, though it was a sunshiny morning, he thought that, owing to heavy dews, dampness might lurk in the ground —long stood before the stone, sharply leaning over on his staff, spectacles on nose, spelling out the epitaph word by word ; and, afterwards meeting Old Plain Talk in the street, gave a great rap with his stick, and said : "Friend Plain Talk, that epitaph will do very well. Nevertheless, one short sentence is wanting." Upon which, Plain Talk said it was too late, the chiselled words being so arranged, after the usual manner of such inscriptions, that nothing could be interlined. "Then," said Old Prudence, " I will put it in the shape of a post-script." Accordingly, with the approbation of Old Plain Talk, he had the following words chiselled at the left-hand corner of the stone, and pretty low down :—

"The root of all was a friendly loan."'

CHAPTER XLI

ENDING WITH A RUPTURE OF THE HYPOTHESIS

' WITH what heart,' cried Frank, still in character, ' have you told me this story ? A story I can no way approve ; for its moral, if accepted, would drain me of all reliance upon my last stay, and, therefore, of my last courage in life. For, what was that bright view of China Aster but a cheerful trust that, if he but kept up a brave heart, worked hard, and ever hoped for the best, all at last would go well ? If your purpose, Charlie, in telling me this story, was to pain me, and keenly, you have succeeded ; but, if it was to destroy my last confidence, I praise God you have not.'

' Confidence ? ' cried Charlie, who, on his side, seemed with his whole heart to enter into the spirit of the thing, ' what has confidence to do with the matter ? That moral of the story, which I am for commending to you, is this : the folly, on both sides, of a friend's helping a friend. For was not that loan of Orchis to China Aster the first step toward their estrangement ? And did it not bring about what in effect was the enmity of Orchis ? I tell you, Frank, true friendship, like other precious things, is not rashly to be meddled with. And what more meddlesome between friends than a loan ? A regular marplot. For how can you help that the helper must turn out a creditor ? And creditor and friend, can they ever be one ? no, not in the most lenient case ; since, out of lenity to forgo one's claim, is less to be a friendly creditor than to cease to be a creditor at all. But it will not do to rely upon this lenity, no, not in the best man ; for the best man, as the worst, is subject to all mortal contingencies. He may travel, he may marry, he may join the Come-Outers, or some equally untoward school or sect, not to speak of other things that more or less tend to new-cast the character. And were there nothing else, who shall answer for his digestion, upon which so much depends ? '

' But Charlie, dear Charlie——'

' Nay, wait.—You have hearkened to my story in vain, if you do not see that, however indulgent and right-minded I may seem to you now, that is no guarantee for the future. And into the power of that uncertain personality which, through the mutability of my humanity, I may hereafter become, should not common sense dissuade you, my dear Frank, from putting yourself ? Consider. Would you, in your present need, be willing to accept a loan from a friend, securing him by a mortgage on your homestead, and do so, knowing that you had no reason to feel satisfied that the mortgage might not eventually be transferred into the hands of a foe ? Yet the difference between this man and that man is not so great as the difference between what the same man be to-day, and what he may be in days to come. For there is no bent of heart or turn of thought which any man holds by virtue of an unalterable nature or will. Even those feelings and opinions deemed most identical with eternal right and truth, it is not impossible but that, as personal persuasions, they may in reality be but the result of some chance tip of Fate's elbow in throwing her dice. For, not to go into the first seeds of things, and passing by the accident of parentage predisposing to this or that habit of mind, descend below these, and tell me, if you change this man's experiences or that man's books, will wisdom go surety for his unchanged convictions ? As particular food begets particular dreams, so particular experiences or books particular feelings or beliefs. I will hear nothing of that fine babble about development and its laws ; there is no development in opinion and feeling but the developments of time and tide. You may deem all this talk idle, Frank ; but conscience bids me show you how fundamental the reasons for treating you as I do.'

'But Charlie, dear Charlie, what new notions are these ? I thought that man was no poor drifting weed of the universe, as you phrased it ; that, if so minded, he could have a will, a way, a thought, and a heart of his own ? But now you have turned everything upside down again, with an inconsistency that amazes and shocks me.'

'Inconsistency ? Bah ! '

'There speaks the ventriloquist again,' sighed Frank, in bitterness.

Illy pleased, it may be, by this repetition of an allusion little flattering to his originality, however much so to his docility, the disciple sought to carry it off by exclaiming : 'Yes, I turn over day and night, with indefatigable pains, the sublime pages of my master, and unfortunately for you, my dear friend, I find nothing *there* that leads me to think otherwise than I do. But enough : in this matter the experience of China Aster teaches a moral more to the point than anything Mark Winsome can offer, or I either.'

'I cannot think so, Charlie ; for neither am I China Aster, nor do I stand in his position. The loan to China Aster was to extend his business with ; the loan I seek is to relieve my necessities.'

'Your dress, my dear Frank, is respectable ; your cheek is not gaunt. Why talk of necessities when nakedness and starvation beget the only real necessities ? '

' But I need relief, Charlie ; and so sorely, that I now
conjure you to forget that I was ever your friend, while
I apply to you only as a fellow-being, whom, surely, you
will not turn away.'

' That I will not. Take off your hat, bow over to the
ground, and supplicate an alms of me in the way of
London streets, and you shall not be a sturdy beggar in
vain. But no man drops pennies into the hat of a friend,
let me tell you. If you turn beggar, then, for the honour
of noble friendship, I turn stranger.'

' Enough,' cried the other, rising, and with a toss of
his shoulders seeming disdainfully to throw off the character he had assumed. ' Enough. I have had my fill
of the philosophy of Mark Winsome as put into action.
And moonshiny as it in theory may be, yet a very practical philosophy it turns out in effect, as he himself engaged I should find. But, miserable for my race should
I be, if I thought he spoke truth when he claimed, for
proof of the soundness of his system, that the study of
it tended to much the same formation of character with
the experiences of the world.—Apt disciple ! Why
wrinkle the brow, and waste the oil both of life and the
lamp, only to turn out a head kept cool by the under
ice of the heart ? What your illustrious magian has
taught you, any poor, old, broken-down, heart-shrunken
dandy might have lisped. Pray, leave me, and with
you take the last dregs of your inhuman philosophy.
And here, take this shilling, and at the first wood-landing
buy yourself a few chips to warm the frozen natures of
you and your philosopher by.'

With these words and a grand scorn the cosmopolitan
turned on his heel, leaving his companion at a loss to
determine where exactly the fictitious character had
been dropped, and the real one, if any, resumed. If
any, because, with pointed meaning, there occurred to

him, as he gazed after the cosmopolitan, these familiar
lines :—

> ' All the world 's a stage,
> And all the men and women merely players,
> Who have their exits and their entrances,
> And one man in his time plays many parts.'*

CHAPTER XLII

'BLESS you, barber!'

Now, owing to the lateness of the hour, the barber
had been all alone until within the ten minutes last
past ; when, finding himself rather dullish company to
himself, he thought he would have a good time with
Souter John and Tam O'Shanter,* otherwise called
Somnus and Morpheus, two very good fellows, though
one was not very bright, and the other an arrant rattle-
brain, who, though much listened to by some, no wise
man would believe under oath.

In short, with back presented to the glare of his lamps,
and so to the door, the honest barber was taking what
are called cat-naps, and dreaming in his chair ; so that,
upon suddenly hearing the benediction above, pronounced
in tones not unangelic, starting up, half awake, he stared
before him, but saw nothing, for the stranger stood behind. What with cat-naps, dreams, and bewilderments,
therefore, the voice seemed a sort of spiritual manifesta-
tion to him ; so that, for the moment, he stood all agape,
eyes fixed, and one arm in the air.

'Why, barber, are you reaching up to catch birds
there with salt ?'

'Ah!' turning round disenchanted, 'it is only a man,
then.'

'*Only* a man ? As if to be but man were nothing.
But don't be too sure what I am. You call me *man*,

just as the townsfolk called the angels who, in man's form, came to Lot's house ;* just as the Jew rustics called the devils who, in man's form, haunted the tombs.* You can conclude nothing absolute from the human form, barber.'

'But I can conclude something from that sort of talk, with that sort of dress,' shrewdly thought the barber, eyeing him with regained self-possession, and not without some latent touch of apprehension at being alone with him. What was passing in his mind seemed divined by the other, who now, more rationally and gravely, and as if he expected it should be attended to, said : ' Whatever else you may conclude upon, it is my desire that you conclude to give me a good shave,' at the same time loosening his neck-cloth. 'Are you competent to a good shave, barber ? '

'No broker more so, sir,' answered the barber, whom the business-like proposition instinctively made confine to business ends his views of the visitor.

'Broker ? What has a broker to do with lather ? A broker I have always understood to be a worthy dealer in certain papers and metals.'

'He, he ! ' taking him now for some dry sort of joker, whose jokes, he being a customer, it might be as well to appreciate—' he, he ! You understand well enough, sir. Take this seat, sir,' laying his hand on a great stuffed chair, high-backed and high-armed, crimson-covered, and raised on a sort of dais, and which seemed but to lack a canopy and quarterings, to make it in aspect quite a throne ; ' take this seat, sir.'

'Thank you,' sitting down ; ' and now, pray, explain that about the broker. But look, look—what 's this ? ' suddenly rising, and pointing, with his long pipe, toward a gilt notification swinging among coloured fly-papers from the ceiling, like a tavern sign, ' *No Trust* ? No trust means distrust; distrust means no confidence. Barber,' turning upon him excitedly, ' what fell suspiciousness prompts this scandalous confession ? My life ! ' stamping his foot, ' if but to tell a dog that you have no confidence in him be matter for affront to the dog, what an insult to take that way the whole haughty race of man by the beard ! By my heart, sir ! but at least you are valiant ; backing the spleen of Thersites* with the pluck of Agamemnon.'

' Your sort of talk, sir, is not exactly in my line,' said the barber, rather ruefully, being now again hopeless of his customer, and not without return of uneasiness ; ' not in my line, sir,' he emphatically repeated.

' But the taking of mankind by the nose is ; a habit, barber, which I sadly fear has insensibly bred in you a disrespect for man. For how, indeed, may respectful conceptions of him coexist with the perpetual habit of taking him by the nose ? But, tell me, though I, too, clearly see the import of your notification, I do not, as yet, perceive the object. What is it ? '

' Now you speak a little in my line, sir,' said the barber, not unrelieved at this return to plain talk ; ' that notification I find very useful, sparing me much work which would not pay. Yes, I lost a good deal, off and on, before putting that up,' gratefully glancing toward it.

' But what is its object ? Surely, you don't mean to say, in so many words, that you have no confidence ? For instance, now,' flinging aside his neck-cloth, throwing back his blouse, and reseating himself on the tonsorial throne, at sight of which proceeding the barber mechanically filled a cup with hot water from a copper vessel over a spirit-lamp, ' for instance, now, suppose I say to you, " Barber, my dear barber, unhappily I have no small change by me to-night, but shave me, and depend upon your money to-morrow "—suppose I should say

that now, you would put trust in me, wouldn't you ?
You would have confidence ? '

' Seeing that it is you, sir,' with complaisance replied
the barber, now mixing the lather, ' seeing that it is *you*,
sir, I won't answer that question. No need to.'

' Of course, of course—in that view. But, as a supposition—you would have confidence in me, wouldn't
you ? '

' Why—yes, yes.'

' Then why that sign ? '

' Ah, sir, all people ain't like you,' was the smooth
reply, at the same time, as if smoothly to close the debate, beginning smoothly to apply the lather, which
operation, however, was, by a motion, protested against
by the subject, but only out of a desire to rejoin, which
was done in these words :—

' All people ain't like me. Then I must be either
better or worse than most people. Worse, you could
not mean ; no, barber, you could not mean that ; hardly
that. It remains, then, that you think me better than
most people. But that I ain't vain enough to believe ;
though from vanity, I confess, I could never yet, by
my best wrestlings, entirely free myself ; nor, indeed, to
be frank, am I at bottom over anxious to—this same
vanity, barber, being so harmless, so useful, so comfortable,
so pleasingly preposterous a passion.'

' Very true, sir ; and upon my honour, sir, you talk
very well. But the lather is getting a little cold, sir.'

' Better cold lather, barber, than a cold heart. Why
that cold sign ? Ah, I don't wonder you try to shirk
the confession. You feel in your soul how ungenerous
a hint is there. And yet, barber, now that I look into
your eyes—which somehow speak to me of the mother
that must have so often looked into them before me—
I dare say, though you may not think it, that the spirit

of that notification is not one with your nature. For
look now, setting business views aside, regarding the
thing in an abstract light; in short, supposing a case,
barber; supposing, I say, you see a stranger, his face
accidentally averted, but his visible part very respectable-looking; what now, barber—I put it to your conscience, to your charity—what would be your impression
of that man, in a moral point of view? Being in a signal
sense a stranger, would you, for that, signally set him
down for a knave?'

'Certainly not, sir; by no means,' cried the barber,
humanely resentful.

'You would upon the face of him——'

'Hold, sir,' said the barber, 'nothing about the face;
you remember, sir, that is out of sight.'

'I forgot that. Well then, you would, upon the *back*
of him, conclude him to be, not improbably, some worthy
sort of person; in short, an honest man; wouldn't
you?'

'Not unlikely I should, sir.'

'Well now—don't be so impatient with your brush,
barber—suppose that honest man meet you by night in
some dark corner of the boat where his face would still
remain unseen, asking you to trust him for a shave—
how then?'

'Wouldn't trust him, sir.'

'But is not an honest man to be trusted?'

'Why—why—yes, sir.'

'There! don't you see, now?'

'See what?' asked the disconcerted barber, rather
vexedly.

'Why, you stand self-contradicted, barber; don't
you?'

'No,' doggedly.

'Barber,' gravely, and after a pause of concern, 'the

enemies of our race have a saying that insincerity is the most universal and inveterate vice of man—the lasting bar to real amelioration, whether of individuals or of the world. Don't you now, barber, by your stubbornness on this occasion, give colour to such a calumny ? '

' Hity-tity ! ' cried the barber, losing patience, and with it respect ; ' stubbornness ? ' Then clattering round the brush in the cup, ' Will you be shaved, or won't you ? '

' Barber, I will be shaved, and with pleasure ; but, pray, don't raise your voice that way. Why, now, if you go through life gritting your teeth in that fashion, what a comfortless time you will have.'

' I take as much comfort in this world as you or any other man,' cried the barber, whom the other's sweetness of temper seemed rather to exasperate than soothe.

' To resent the imputation of anything like unhappiness I have often observed to be peculiar to certain orders of men,' said the other pensively, and half to himself, ' just as to be indifferent to that imputation, from holding happiness but for a secondary good and inferior grace, I have observed to be equally peculiar to other kinds of men. Pray, barber,' innocently looking up, ' which think you is the superior creature ? '

' All this sort of talk,' cried the barber, still unmollified, ' is, as I told you once before, not in my line. In a few minutes I shall shut up this shop. Will you be shaved ? '

' Shave away, barber. What hinders ? ' turning up his face like a flower.

The shaving began, and proceeded in silence, till at length it became necessary to prepare to relather a little—affording an opportunity for resuming the subject, which, on one side, was not let slip.

' Barber,' with a kind of cautious kindliness, feeling his way, ' barber, now have a little patience with me ;

do ; trust me, I wish not to offend. I have been thinking over that supposed case of the man with the averted
face, and I cannot rid my mind of the impression that,
by your opposite replies to my questions at the time,
you showed yourself much of a piece with a good many
other men—that is, you have confidence, and then again,
you have none. Now, what I would ask is, do you think
it sensible standing for a sensible man, one foot on confidence and the other on suspicion ? Don't you think,
barber, that you ought to elect ? Don't you think consistency requires that you should either say, "I have
confidence in all men," and take down your notification ;
or else say, "I suspect all men," and keep it up.'

This dispassionate, if not deferential, way of putting
the case, did not fail to impress the barber, and pro-
portionately conciliate him. Likewise, from its pointed-
ness, it served to make him thoughtful ; for, instead of
going to the copper vessel for more water, as he had
purposed, he halted half-way toward it, and, after a
pause, cup in hand, said : ' Sir, I hope you would not do
me injustice. I don't say, and can't say, and wouldn't
say, that I suspect all men ; but I *do* say that strangers
are not to be trusted, and so,' pointing up to the sign,
' no trust.'

' But look, now, I beg, barber,' rejoined the other
deprecatingly, not presuming too much upon the barber's
changed temper ; ' look, now ; to say that strangers
are not to be trusted, does not that imply something like
saying that mankind is not to be trusted : for the mass
of mankind, are they not necessarily strangers to each
individual man ? Come, come, my friend,' winningly,
' you are no Timon to hold the mass of mankind untrust-
worthy. Take down your notification ; it is misanthropical ; much the same sign that Timon traced*with
charcoal on the forehead of a skull stuck over his cave.

Take it down, barber ; take it down to-night. Trust
men. Just try the experiment of trusting men for this
one little trip. Come now, I 'm a philanthropist, and will
ensure you against losing a cent.'

The barber shook his head dryly, and answered, ' Sir,
you must excuse me. I have a family.'

CHAPTER XLIII

VERY CHARMING

' So you are a philanthropist, sir,' added the barber with
an illuminated look ; ' that accounts, then, for all. Very
odd sort of man the philanthropist. You are the second
one, sir, I have seen. Very odd sort of man, indeed, the
philanthropist. Ah, sir,' again meditatively stirring in
the shaving-cup, ' I sadly fear, lest you philanthropists
know better what goodness is, than what men are.'
Then, eyeing him as if he were some strange creature
behind cage-bars, ' So you are a philanthropist, sir.'

' I am Philanthropos, and love mankind.* And, what
is more than you do, barber, I trust them.'

Here the barber, casually recalled to his business,
would have replenished his shaving-cup, but finding now
that on his last visit to the water-vessel he had not replaced it over the lamp, he did so now ; and, while waiting for it to heat again, became almost as sociable as if
the heating water were meant for whisky-punch ; and
almost as pleasantly garrulous as the pleasant barbers
in romances.

' Sir,' said he, taking a throne beside his customer
(for in a row there were three thrones on the dais, as for
the three kings of Cologne,* those patron saints of the
barber), ' sir, you say you trust men. Well, I suppose
I might share some of your trust, were it not for this
trade, that I follow, too much letting me in behind the
scenes.'

' I think I understand,' with a saddened look ; ' and

much the same thing I have heard from persons in pursuits different from yours—from the lawyer, from the congressman, from the editor, not to mention others, each, with a strange kind of melancholy vanity, claiming for his vocation the distinction of affording the surest inlets to the conviction that man is no better than he should be. All of which testimony, if reliable, would, by mutual corroboration, justify some disturbance in a good man's mind. But no, no ; it is a mistake—all a mistake.'

'True, sir, very true,' assented the barber.

'Glad to hear that,' brightening up.

'Not so fast, sir,' said the barber ; 'I agree with you in thinking that the lawyer, and the congressman, and the editor, are in error, but only in so far as each claims peculiar facilities for the sort of knowledge in question ; because, you see, sir, the truth is, that every trade or pursuit which brings one into contact with the facts, sir, such trade or pursuit is equally an avenue to those facts.'

'*How* exactly is that ?'

'Why, sir, in my opinion—and for the last twenty years I have, at odd times, turned the matter over some in my mind—he who comes to know man, will not remain in ignorance of man. I think I am not rash in saying that ; am I, sir ?'

'Barber, you talk like an oracle—obscurely, barber, obscurely.'

'Well, sir,' with some self-complacency, 'the barber has always been held an oracle, but as for the obscurity, that I don't admit.'

'But pray, now, by your account, what precisely may be this mysterious knowledge gained in your trade ? I grant you, indeed, as before hinted, that your trade, imposing on you the necessity of functionally tweaking

the noses of mankind, is, in that respect, unfortunate,
very much so ; nevertheless, a well-regulated imagination should be proof even to such a provocation to
improper conceits. But what I want to learn from you,
barber, is, how does the mere handling of the outside of
men's heads lead you to distrust the inside of their
hearts ? '

' What, sir, to say nothing more, can one be forever
dealing in macassar oil, hair dyes, cosmetics, false mous-
taches, wigs, and toupees, and still believe that men are
wholly what they look to be ? What think you, sir,
are a thoughtful barber's reflections, when, behind a
careful curtain, he shaves the thin, dead stubble off a
head, and then dismisses it to the world, radiant in curl-
ing auburn ? To contrast the shamefaced air behind
the curtain, the fearful looking forward to being possibly
discovered there by a prying acquaintance, with the
cheerful assurance and challenging pride with which
the same man steps forth again, a gay deception, into the
street, while some honest, shock-headed fellow humbly
gives him the wall. Ah, sir, they may talk of the courage
of truth, but my trade teaches me that truth sometimes
is sheepish. Lies, lies, sir, brave lies are the lions ! '

' You twist the moral, barber ; you sadly twist it.
Look, now ; take it this way : A modest man thrust out
naked into the street, would he not be abashed ? Take
him in and clothe him ; would not his confidence be
restored ? And in either case, is any reproach involved ?
Now, what is true of the whole, holds proportionably
true of the part. The bald head is a nakedness which
the wig is a coat to. To feel uneasy at the possibility
of the exposure of one's nakedness at top, and to feel
comforted by the consciousness of having it clothed—
these feelings, instead of being dishonourable to a bold
man, do, in fact, but attest a proper respect for himself

and his fellows. And as for the deception, you may as well call the fine roof of a fine château a deception, since, like a fine wig, it also is an artificial cover to the head, and equally, in the common eye, decorates the wearer.—I have confuted you, my dear barber; I have confounded you.'

'Pardon,' said the barber, 'but I do not see that you have. His coat and his roof no man pretends to palm off as a part of himself, but the bald man palms off hair, not his, for his own.'

'Not *his*, barber? If he have fairly purchased his hair, the law will protect him in its ownership, even against the claims of the head on which it grew. But it cannot be that you believe what you say, barber; you talk merely for the humour. I could not think so of you as to suppose that you would contentedly deal in the impostures you condemn.'

'Ah, sir, I must live.'

'And can't you do that without sinning against your conscience, as you believe? Take up some other calling.'

'Wouldn't mend the matter much, sir.'

'Do you think, then, barber, that, in a certain point, all the trades and callings of men are much on a par? Fatal, indeed,' raising his hand, 'inexpressibly dreadful, the trade of the barber, if to such conclusions it necessarily leads. Barber,' eyeing him not without emotion, 'you appear to me not so much a misbeliever, as a man misled. Now, let me set you on the right track; let me restore you to trust in human nature, and by no other means than the very trade that has brought you to suspect it.'

'You mean, sir, you would have me try the experiment of taking down that notification,' again pointing to it with his brush; 'but, dear me, while I sit chatting here, the water boils over.'

With which words, and such a well-pleased, sly, smug expression, as they say some men have when they think their little stratagem has succeeded, he hurried to the copper vessel, and soon had his cup foaming up with white bubbles, as if it were a mug of new ale.

Meantime, the other would have fain gone on with the discourse ; but the cunning barber lathered him with so generous a brush, so piled up the foam on him, that his face looked like the yeasty crest of a billow, and vain to think of talking under it, as for a drowning priest in the sea to exhort his fellow-sinners on a raft. Nothing would do, but he must keep his mouth shut. Doubtless, the interval was not, in a meditative way, unimproved ; for, upon the traces of the operation being at last removed, the cosmopolitan rose, and, for added refreshment, washed his face and hands ; and having generally readjusted himself, began, at last, addressing the barber in a manner different, singularly so, from his previous one. Hard to say exactly what the manner was, any more than to hint it was a sort of magical ; in a benign way, not wholly unlike the manner, fabled or otherwise, of certain creatures in nature, which have the power of persuasive fascination—the power of holding another creature by the button of the eye, as it were, despite the serious disinclination, and, indeed, earnest protest, of the victim. With this manner the conclusion of the matter was not out of keeping ; for, in the end, all argument and expostulation proved vain, the barber being irresistibly persuaded to agree to try, for the remainder of the present trip, the experiment of trusting men, as both phrased it. True, to save his credit as a free agent, he was loud in averring that it was only for the novelty of the thing that he so agreed, and he required the other, as before volunteered, to go security to him against any loss that might ensue ; but still the fact remained, that

he engaged to trust men, a thing he had before said he
would not do, at least not unreservedly. Still the more
to save his credit, he now insisted upon it, as a last point,
that the agreement should be put in black and white,
especially the security part. The other made no demur ;
pen, ink, and paper were provided, and grave as any
notary the cosmopolitan sat down, but, ere taking the
pen, glanced up at the notification, and said : ' First
down with that sign, barber—Timon's sign, there ; down
with it.'

This, being in the agreement, was done—though a
little reluctantly—with an eye to the future, the sign
being carefully put away in a drawer.

' Now, then, for the writing,' said the cosmopolitan,
squaring himself. ' Ah,' with a sigh, ' I shall make a
poor lawyer, I fear. Ain't used, you see, barber, to a
business which, ignoring the principle of honour, holds
no nail fast till clinched. Strange, barber,' taking up
the blank paper, ' that such flimsy stuff as this should
make such strong hawsers ; vile hawsers, too. Barber,'
starting up, ' I won't put it in black and white. It were
a reflection upon our joint honour. I will take your
word, and you shall take mine.'

' But your memory may be none of the best, sir. Well
for you, on your side, to have it in black and white, just
for a memorandum like, you know.'

' That, indeed ! Yes, and it would help *your* memory,
too, wouldn't it, barber ? Yours, on your side, being a
little weak, too, I dare say. Ah, barber ! how ingenious
we human beings are ; and how kindly we reciprocate
each other's little delicacies, don't we ? What better
proof, now, that we are kind, considerate fellows, with
responsive fellow-feelings—eh, barber ? But to business.
Let me see. What 's your name, barber ? '

' William Cream, sir.'

Pondering a moment, he began to write; and, after some corrections, leaned back, and read aloud the following:—

'AGREEMENT

between

FRANK GOODMAN, Philanthropist, and Citizen of the World,

and

WILLIAM CREAM, Barber of the Mississippi steamer *Fidèle*.

'The first hereby agrees to make good to the last any loss that may come from his trusting mankind, in the way of his vocation, for the residue of the present trip; PROVIDED that William Cream keep out of sight, for the given term, his notification of "No TRUST," and by no other mode convey any, the least hint or intimation, tending to discourage men from soliciting trust from him, in the way of his vocation, for the time above specified; but, on the contrary, he do, by all proper and reasonable words, gestures, manners, and looks, evince a perfect confidence in all men, especially strangers: otherwise, this agreement to be void.

'Done, in good faith, this 1st day of April, 18—, at a quarter to twelve o'clock P.M., in the shop of said William Cream, on board the said boat *Fidèle*.'

'There, barber; will that do?'

'That will do,' said the barber, 'only now put down your name.'

Both signatures being affixed, the question was started by the barber, who should have custody of the instrument; which point, however, he settled for himself, by proposing that both should go together to the captain, and give the document into his hands—the barber hinting that this would be a safe proceeding, because the captain was necessarily a party disinterested, and, what was more, could not, from the nature of the present case, make anything by a breach of trust. All of which was listened to with some surprise and concern.

' Why, barber,' said the cosmopolitan, ' this don't show the right spirit ; for me, I have confidence in the captain purely because he is a man ; but he shall have nothing to do with our affair ; for if you have no confidence in me, barber, I have in you. There, keep the paper yourself,' handing it magnanimously.

' Very good,' said the barber, ' and now nothing remains but for me to receive the cash.'

Though the mention of that word, or any of its singularly numerous equivalents, in serious neighbourhood to a requisition upon one's purse, is attended with a more or less noteworthy effect upon the human countenance, producing in many an abrupt fall of it—in others, a writhing and screwing up of the features to a point not undistressing to behold, in some, attended with a blank pallor and fatal consternation—yet no trace of any of these symptoms was visible upon the countenance of the cosmopolitan, notwithstanding nothing could be more sudden and unexpected than the barber's demand.

' You speak of cash, barber ; pray in what connection ? '

' In a nearer one, sir,' answered the barber, less blandly, ' than I thought the man with the sweet voice stood, who wanted me to trust him once for a shave, on the score of being a sort of thirteenth cousin.'

' Indeed, and what did you say to him ? '

' I said, " Thank you, sir, but I don't see the connection." '

' How could you so unsweetly answer one with a sweet voice ? '

' Because, I recalled what the son of Sirach says in the True Book : " An enemy speaketh sweetly with his lips " ;* and so I did what the son of Sirach advises in such cases : " I believed not his many words." '*

'What, barber, do you say that such cynical sort of things are in the True Book, by which, of course, you mean the Bible?'

'Yes, and plenty more to the same effect. Read the Book of Proverbs.'

'That's strange, now, barber; for I never happen to have met with those passages you cite. Before I go to bed this night, I'll inspect the Bible I saw on the cabin-table, to-day. But mind, you mustn't quote the True Book that way to people coming in here; it would be impliedly a violation of the contract. But you don't know how glad I feel that you have for one while signed off all that sort of thing.'

'No, sir; not unless you down with the cash.'

'Cash again! What do you mean?'

'Why, in this paper here, you engage, sir, to insure me against a certain loss, and——'

'Certain? Is it so *certain* you are going to lose?'

'Why, that way of taking the word may not be amiss, but I didn't mean it so. I meant a *certain* loss; you understand, a CERTAIN loss; that is to say, a certain loss. Now then, sir, what use your mere writing and saying you will insure me, unless beforehand you place in my hands a money-pledge, sufficient to that end?'

'I see; the material pledge.'

'Yes, and I will put it low; say fifty dollars.'

'Now what sort of a beginning is this? You, barber, for a given time engage to trust man, to put confidence in men, and, for your first step, make a demand imply-ing no confidence in the very man you engage with. But fifty dollars is nothing, and I would let you have it cheerfully, only I unfortunately happen to have but little change with me just now.'

'But you have money in your trunk, though?'

'To be sure. But you see—in fact, barber, you must

be consistent. No, I won't let you have the money now ;
I won't let you violate the inmost spirit of our contract,
that way. So good-night, and I will see you again.'

'Stay, sir '—humming and hawing—' you have forgotten something.'

'Handkerchief ?—gloves ? No, forgotten nothing.
Good-night.'

'Stay, sir—the—the shaving.'

'Ah, I *did* forget that. But now that it strikes me, I
shan't pay you at present. Look at your agreement ;
you must trust. Tut ! against loss you hold the guarantee. Good-night, my dear barber ! '

With which words he sauntered off, leaving the barber
in a maze, staring after.

But it holding true in fascination as in natural philosophy, that nothing can act where it is not, so the barber
was not long now in being restored to his self-possession
and senses ; the first evidence of which perhaps was,
that, drawing forth his notification from the drawer, he
put it back where it belonged ; while, as for the agreement, that he tore up ; which he felt the more free to do
from the impression that in all human probability he
would never again see the person who had drawn it.
Whether that impression proved well founded or not,
does not appear. But in after days, telling the night's
adventure to his friends, the worthy barber always spoke
of his queer customer as the man-charmer—as certain
East Indians are called snake-charmers—and all his
friends united in thinking him QUITE AN ORIGINAL.

CHAPTER XLIV

'QUITE AN ORIGINAL': a phrase, we fancy, rather oftener used by the young, or the unlearned, or the untravelled, than by the old, or the well-read, or the man who has made the grand tour. Certainly, the sense of originality exists at its highest in an infant, and probably at its lowest in him who has completed the circle of the sciences.

As for original characters in fiction, a grateful reader will, on meeting with one, keep the anniversary of that day. True, we sometimes hear of an author who, at one creation, produces some two or three score such characters ; it may be possible. But they can hardly be original in the sense that Hamlet is, or Don Quixote, or Milton's Satan.* That is to say, they are not, in a thorough sense, original at all. They are novel, or singular, or striking, or captivating, or all four at once.

More likely, they are what are called odd characters ; but for that, are no more original, than what is called an odd genius, in his way, is. But, if original, whence came they ? Or where did the novelist pick them up ?

Where does any novelist pick up any character ? For the most part, in town, to be sure. Every great town is a kind of man-show, where the novelist goes for his stock, just as the agriculturist goes to the cattle-show for his. But in the one fair, new species of quadrupeds are hardly more rare, than in the other are new species of characters —that is, original ones.   Their rarity may still the more appear from this, that, while characters, merely singular, imply but singular forms, so to speak, original ones, truly so, imply original instincts.

In short, a due conception of what is to be held for this sort of personage in fiction would make him almost as much of a prodigy there, as in real history is a new law-giver, a revolutionising philosopher, or the founder of a new religion.

In nearly all the original characters, loosely accounted such in works of invention, there is discernible something prevailingly local, or of the age ; which circumstance, of itself, would seem to invalidate the claim, judged by the principles here suggested.

Furthermore, if we consider, what is popularly held to entitle characters in fiction to being deemed original, is but something personal—confined to itself.   The char- acter sheds not its characteristic on its surroundings, whereas, the original character, essentially such, is like a revolving Drummond light,* raying away from itself all round it—everything is lit by it, everything starts up to it (mark how it is with Hamlet), so that, in certain minds, there follows upon the adequate conception of such a character, an effect, in its way, akin to that which in Genesis* attends upon the beginning of things.

For much the same reason that there is but one planet to one orbit, so can there be but one such original char- acter to one work of invention.   Two would conflict to chaos.   In this view, to say that there are more than one to a book, is good presumption there is none at all. But for new, singular, striking, odd, eccentric, and all sorts of entertaining and instructive characters, a good

fiction may be full of them. To produce such characters, an author, beside other things, must have seen
much, and seen through much : to produce but one
original character, he must have had much luck.

There would seem but one point in common between
this sort of phenomenon in fiction and all other sorts :
it cannot be born in the author's imagination—it being
as true in literature as in zoology, that all life is from
the egg.

In the endeavour to show, if possible, the impropriety
of the phrase, *Quite an Original*, as applied by the barber's
friends, we have, at unawares, been led into a dissertation bordering upon the prosy, perhaps upon the smoky.
If so, the best use the smoke can be turned to, will be,
by retiring under cover of it, in good trim as may be, to
the story.

CHAPTER XLV

THE COSMOPOLITAN INCREASES IN SERIOUSNESS

In the middle of the gentlemen's cabin burned a solar lamp,* swung from the ceiling, and whose shade of ground glass was all round fancifully variegated, in transparency, with the image of a horned altar,* from which flames rose, alternate with the figure of a robed man, his head encircled by a halo. The light of this lamp, after dazzlingly striking on marble, snow-white and round—the slab of a centre-table beneath—on all sides went rippling off with ever-diminishing distinctness, till, like circles from a stone dropped in water, the rays died dimly away in the furthest nook of the place.

Here and there, true to their place, but not to their function, swung other lamps, barren planets, which had either gone out from exhaustion, or been extinguished by such occupants of berths as the light annoyed, or who wanted to sleep, not see.

By a perverse man, in a berth not remote, the remaining lamp would have been extinguished as well, had not a steward forbade, saying that the commands of the captain required it to be kept burning till the natural light of day should come to relieve it. This steward, who, like many in his vocation, was apt to be a little free-spoken at times, had been provoked by the man's pertinacity to remind him, not only of the sad consequences which might, upon occasion, ensue from the cabin being left in darkness, but, also, of the circumstance that, in a place full of strangers, to show one's self anxious to produce darkness there, such an anxiety was, to say the least, not becoming. So the lamp—last survivor of many—burned on, inwardly blessed by those in some berths, and inwardly execrated by those in others.

Keeping his lone vigils beneath his lone lamp, which lighted his book on the table, sat a clean, comely, old man, his head snowy as the marble, and a countenance like that which imagination ascribes to good Simeon[*], when, having at last beheld the Master of Faith, he blessed him and departed in peace. From his hale look of greenness in winter, and his hands ingrained with the tan, less, apparently, of the present summer, than of accumulated ones past, the old man seemed a well-to-do farmer, happily dismissed, after a thrifty life of activity, from the fields to the fireside—one of those who, at threescore-and-ten, are fresh-hearted as at fifteen; to whom seclusion gives a boon more blessed than knowledge, and at last sends them to heaven untainted by the world, because ignorant of it; just as a countryman putting up at a London inn, and never stirring out of it as a sight-seer, will leave London at last without once being lost in its fog, or soiled by its mud.

Redolent from the barber's shop, as any bridegroom tripping to the bridal chamber might come, and by his look of cheeriness seeming to dispense a sort of morning through the night, in came the cosmopolitan; but marking the old man, and how he was occupied, he toned himself down, and trod softly, and took a seat on the other side of the table, and said nothing. Still, there was a kind of waiting expression about him.

'Sir,' said the old man, after looking up puzzled at him a moment, 'sir,' said he, 'one would think this was a coffee-house, and it was war-time, and I had a newspaper here with great news, and the only copy to be had, you sit there looking at me so eager.'

'And so you *have* good news there, sir—the very best of good news.'

'Too good to be true,' here came from one of the curtained berths.

'Hark!' said the cosmopolitan. 'Someone talks in his sleep.'

'Yes,' said the old man, 'and you—*you* seem to be talking in a dream. Why speak you, sir, of news, and all that, when you must see this is a book I have here— the Bible, not a newspaper?'

'I know that; and when you are through with it— but not a moment sooner—I will thank you for it. It belongs to the boat, I believe—a present from a society.'

'Oh, take it, take it!'

'Nay, sir, I did not mean to touch you at all. I simply stated the fact in explanation of my waiting here—nothing more. Read on, sir, or you will distress me.'

This courtesy was not without effect. Removing his spectacles, and saying he had about finished his chapter, the old man kindly presented the volume, which was received with thanks equally kind. After reading for some minutes, until his expression merged from attentiveness into seriousness, and from that into a kind of pain, the cosmopolitan slowly laid down the book, and turning to the old man, who thus far had been watching him with benign curiosity, said: 'Can you, my aged friend, resolve me a doubt—a disturbing doubt?'

'There are doubts, sir,' replied the old man, with a changed countenance, 'there are doubts, sir, which, if man have them, it is not man that can solve them.'

'True; but look, now, what my doubt is. I am one who thinks well of man. I love man. I have confidence in man. But what was told me not a half-hour since? I was told that I would find it written—" Be-

lieve not his many words—an enemy speaketh sweetly
with his lips "—and also I was told that I would find a
good deal more to the same effect, and all in this book.
I could not think it ; and, coming here to look for myself,
what do I read ?   Not only just what was quoted, but
also, as was engaged, more to the same purpose, such as
this : "With much communication he will tempt thee*;
he will smile upon thee, and speak thee fair, and say
What wantest thou ?   If thou be for his profit he will
use thee ; he will make thee bear, and will not be sorry
for it.   Observe and take good heed.   When thou hearest
these things, awake in thy sleep." '

'Who 's that describing the confidence-man ? ' here
came from the berth again.

'Awake in his sleep, sure enough, ain't he ? ' said the
cosmopolitan, again looking off in surprise.   'Same voice
as before, ain't it ?   Strange sort of dreamy man, that.
Which is his berth, pray ? '

'Never mind *him*, sir,' said the old man anxiously,
' but tell me truly, did you, indeed, read from the book
just now ? '

'I did,' with changed air, ' and gall and wormwood it
is to me, a truster in man ; to me, a philanthropist.'

'Why,' moved, ' you don't mean to say, that what you
repeated is really down there ?   Man and boy, I have
read the good book this seventy years, and don't remember seeing anything like that.   Let me see it,'
rising earnestly, and going round to him.

'There it is ; and there—and there '—turning over
the leaves, and pointing to the sentences one by one ;
' there—all down in the " Wisdom of Jesus, the Son of
Sirach." '*

'Ah ! ' cried the old man, brightening up, ' now I
know.   Look,' turning the leaves forward and back,
till all the Old Testament lay flat on one side, and all the

New Testament flat on the other, while in his fingers he supported vertically the portion between, ' look, sir, all this to the right is certain truth, and all this to the left is certain truth, but all I hold in my hand here is apocrypha.'

' Apocrypha ? '

' Yes ; and there 's the word in black and white,' pointing to it. ' And what says the word ? It says as much as " not warranted " ; for what do college men say of anything of that sort ? They say it is apocryphal. The word itself, I 've heard from the pulpit, implies something of uncertain credit. So if your disturbance be raised from aught in this apocrypha,' again taking up the pages, ' in that case, think no more of it, for it 's apocrypha.'

' What 's that about the Apocalypse ? '* here, a third time, came from the berth.

' He 's seeing visions now, ain't he ? ' said the cosmopolitan, once more looking in the direction of the interruption. ' But, sir,' resuming, ' I cannot tell you how thankful I am for your reminding me about the apocrypha here. For the moment, its being such escaped me. Fact is, when all is bound up together, it 's sometimes confusing. The uncanonical part should be bound distinct. And, now that I think of it, how well did those learned doctors who rejected for us this whole book of Sirach. I never read anything so calculated to destroy man's confidence in man. This Son of Sirach even says —I saw it but just now : " Take heed of thy friends;" not, observe, thy seeming friends, thy hypocritical friends, thy false friends, but thy *friends*, thy real friends—that is to say, not the truest friend in the world is to be implicitly trusted. Can Rochefoucauld equal that ? I should not wonder if his view of human nature, like Machiavelli's, was taken from this Son of Sirach. And

to call it wisdom—the Wisdom of the Son of Sirach !
Wisdom, indeed ! What an ugly thing wisdom must
be ! Give me the folly that dimples the cheek, say I,
rather than the wisdom that curdles the blood. But no,
no ; it ain't wisdom ; it 's apocrypha, as you say, sir.
For how can that be trustworthy that teaches distrust ? '

' I tell you what it is,' here cried the same voice as
before, only more in less of mockery, ' if you two don't
know enough to sleep, don't be keeping wiser men awake.
And if you want to know what wisdom is, go find it under
your blankets.'

' Wisdom ? ' cried another voice with a brogue ;
' arrah, and is 't wisdom the two geese are gabbling
about all this while ? To bed with ye, ye divils, and
don't be after burning your fingers with the likes of
wisdom.'

' We must talk lower,' said the old man ; ' I fear we
have annoyed these good people.'

' I should be sorry if wisdom annoyed anyone,' said
the other ; ' but we will lower our voices, as you say.
To resume : taking the thing as I did, can you be surprised at my uneasiness in reading passages so charged
with the spirit of distrust ? '

' No, sir, I am not surprised,' said the old man ; then
added : ' from what you say, I see you are something
of my way of thinking—you think that to distrust the
creature, is a kind of distrusting of the Creator. Well,
my young friend, what is it ? This is rather late for you
to be about. What do you want of me ? '

These questions were put to a boy in the fragment of
an old linen coat, bedraggled and yellow, who, coming
in from the deck barefooted on the soft carpet, had been
unheard. All pointed and fluttering, the rags of the
little fellow's red-flannel shirt, mixed with those of his
yellow coat, flamed about him like the painted flames in

the robes of a victim in *auto-da-fé.** His face, too, wore
such a polish of seasoned grime, that his sloe-eyes sparkled
from out it like lustrous sparks in fresh coal. He was a
juvenile peddler, or *marchand*, as the polite French might
have called him, of travellers' conveniences ; and, having
no allotted sleeping-place, had, in his wanderings about
the boat, spied, through glass doors, the two in the cabin ;
and, late though it was, thought it might never be too
much so for turning a penny.

Among other things, he carried a curious affair—a
miniature mahogany door, hinged to its frame, and suitably furnished in all respects but one, which will shortly
appear. This little door he now meaningly held before
the old man, who, after staring at it a while, said : ' Go
thy ways with thy toys, child.'

' Now, may I never get so old and wise as that comes
to,' laughed the boy through his grime ; and, by so doing,
disclosing leopard-like teeth, like those of Murillo's wild
beggar boys.*

' The divils are laughing now, are they ? ' here came
the brogue from the berth. ' What do the divils find to
laugh about in wisdom, begorrah ? To bed with ye, ye
divils, and no more of ye.'

' You see, child, you have disturbed that person,'
said the old man ; ' you mustn't laugh any more.'

' Ah, now,' said the cosmopolitan, ' don't, pray, say
that ; don't let him think that poor Laughter is perse-
cuted for a fool in this world.'

' Well,' said the old man to the boy, ' you must, at any
rate, speak very low.'

' Yes, that wouldn't be amiss, perhaps,' said the cosmopolitan ; ' but, my fine fellow, you were about saying
something to my aged friend here ; what was it ? '

' Oh,' with a lowered voice, coolly opening and shutting
his little door, ' only this : when I kept a toy-stand at the

fair in Cincinnati last month, I sold more than one old man a child's rattle.'

'No doubt of it,' said the old man. 'I myself often buy such things for my little grandchildren.'

'But these old men I talk of were old bachelors.'

The old man stared at him a moment; then, whispering to the cosmopolitan: 'Strange boy, this; sort of simple, ain't he? Don't know much, hey?'

'Not much,' said the boy, 'or I wouldn't be so ragged.'

'Why, child, what sharp ears you have!' exclaimed the old man.

'If they were duller, I would hear less ill of myself,' said the boy.

'You seem pretty wise, my lad,' said the cosmopolitan; 'why don't you sell your wisdom, and buy a coat?'

'Faith,' said the boy, 'that's what I did to-day, and this is the coat that the price of my wisdom bought. But won't you trade? See, now, it is not the door I want to sell; I only carry the door round for a specimen like. Look now, sir,' standing the thing up on the table, 'supposing this little door is your state-room door; well,' opening it, 'you go in for the night; you close your door behind you—thus. Now, is all safe?'

'I suppose so, child,' said the old man.

'Of course it is, my fine fellow,' said the cosmopolitan.

'All safe. Well, now, about two o'clock in the morning, say, a soft-handed gentleman comes softly and tries the knob here—thus; in creeps my soft-handed gentleman; and hey, presto! he comes on the soft cash?'

'I see, I see, child,' said the old man; 'your fine gentleman is a fine thief, and there's no lock to your little door to keep him out'; with which words he peered at it more closely than before.

'Well, now,' again showing his white teeth, 'well,

now, some of you old folks are knowing 'uns, sure enough ; but now comes the great invention,' producing a small steel contrivance, very simple but ingenious, and which, being clapped on the inside of the little door, secured it as with a bolt. 'There now,' admiringly holding it off at arm's-length, 'there now, let that soft-handed gentleman come now a softly trying this little knob here, and let him keep a trying till he finds his head as soft as his hand. Buy the traveller's patent lock, sir, only twenty-five cents.'

'Dear me,' cried the old man, 'this beats printing. Yes, child, I will have one, and use it this very night.'

With the phlegm of an old banker pouching the change, the boy now turned to the other : 'Sell you one, sir ? '

'Excuse me, my fine fellow, but I never use such black-smiths' things.'

'Those who give the blacksmith most work seldom do,' said the boy, tipping him a wink expressive of a degree of indefinite knowingness, not uninteresting to consider in one of his years. But the wink was not marked by the old man, nor, to all appearances, by him for whom it was intended.

'Now then,' said the boy, again addressing the old man. 'With your traveller's lock on your door to-night, you will think yourself all safe, won't you ? '

'I think I will, child.'

'But how about the window ? '

'Dear me, the window, child. I never thought of that. I must see to that.'

'Never you mind about the window,' said the boy, 'nor, to be honour bright, about the traveller's lock either (though I ain't sorry for selling one) ; do you just buy one of these little jokers,' producing a number of suspender-like objects, which he dangled before the old man ; 'money-belts, sir ; only fifty cents.'

'Money-belt ? never heard of such a thing.'

'A sort of pocket-book,' said the boy, 'only a safer sort. Very good for travellers.'

'Oh, a pocket-book. Queer-looking pocket-books though, seems to me. Ain't they rather long and narrow for pocket-books ? '

'They go round the waist, sir, inside,' said the boy ; 'door open or locked, wide awake on your feet or fast asleep in your chair, impossible to be robbed with a money-belt.'

'I see, I see. It *would* be hard to rob one's money-belt. And I was told to-day the Mississippi is a bad river for pick-pockets. How much are they ? '

'Only fifty cents, sir.'

'I 'll take one. There ! '

'Thank-ee. And now there 's a present for ye,' with which, drawing from his breast a batch of little papers, he threw one before the old man, who, looking at it, read ' *Counterfeit Detector*.'*

'Very good thing,' said the boy. 'I give it to all my customers who trade seventy-five cents' worth ; best present can be made them. Sell you a money-belt, sir ? ' turning to the cosmopolitan.

'Excuse me, my fine fellow, but I never use that sort of thing ; my money I carry loose.'

'Loose bait ain't bad,' said the boy, 'look a lie and find the truth ;* don't care about a Counterfeit Detector, do ye ? or is the wind East, d' ye think ? '

'Child,' said the old man in some concern, 'you mustn't sit up any longer, it affects your mind ; there, go away, go to bed.'

'If I had some people's brains to lie on, I would,' said the boy, 'but planks is hard, you know.'

'Go, child—go, go ! '

'Yes, child—yes, yes,' said the boy, with which roguish

parody, by way of congé, he scraped back his hard foot on the woven flowers of the carpet, much as a mischievous steer in May scrapes back his horny hoof in the pasture ; and then with a flourish of his hat—which, like the rest of his tatters, was, thanks to hard times, a belonging beyond his years, though not beyond his experience, being a grown man's cast-off beaver—turned, and with the air of a young Caffre, quitted the place.

'That's a strange boy,' said the old man, looking after him. 'I wonder who's his mother ; and whether she knows what late hours he keeps ? '

'The probability is,' observed the other, 'that his mother does not know. But if you remember, sir, you were saying something, when the boy interrupted you with his door.'

'So I was.—Let me see,' unmindful of his purchases for the moment, ' what, now, was it ? What was that I was saying ? Do *you* remember ? '

'Not perfectly, sir ; but, if I am not mistaken, it was something like this : you hoped you did not distrust the creature ; for that would imply distrust of the Creator.'

'Yes, that was something like it,' mechanically and unintelligently letting his eye fall now on his purchases.

'Pray, will you put your money in your belt to-night ? '

'It's best, ain't it ? ' with a slight start. 'Never too late to be cautious. "Beware of pick-pockets" is all over the boat.'

'Yes, and it must have been the Son of Sirach, or some other morbid cynic, who put them there. But that's not to the purpose. Since you are minded to it, pray, sir, let me help you about the belt. I think that, between us, we can make a secure thing of it.'

'Oh no, no, no ! ' said the old man, not unperturbed, ' no, no, I wouldn't trouble you for the world,' then,

nervously folding up the belt, ' and I won't be so impolite
as to do it for myself, before you, either.   But, now that
I think of it,' after a pause, carefully taking a little wad
from a remote corner of his vest pocket, ' here are two
bills they gave me at St. Louis, yesterday. No doubt
they are all right ; but just to pass time, I 'll compare
them with the Detector here. Blessed boy to make me
such a present. Public benefactor, that little boy ! '

Laying the Detector square before him on the table, he
then, with something of the air of an officer bringing by
the collar a brace of culprits to the bar, placed the two
bills opposite the Detector, upon which, the examination
began, lasting some time, prosecuted with no small
research and vigilance, the forefinger of the right hand
proving of lawyer-like efficacy in tracing out and pointing the evidence, whichever way it might go.

After watching him a while, the cosmopolitan said in a
formal voice, ' Well, what say you, Mr. Foreman ; guilty,
or not guilty ?—Not guilty, ain't it ? '

' I don't know, I don't know,' returned the old man,
perplexed. ' There 's so many marks of all sorts to go
by, it makes it kind of uncertain. Here, now, is this
bill,' touching one, ' it looks to be a three-dollar bill on
the Vicksburgh Trust and Insurance Banking Company.*
Well, the Detector says——'

' But why, in this case, care what it says ?   Trust and
Insurance !   What more would you have ? '

' No ; but the Detector says, among fifty other things,
that, if a good bill, it must have, thickened here and
there into the substance of the paper, little wavy spots
of red ; and it says they must have a kind of silky feel,
being made by the lint of a red silk handkerchief stirred
up in the paper-maker's vat—the paper being made to
order for the company.'

' Well, and is——'

'Stay. But then it adds, that sign is not always to be relied on; for some good bills get so worn, the red marks get rubbed out. And that's the case with my bill here—see how old it is—or else it's a counterfeit, or else—I don't see right—or else—dear, dear me—I don't know what else to think.'

'What a peck of trouble that Detector makes for you now; believe me, the bill is good; don't be so distrustful. Proves what I've always thought, that much of the want of confidence, in these days, is owing to these Counterfeit Detectors you see on every desk and counter. Puts people up to suspecting good bills. Throw it away, I beg, if only because of the trouble it breeds you.'

'No; it's troublesome, but I think I'll keep it.—Stay, now, here's another sign. It says that, if the bill is good, it must have in one corner, mixed in with the vignette, the figure of a goose, very small, indeed, all but microscopic; and, for added precaution, like the figure of Napoleon outlined by the tree, not observable, even if magnified, unless the attention is directed to it. Now, pore over it as I will, I can't see this goose.'

'Can't see the goose? why, I can; and a famous goose it is. There' (reaching over and pointing to a spot in the vignette).

'I don't see it—dear me—I don't see the goose. Is it a real goose?'

'A perfect goose;* beautiful goose.'

'Dear, dear, I don't see it.'

'Then throw that Detector away, I say again; it only makes you purblind; don't you see what a wild-goose chase it has led you? The bill is good. Throw the Detector away.'

'No, it ain't so satisfactory as I thought for, but I must examine this other bill.'

' As you please, but I can't in conscience assist you
any more ; pray, then, excuse me.'

So, while the old man with much painstakings resumed
his work, the cosmopolitan, to allow him every facility,
resumed his reading.   At length, seeing that he had given
up his undertaking as hopeless, and was at leisure again,
the cosmopolitan addressed some gravely interesting
remarks to him about the book before him, and, presently,
becoming more and more grave, said, as he turned the
large volume slowly over on the table, and with much
difficulty traced the faded remains of the gilt inscription
giving the name of the society who had presented it to
the boat, ' Ah, sir, though everyone must be pleased at
the thought of the presence in public places of such a
book, yet there is something that abates the satisfaction.
Look at this volume ; on the outside, battered as any
old valise in the baggage-room ; and inside, white and
virgin as the hearts of lilies in bud.'

' So it is, so it is,' said the old man sadly, his attention
for the first directed to the circumstance.

' Nor is this the only time,' continued the other, ' that
I have observed these public Bibles in boats and hotels.
All much like this—old without, and new within.   True,
this aptly typifies that internal freshness, the best mark
of truth, however ancient ; but then, it speaks not so
well as could be wished for the good book's esteem in
the minds of the travelling public.   I may err, but it
seems to me that if more confidence was put in it by the
travelling public, it would hardly be so.'

With an expression very unlike that with which he
had bent over the Detector, the old man sat meditating
upon his companion's remarks a while ; and, at last, with
a rapt look, said : ' And yet, of all people, the travelling
public most need to put trust in that guardianship which
is made known in this book.'

'True, true,' thoughtfully assented the other.

'And one would think they would want to, and be glad to,' continued the old man, kindling; 'for, in all our wanderings through this vale, how pleasant, not less than obligatory, to feel that we need start at no wild alarms, provide for no wild perils; trusting in that Power which is alike able and willing to protect us when we cannot ourselves.'

His manner produced something answering to it in the cosmopolitan, who, leaning over toward him, said sadly: 'Though this is a theme on which travellers seldom talk to each other, yet, to you, sir, I will say, that I share something of your sense of security. I have moved much about the world, and still keep at it; nevertheless, though in this land, and especially in these parts of it, some stories are told about steamboats and railroads fitted to make one a little apprehensive, yet, I may say that, neither by land nor by water, am I ever seriously disquieted, however, at times, transiently uneasy; since, with you, sir, I believe in a Committee of Safety,* holding silent sessions over all, in an invisible patrol, most alert when we soundest sleep, and whose beat lies as much through forests as towns, along rivers as streets. In short, I never forget that passage of Scripture which says, "Jehovah shall be thy confidence."* The traveller who has not this trust, what miserable misgivings must be his; or, what vain, short-sighted care must he take of himself.'

'Even so,' said the old man, lowly.

'There is a chapter,' continued the other, again taking the book, 'which, as not amiss, I must read you. But this lamp, solar lamp as it is, begins to burn dimly.'

'So it does, so it does,' said the old man with changed air; 'dear me, it must be very late. I must to bed, to bed! Let me see,' rising and looking wistfully all round,

first on the stools and settees, and then on the carpet,
' let me see, let me see ;—is there anything I have forgot,
—forgot ? Something I a sort of dimly remember.
Something, my son—careful man—told me at starting
this morning, this very morning. Something about
seeing to—something before I got into my berth. What
could it be ? Something for safety. Oh, my poor old
memory ! '

' Let me give a little guess, sir. Life-preserver ? '*

' So it was. He told me not to omit seeing I had a
life-preserver in my state-room ; said the boat supplied
them, too. But where are they ? I don't see any.
What are they like ? '

' They are something like this, sir, I believe,' lifting a
brown stool with a curved tin compartment*underneath ;
' yes, this, I think, is a life-preserver, sir ; and a very
good one, I should say, though I don't pretend to know
much about such things, never using them myself.'

' Why, indeed, now ! Who would have thought it ?
that a life-preserver ? That 's the very stool I was sitting
on, ain't it ? '

' It is. And that shows that one's life is looked out
for, when he ain't looking out for it himself. In fact,
any of these stools here will float you, sir, should the boat
hit a snag, and go down in the dark. But, since you
want one in your room, pray take this one,' handing it
to him. ' I think I can recommend this one ; the tin
part,' rapping it with his knuckles, ' seems so perfect—
sounds so very hollow.'

' Sure it 's *quite* perfect, though ? ' Then, anxiously
putting on his spectacles, he scrutinised it pretty closely
—' well soldered ? quite tight ? '

' I should say so, sir ; though, indeed, as I said, I
never use this sort of thing, myself. Still, I think that
in case of a wreck, barring sharp-pointed timbers, you

could have confidence in that stool for a special providence.'*

'Then, good-night, good-night ; and Providence have both of us in its good keeping.'

'Be sure it will,' eyeing the old man with sympathy, as for the moment he stood, money-belt in hand, and life-preserver under arm, 'be sure it will, sir, since in Providence, as in man, you and I equally put trust. But, bless me, we are being left in the dark here. Pah ! what a smell, too.'

'Ah, my way now,' cried the old man, peering before him, 'where lies my way to my state-room ? '

'I have indifferent eyes, and will show you ; but, first, for the good of all lungs, let me extinguish this lamp.'

The next moment, the waning light expired, and with it the waning flames of the horned altar, and the waning halo round the robed man's brow ; while in the darkness which ensued, the cosmopolitan kindly led the old man away. Something further may follow of this Masquerade.

APPENDIX A

Black Guinea's List

Black Guinea's list of gentlemen who will speak for him (p. 14) is generally agreed to be a list of the confidence men, or versions of the Confidence-Man, on the *Fidèle*. It is, however, the trickiest passage in the novel, as some of those he mentions do not appear exactly as described, and some 'avatars' of the Confidence-Man (including the crucial figure of the Cosmopolitan) are not mentioned, unless identifications are forced. Thus the text includes a yarb-doctor (herb-doctor), first seen in Chapter 16, and gentlemen with a weed (Chapter 4), a gray coat and white tie (Chapter 6), a big book (Chapter 9), and a brass plate (Chapter 22); there is a soldier, the pretended veteran of the Mexican War (Chapter 19), although he encounters and is duped by the herb-doctor. This leaves the two gentlemen who wear a 'yaller west' and a 'wiolet robe', with the only possible candidates consisting of Charlie Noble with his 'violet vest' (waistcoat), the boy with the yellow coat in the final chapter, and the Cosmopolitan, who wears a predominantly red costume with a purple smoking-cap. Considering these discrepancies, Foster observes (1954): 'It seems most likely that Melville changed or forgot his earlier intentions regarding some of the subordinate arrangements of the story. It will be remembered that Melville did not see the novel through the press. Ill and sorely troubled with his eyes, perhaps he did not even read the whole manuscript before or after Augusta [his sister] copied it.' Franklin (1967) argues that most of Black Guinea's descriptions could apply to more than one figure in the novel; that 'one must read his list artfully', and recognize that it 'ultimately includes everybody'. Although some of his suggestions seem over-ingenious, it is at least equally arguable that Melville is indeed providing a model for the difficulties of reading the signs of character, or of the presence of the Devil or the Redeemer. Black Guinea's list would thus resemble the Counterfeit Detector for identifying false currency in the last chapter; as the baffled old man says, 'there's so many marks of all sorts to go by, it makes it a kind of uncertain'.

APPENDIX B

Missouri and slavery

Missouri, on the right-hand or western bank as the *Fidèle* travels in the direction of New Orleans, was admitted to the Union as a state permitting slavery in 1821. By the 'Missouri Compromise', Maine was simultaneously admitted as a 'free' state banning slavery, and further extension of slavery was forbidden in territory north of 36 ° 30 '. The fact that Missouri fought with the Union is indicative of its critical and unstable status. *The Confidence-Man*, which describes a journey towards the south, was written and is set in the decade in which the issue of slavery came to split the Union in two. It is worth noting some of the most significant developments in this period of escalation.

1852 Harriet Beecher Stowe's *Uncle Tom's Cabin*, the great abolitionist novel.

1854 Kansas–Nebraska Act, allowing self-determination to these new territories, leads to bloody battles in Kansas between pro- and anti-slavery forces. Republican Party formed with anti-slavery policy.

1857 Dred–Scott decision by Supreme Court, returning slave to his master, also declares 'Missouri Compromise' unconstitutional, raising possibility of slavery as national rather than Southern institution.

1858 Lincoln–Douglas debates on slavery.

1861 Formation of Confederacy, after election of Lincoln as President, renders Civil War (1861–5) inevitable.

EXPLANATORY NOTES

1 *a first of April*: All Fools' or April Fools' Day.

suddenly as Manco Capac at the lake Titicaca: the mythical founder of the imperial Inca dynasty of Peru, sent to earth to redeem man by his father the Sun.

St. Louis: busy commercial city near the junction of the Mississippi and the Missouri. Connected the North to the South, as a river port, and the East to the West, as the terminus of the main westward trails; hence the symbolic centre of a young nation not yet fully extended across the continent.

Fidèle: Fr. faithful; also the name adopted by Imogen in Shakespeare's *Cymbeline*.

2 *chevaliers*: Fr. 'chevaliers d'industrie', pickpockets, swindlers.

Measan . . . Murrel . . . the brothers Harpe: famous criminals associated with murder for its own sake.

Thugs: Indian followers of the goddess Kali feared for the ritual killing of travellers.

Charity thinketh no evil: 1 Corinthians 13.

4 *NO TRUST*: no credit given.

6 *Casper Hauser*: Kaspar Hauser (1812?–33), the mysterious 'wild boy' with no recollection of his past discovered at Nuremberg in 1828, also referred to by Melville in *Moby-Dick* and *Billy Budd*. The subject of Werner Herzog's film *The Enigma of Kaspar Hauser*.

Green prophet from Utah: the Mormons were led by Brigham Young in 1847 to Utah, where they founded Salt Lake City. In 1858, after bloodshed in the Mormon community, a force of US troops was sent against them.

Spirit-rapper: spiritualist.

Moon-calf: abortion, or dolt.

Endymion: in Greek myth, the shepherd lover of the moon goddess Selene, allowed by Zeus to sleep perpetually.

Jacob dreaming at Luz: the position of the lamb-like mute leads the onlookers to compare him to Jacob's dream in Genesis 28: 12–15 of a ladder leading to heaven, with angels ascending and descending it.

 7 *the great ship canal of Ving-King-Ching*: the Grand Canal of China.

on 'change': at the Stock Exchange.

 9 *blacklegs*: professional gamblers.

hard-shell: rigidly orthodox.

clay-eaters: a practice particularly associated with the South, exemplified by Goneril in Chapter 12.

an Anarcharsis Cloots congress: as described in Carlyle's *The French Revolution* (1837), de Clootz was a Prussian nobleman who led a delegation including representatives from several countries to the National Assembly in 1790. See *Moby-Dick*, ch. 27.

Tartar-like: properly Tatar; a term generally extended to all of the Asiatic warriors who swept across Europe in the thirteenth century.

13 *The will of man is by his reason swayed*: *A Midsummer Night's Dream*, II. ii. 121. The scene in fact shows mortals as fools; Lysander has been led to love Helena, not by reason, but by Puck's magic juice.

14 *Oh yes, oh yes, dar is aboard here* . . . : see Appendix A.

17 *timber-toe*: wooden leg.

ship of fools: the literary trope of the ship as microcosm, so important to Melville, derives from Sebastian Brant's *Das Narrenschiff* (1494), roughly translated into English as *The Ship of Fools*.

18 *Timon*: the hero of *Timon of Athens*, who turns on his friends and chooses to live in a cave; the epitome of misanthropy and cynicism throughout *The Confidence-Man*.

19 *Jeremy Diddler*: the name of the swindler hero in a popular farce of 1803; the likely origin of the word 'diddle' (see Introduction, p. xi).

21 *weed*: covering of black cloth signifying mourning.

22 *Werter's Charlotte*: the hero of Goethe's Romantic novel *The Sorrows of Young Werther* (1774) falls in love with Charlotte when he sees her serving tea to her brothers and sisters.

24 *we are but clay*: echo of Isaiah 64: 8.

25 *you are a mason*: as recorded in Melville's local journal, the *Springfield Republican*, 5 May 1855, a man assumed to be the original 1849 'Confidence Man' (see Introduction, pp. xi-xii) made exactly this form of approach to the owner of a Broadway jewellery store (Foster).

27 *to fear no second fate*: echo of Satan's speech in Milton's *Paradise Lost*, ii. 14–17.

31 *sophomore*: second-year student.

32 *Tacitus*: Roman historian (c.55–120), author of the *Histories* and the *Annals*, which together formed a history of the Empire from Tiberius to Domitian.

33 *There is a subtle man*: condensation of verses in chs. 19 and 20 of the book of Ecclesiasticus in the Apocrypha.

the cemeteries of Auburn and Greenwood: cemeteries were much frequented by the 'sentimentalists' of the late eighteenth century; these were in Cambridge, Massachusetts and Brooklyn, New York, respectively.

Akenside: the man with the weed aligns himself with the optimism of the tradition that runs from the philosopher Lord Shaftesbury (1671–1713) to his disciple Mark Akenside, author of the long didactic poem *The Pleasures of Imagination* (1744).

34 *Ovid, Horace, Anacreon*: lyric poets sometimes regarded as licentious.

Aeschylus: the father of Greek tragedy (525 BC–456 BC).

Thucydides, Juvenal, Lucian . . . Tacitus: this group of

classical authors mixes the historians, Thucydides and Tacitus, with two satirists.

Astraea: goddess who dwelt on earth during the Golden Age, but was subsequently driven away and transformed into the constellation Virgo.

36 *the Seminoles*: the only American Indian tribe to resist the 'removals' of the 1830s. After the second Seminole War (1835–42) the remnants of the tribe were moved from Florida to present-day Oklahoma.

39 *Benedicts*: sworn bachelors who marry, after the hero of *Much Ado About Nothing*.

41 *Caffre*: kaffir, African negro.

47 *the Hebrew governor*: Pontius Pilate in Matthew 27: 24, washing his hands to symbolize his innocence of the decision to crucify Christ.

Wilberforce: William Wilberforce (1759–1833), English philanthropist who achieved the abolition of the slave trade in Britain in 1807.

scarcely for a righteous man: Romans 5: 7.

49 *that notion of Socrates*: employed by him in several works of Plato, notably the *Republic*; the harmony is between the rational part, the irrational part, and the will.

the World's Fair in London: the Great Exhibition at the Crystal Palace, Hyde Park, 1851.

50 *Protean*: shape-changing, like the Greek sea god Proteus.

51 *Fourier*: François Fourier (1772–1837), French social theorist, who advocated the reorganization of society into communes. Brook Farm, a Utopian community influenced by Fourier's ideas, involved such figures as Nathaniel Hawthorne and Margaret Fuller in the 1840s.

53 *Archimedean*: Archimedes invented the lever, and the saying 'Give me a firm spot on which to stand, and I will move the earth' is attributed to him.

54 *kraken*: legendary sea monster.

Abraham reviling the angel: when told that his aged wife Sarah would bear a child, in Genesis 17: 7.

55 *the millenial promise*: in Revelation 20, of the resurrection of the dead and the appearance of the New Jerusalem, after Satan had been imprisoned for a thousand years.

gestures that were a Pentecost: at Pentecost the Holy Spirit gave Christ's disciples the gift of tongues (other languages); Acts 2: 1–40.

57 *confidence*: faith, in this usage.

59 *I rejoice that I have confidence*: 2 Corinthians 7: 16.

62 *bears*: those who sell stocks in the expectation of a fall in price.

63 *spurious Jeremiahs . . . sham Heraclituses*: Jeremiah is the gloomiest Old Testament prophet, Heraclitus the gloomiest Greek philosopher.

sham Lazaruses: in the general sense of 'diseased beggars'.

Good-Enough-Morgan: an adequate substitute or pretext for obtaining advantage. The anti-Masonic writer William Morgan disappeared in 1826. When the identification of a body in the Niagara as his was disputed, another anti-Mason, Thurlow Weed, called it 'a good enough Morgan' (for them to make political capital).

64 *a musty old Seneca*: Lucius Annaeus Seneca (*c*.5 BC–AD 65), Roman statesman, tragedian and Stoic philosopher.

croaker: one who grumbles or forebodes evil.

65 *come home to my business and bosom*: Bacon's essays, according to the dedication to the 1625 edition, 'come home to men's business and bosoms'.

New Jerusalem: compare the fraudulent sale of land near Cairo, Illinois to the hero in Dickens's *Martin Chuzzlewit* (1842–3), Chapter 21. (See Introduction p. xvii.)

lyceums: organizations for instruction by lectures.

66 *two fugitives, who had swum over*: probable allusion to Bunyan's *The Pilgrim's Progress* (1678), in which Christian

and Hopeful swim across a river to reach the Heavenly City (though 'naked' suggests Adam and Eve).

Ariamius: Arimanius, the principle of evil in the Persian religion of Zoroastrianism.

67 *philosophes*: Fr. philosophers.

ODE ON THE INTIMATIONS OF DISTRUST: allusion to Wordsworth's 'Ode: Intimations of Immortality'.

69 *Philomel*: nightingale, from the Greek legend of Philomela.

71 *locust-tree*: carob.

75 *Nature . . . had meal and bran*: echo of *Cymbeline*, IV. ii. 27.

Zimmermann: Johann Georg Ritter von Zimmermann, author of the sentimental work *On Solitude* (1755, 1785), which was successful throughout Europe and remained popular with the Romantics.

Torquemada: Tomas de Torquemada (1420–98) became the first inquisitor-general of the Church in Spain in 1483; his name is a byword for ruthless torture and murder.

77 *Thrasea*: Stoic and Roman senator, killed by Nero for opposing him in AD 66; the saying is attribted to him by Pliny.

Goneril: the name of one of the evil daughters of King Lear; it has been argued that aspects of the character are derived from the Shakespearian actress Fanny Kemble, a neighbour of Melville's in the Berkshire Hills in Massachusets.

82 *savan*: savant, learned man.

Sir Humphrey Davy: English chemist (1778–1829) who discovered several metals and invented the safety lamp. No source of the story has been traced.

85 *Malakoff*: supposedly secure fortress protecting Sebastopol during the Crimean War, which was in fact taken by the French on 5 September 1855.

87 *In vino veritas*: Lat. (there is) truth in wine.

Irish Rebellion: the most recent nationalist activity was the abortive attempted rising by the 'Young Ireland' movement in 1848.

89 *rara avis*: Lat. rare bird.

90 *expect to run and read*: echo of Habakkuk 2: 2.

caterpillar . . . butterfly: terms reversed in the original text.

91 *fearfully and wonderfully made*: Psalms 139: 14.

93 *pine barrens*: semi-deserted region with pine trees.

94 *Philadelphian regularity*: referring to the geometrical grid of that city's streets.

Procrustean beds: from Procrustes, a Greek robber who forcibly altered the bodies of his victims to fit his bed of torture.

95 *Orpheus in his gay descent*: Orpheus in Greek myth descended into the underworld to recover his wife Eurydice; the story is told in Ovid's *Metamorphoses*, x.

a wail like that of Dives: the rich man suffering in hell in the parable told in Luke 16: 19–31; cf. 'Dives and Lazarus' in the description of the *Fidèle*'s passengers at the end of Chapter 2.

hunks: miserly curmudgeon.

96 *Cant, gammon!*: the miser regards talk of confidence as cant (meaningless words) and gammon (humbug); but also employs 'cant', the secret language of the underworld: gammon-pickpocket's assistant; bubble-dupe; fetch-steal; gouge-cheat.

98 *help, friend, my distrust!*: modifying Mark 9: 24, 'help thou my unbelief'.

100 *seventy-four*: warship with seventy-four guns, like the *Bellipotent* in *Billy Budd*.

daedal: ingeniously made, as if by Daedalus, the artificer of Greek myth.

surtout: close-bodied frock-coat.

101 *good Samaritans*: refers to the parable in Luke 10: 30–7.

Calvin Edson: a 'living skeleton' in P. T. Barnum's American Museum.

102 *Pharaoh's vain sorcerers*: those whose magic was defeated by that of Moses and Aaron in Exodus 7–9.

provoked to anger with their inventions: echo of Psalms 106: 29.

103 *the hyssop on the wall*: echo of 1 Kings 4: 33.

Medea gathered: quoting *The Merchant of Venice*, v. i. 13–14.

Aeson . . . Medea: in Ovid, as recalled by Shakespeare, the mythical sorceress Medea revives and rejuvenates Aeson, the father of her husband Jason.

104 *Preisnitz!*: Vincenz Preissnitz (1799–1851), a German advocate of water cures.

to get strength by confidence: echo of Isaiah 30: 15.

106 *Nature in Disease*: book on various medical topics (1843) by Joseph Bigelow.

109 *prove all the vials*: cf. 1 Thessalonians 5: 21, 'Prove all things; hold fast that which is good'. 'Prove' means 'test'.

Japus in Virgil: Virgil, *Aeneid*, iii. 427–9.

110 *tic-douloureux*: affliction involving paroxysms of pain in the face and forehead.

112 *haunted Cock Lane*: the ghost here was exposed as a hoax in 1762 by a committee which included Dr Johnson.

a kind of invalid Titan: in Greek mythology the Titans were a race of lawless giants. The myth of the Titan Enceladus is invoked in Melville's *Pierre*.

a little Cassandra: the wild prophetess, accurate but ignored, of Homer's *Iliad*.

117 *Bourse*: Stock Exchange.

Asmodeus: demon in the book of *Tobit* in the Apocrypha, who in Le Sage's novel *Le Diable Boiteux* (1707) is capable of flight and revealing the secrets of men's lives.

as Hamlet says: Horatio in *Hamlet*, v, i. 207.

121 *Jesuit emissaries prowling all over our country*: scares about excessive Jesuit influence gave rise to the secret 'Know-Nothing movement' of the 1840s, which had gone public by 1856, backing Fillmore for President.

122 *Molino del Rey? Resaca de la Palma?*: two battles of the Mexican War (1846–7), which enabled the USA to acquire both Texas and California.

Tombs!: the Tombs was a prison in New York, to which the hero of Melville's 'Bartleby' (1853) was taken.

123 *the other Lazarus*: i.e. the beggar of Luke 16, not the Lazarus who returns from the dead in John 11–12.

Epictetus: Stoic philosopher, born in Rome around AD 50.

124 *Mrs Fry*: Elizabeth Fry (1780–1845), English prison reformer.

125 *pavior*: a layer of pavements.

128 *Buena Vista . . . Contreras*: further battles in the Mexican War.

130 *those who are loved are chastened*: cf. Hebrews 12:6, Proverbs 13:24.

134 *eagles*: ten-dollar coins.

137 *the Mammoth Cave*: a famous cave in Kentucky briefly occupied in 1843 by consumptives hoping to be cured by its atmosphere.

138 *pistareens*: coins of low value.

clipped . . . sweated: cut and heated to remove precious metal.

140 *file*: wretch.

spencer: short overcoat.

Hoosier: rustic; usually an inhabitant of Indiana.

141 *good Queen Bess*: a wiser ruler, after Elizabeth I of England.

teamster: one who drives a team of horses.

Peter the Wild Boy: a boy of about 12 found living as an animal in Hanover in 1725, who, like Kaspar Hauser (ch. 2) became a subject of discussion amongst intellectuals.

142 *that soil will come back after many days*: echo of Ecclesiastes 11: 1.

143 *the Siamese twins*: Barnum's American Museum included the famous Siamese twins Chang and Eng.

144 *lint her out*: by using lint as insulation.

146 *the dungeoned Italian*: the Abbé Faria in Dumas's *The Count of Monte Cristo*, published in 1846 (Foster).

149 *You are an abolitionist, ain't you?*: the campaign to abolish slavery in the USA became an organized movement in the 1830s.

    you, a Missourian, though living in a slave state: see Appendix B.

151 *IN THE POLITE SPIRIT OF THE TUSCULAN DISPU-TATIONS*: an ironical chapter heading; the *Disputations* is a late work by Cicero (106–43 BC) of leisurely philosophical conversations.

    Intelligence Office: employment agency.

    baker-kneed: knock-kneed.

152 *the free state we now pass*: Illinois, on the left or eastern bank. The plot of Mark Twain's *The Adventures of Huckleberry Finn* (1884), which is also set on the Mississippi, presumably in the 1840s or early 1850s, depends on the contrasting laws of the states on either side of the river. Huck and the fugitive slave Jim, travelling south on a raft, aim to get to the junction of the Mississippi and the Ohio at Cairo, Illinois, so they can go 'way up the river among the free states'. Below Cairo there were slave states (Missouri and Kentucky, Arkansas and Tennessee) on both sides of the river.

    I'm a Mede and a Persian: unalterable, like the laws of the Medes and Persians in Daniel 6: 8.

154 *patient continuance in well-doing*: echo of Romans 2: 7.

    Praise-God-Barebones: fervent Anabaptist and member of

Cromwell's 'Little Parliament' of 1653 during the English Revolution.

Horace: Quintus Horatius Flaccus (65–8 BC), Roman poet.

156 *a perfect Chesterfield*: the fourth Earl of Chesterfield (1694–1773), an English politician who wrote the famous *Letters to his Son*; used here as the epitome of polished manners.

158 *the child is father to the man*: quoting Wordsworth's 'My Heart Leaps Up'.

159 *Gammon*: nonsense.

A wet sheet and a flowing sea!: title line of a poem by the Scottish poet Allan Cunningham (1784–1842).

166 *the founder of La Trappe*: Abbot de Rancé (1626–1700), a roué as a youth who founded the austere and silent Trappist monastic order, though not the La Trappe monastery.

Ignatius Loyola: formed the Society of Jesus (Jesuits) in 1534, after finding religious enthusiasm at the age of 30.

167 *St Augustine on Original Sin*: not the subject of any particular work by Augustine (354–430), but the Fall is the foundation of his thought.

168 *a very sad dog*: in the *Confessions* Augustine recalls his early attraction to sensuality and heresy.

169 *your marines to whom you may say anything*: like the more recent 'tell it to the marines', the saying assumes them to be more credulous than sailors.

reformado: reformed.

172 *Cairo*: in *The Confidence-Man*, as in *The Adventures of Huckleberry Finn*, the passing of Cairo marks a major transition in the narrative.

Yellow Jack: yellow fever.

has not lost its cunning: echo of Psalms 137: 5.

Typhus: typhoid.

Apemantus: a Cynic—a philosopher contemptuous of wealth and convention—and friend of the hero in *Timon of Athens*. Gk. 'cynic' means 'dog-like'.

173 *Crossbones*: Death.

   Talleyrand: famous French diplomat (1754–1838).

   Machiavelli: Florentine political theorist (1469–1527),
   author of *The Prince*.

   Rosicrucian: member of a secret religious society founded
   in the sixteenth or seventeenth century, based on shared
   mystical knowledge.

174 *windeth his way on his belly*: echo of Genesis 3: 14.

175 *our Fair*: a hint of Vanity Fair in *The Pilgrim's Progress*.

   cochineal: scarlet.

176 *Signor Marzetti in the African pantomime*: Melville may
   have seen this actor perform as described in New York in
   the 1840s.

177 *fortiter in re . . . suaviter in modo*: Lat. resolute in action,
   gentle in manner, a theme of Lord Chesterfield.

   Lunar Mountains: the legendary Mountains of the Moon in
   East Africa.

   Ladrone: Sp. robber.

   London-Dock-Vault: cellars containing the wines of the
   world.

178 *Amontillado*: sherry.

   hide his light under the bushel: echo of Matthew 5: 14.

   Life is a picnic en costume: Foster, who conjectures that the
   novel was begun during the first half of 1855, notes that
   Melville and his family attended a fancy-dress picnic near
   their home in Pittsfield, Massachusetts, on 7 September
   1855.

179 *en confiance*: in confidence.

   Goshen: part of Egypt untouched by the plagues in Exodus,
   hence proverbial place of safety.

   Santa Cruz: West Indies rum.

180 *Tokay*: sweet Hungarian wine.

   megrims: migraine.

181 *Hume's on Suicide*: an essay defending suicide by the Scottish philosopher David Hume (1711–76).

Bacon's on Knowledge: probably no specific work by Francis Bacon (1561–1626) is intended.

Rabelais' pro-wine Koran: *Gargantua* and *Pantagruel*, by the French author François Rabelais (1494?–1553?), mix serious ideas with scenes of debauchery in which wine is always involved.

Mahomet's anti-wine one: the *Koran*, the Islamic sacred text, forbids alcohol.

Jeremy Taylor the divine: English priest and theologian (1613–67); a royalist who wrote most of his eloquent treatises and sermons in seclusion during the period of republican government.

184 *the Piazza, Covent Garden*: an arcade on two sides of London's flower market.

Diogenes: Cynic philosopher (412–323 BC) who took austerity to the point of living in a tub.

merry-andrew: zany, buffoon.

185 *an Ishmael*: an outcast, like the son of Abraham in Genesis; the narrator of *Moby-Dick* gives himself this name.

186 *abord*: Fr. way of approaching someone.

coon: racoon, sly fellow.

187 *eye like Lochiel's*: Sir Ewan Cameron of Lochiel (1629–1719), a fierce Scottish Highland clan leader mentioned in Macaulay's *History of England*.

catamount: mountain cat, i.e. puma, lynx, or similar animal.

188 *I am ready to love Indians*: although Pocahontas (1595–1617), the princess who married a member of the Virginia colony, is the standard example of a 'good Indian', some of the other names have different overtones: Philip of Mount Hope is primarily associated with King Phillip's War (1675–6), a bloody conflict with the New England colonists;

the Shawnee chief Tecumseh attempted to form an independent Indian nation in 1808.

190 *James Hall, the judge*: Hall (1793–1868) was a circuit judge in Illinois who wrote extensively about the American West. The next two chapters are closely based on his *Sketches of History, Life, and Manners, in the West* (1835), which includes the story of Colonel John Moredock, a historical figure.

192 *Rousseau*: Jean-Jacques Rousseau (1712–78), Swiss philosopher, essayist and autobiographer, associated with the idea of the Noble Savage.

193 *ambuscade*: ambush.

Hairy Orson: character in a French medieval romance who is carried off by a bear as a child and grows up as a wild man.

194 *Pathfinder*: one of the names given to James Fenimore Cooper's hero of five novels, Natty Bumppo.

Emperor Julian in Gaul: according to Gibbon, Julian (ruled 361–3) shared the hardships of his soldiers.

Peace Congress: there were several such congresses in the 1840s and 1850s; Franklin cites a pamphlet which describes the 'peace principle' operating in lions and Indians.

the Society of Friends: the pacifist Quakers.

195 *Newgate Calendar*: register of crimes and criminals which first appeared in Britain in 1773. Named after the prison in London.

Annals of Europe: an eighteenth-century almanac of major events.

'*As the twig . . .*': a line from Pope's *Moral Essays* (1732), Epistle 1.

memento mori: Lat. a reminder of mortality.

Moyamensing: prison in Pennsylvania.

a treaty-breaker like an Austrian: a reference to the gains made by the revolution of 1848, which were subsequently rescinded by the imperial government.

Palmer: Dr William Palmer, a British poisoner hanged on 14 June 1856.

Jeffries: George Jeffreys (1648–89), Lord Chancellor of England, most famous for the 'Bloody Assize' after the Monmouth Rebellion in 1688.

Jew: perhaps in the sense of 'crafty person'.

burk: murder, especially by stifling.

Manitou: name used by some Indian tribes for the Great Spirit.

197 *the Bloody Ground, Kentucky*: the Indian word 'kentucky' means 'bloody ground'.

Caesar Borgia: Cesare Borgia (1476–1507), Duke of Valentinois and Romagna, a general who conquered several other Italian city states and was cited in Machiavelli's *The Prince* as the prime example of the ruler's necessary duplicity.

198 *Daniel Boone*: pioneer (1735–1820) who explored the forest area of Kentucky and Missouri.

200 *Hannibal*: Carthaginian general (247–182 BC), forced by his father to swear eternal enmity to Rome when aged nine, who conducted the two Punic Wars.

a Leather-stocking Nemesis: Leather-stocking is another name of Natty Bumppo, hero of five novels by James Fenimore Cooper.

gone to his long home: echo of Ecclesiastes 12: 5.

201 *calenture*: fever involving delusions.

202 *calumet*: Indian peace pipe.

203 *THAT EMINENT ENGLISH MORALIST*: Dr Johnson, as reported by Mrs Piozzi.

204 *Arcadia*: region of Greece associated with simple pastoral life.

205 *Cains*: murderers.

voice calling through the garden: echo of Genesis 3: 8, the passage in which Adam and Eve hide from God after the Fall.

206 *number*: Parker's suggestion (1963) for 'murder' in the original text.

207 *Hull's dubious surrender at Detroit*: ordered to prepare to invade Canada, Brigadier General Hull surrendered to the British without a fight in 1812.

210 *the alleged Lisbon earthquake*: the cause of an intellectual controversy in 1755 between sceptics like Voltaire and believers in God's providential design.

212 *'Let us drink of the wine . . . '*: from Leigh Hunt's 'Bacchus in Tuscany' (1825).

214 *Charlie Arnold Noble*: 'Charlie Noble' is naval slang term for galley funnel (Franklin).

215 *male Brinvillierses*: the Marquise de Brinvilliers (1630–76), who poisoned several members of her own family; the subject of a poem by Melville.

Hebe's cheek: Greek goddess of youth and spring.

217 *Rochefoucaultites*: *Reflexions* by the Duke of Rochfoucauld (1613–80) consists largely of maxims which unmask the self-love in human behaviour.

218 *Sodom*: in Genesis 18–19 God destroys Sodom, after promising Adam that it will be saved if ten good people can be found there.

a man may smile: echo of *Hamlet*, I. v. 108, the hero's observation on his stepfather Claudius.

219 *the voice of the people*: variation of the Latin proverb *vox populi, vox Dei*, the voice of the people is the voice of God.

Aristotle: no such saying occurs in the Greek philosopher's *Politics*.

Phalaris: no such anecdote is told of the tyrant mentioned in the *Politics*; Franklin argues the relevance of the hoax *Epistles of Phalaris* (1695) which were at the centre of the 'battle of the books' involving Swift.

221 *an improvisatore*: entertainer; an Italian word for one who improvises verses or stories.

Jack Cade: leader of a peasant rebellion in England in 1450, who appears in *2 Henry VI*.

Colt's revolver: patented by Samuel Colt in 1835.

Kossuth and Mazzini: the leaders of the short-lived 1848 revolutions in Hungary and Italy respectively.

222 *parhelion*: a false image of the sun.

223 *Praise be unto the press*: the phrasing of the paragraph echoes Proverbs 23: 29–32, a warning against wine; Johann Faust was a fifteenth-century German printer, a partner of Gutenberg; drunkenness was traditionally associated with Noah, after Genesis 9: 20–7.

Madeira or Mytilene: islands famous for their wine.

224 *Sybillic confidence*: the sibyls of the ancient world were prophetesses.

Catawba vine: from the region of the Catawba river in the Carolinas, where wine was produced.

225 *apple . . . ashes*: the proverbial Apples of Sodom are fair on the outside but turn to ashes in the mouth.

226 *the advice of Polonius to Laertes*: the speech of the old palace counsellor as his son departs on a voyage (*Hamlet*, I. iii. 54–81) includes the words 'Neither a borrower nor a lender be'.

227 *old Malvolios*: Malvolio is the conceited steward of *Twelfth Night*, who is described as 'a kind of Puritan'.

228 *sell all thou hast . . .* : Matthew 19: 21, the advice of Christ to the rich young man.

230 *Autolycus*: trickster and pickpocket posing as a peddler in *The Winter's Tale*; 'oh what a fool . . .': *The Winter's Tale*, IV. iv. 606–7.

231 *drules*: drools.

punk: touchwood, tinder.

233 *Why, bless you, Charlie*: corrected from 'Frank' in the original.

234 *blueing-bag*: laundry bag.

235 *free-and-easies*: saloons for drinking.

Pizarro: Francis Pizarro (*c*.1478–1541), Spanish conquistador. The incident the Cosmopolitan later touches on is described in Prescott's *The Conquest of Peru*; Pizarro first accepted the offer of the Inca king Atahualpa to fill a room with gold in return for his life, and then killed him.

Jack Ketch: notoriously inefficient hangman and headsman in seventeenth-century England.

240 *Ovid*: Roman poet (43 BC–AD 17), author of the *Metamorphoses*, versions of classical myths.

241 *Cadmus glided into the snake*: in *Metamorphoses*, iii, Cadmus kills a snake sacred to Mars, and is changed into one.

245 *gazetted*: listed as bankrupt.

250 *a stranger*: a subtle and extended caricature of the American essayist and lecturer Ralph Waldo Emerson (1803–82), the dominant intellectual influence on the New England of the period.

251 *Pitti Palace*: Florentine palace containing numerous art treasures.

Schiller: German Romantic poet, playwright, and essayist (1759–1805).

sidelong crest his head: echo of *Paradise Lost*, ix. 499–525, lines describing Satan's temptation of Eve in the form of a snake (Foster).

252 *Waltz of Death*: in the Dance of Death, an artistic tradition dating from the fourteenth century, Death is shown leading representatives of different parts of society.

who will pity the charmer . . . ?: Ecclesiasticus 12: 13.

253 *Court of Common Pleas*: court generally hearing civil actions brought by one citizen against another.

reductio ad absurdum: Lat. reduction to absurdity; the technique of using an extreme hypothetical example to show an argument to be false.

254 *the page of Hafiz*: a fourteenth-century Persian poet translated by Emerson, who also wrote an essay called 'Persian Poetry'.

255 *I seldom care to be consistent*: glances at the famous declaration in Emerson's 'Self-Reliance' (1841), 'A foolish consistency is the hobgoblin of little minds'.

256 *Proclus*: Greek neo-Platonic philosopher (*c*.412–85) with some influence on Emerson, mocked elsewhere by Melville for writing arcane gibberish.

257 *the stoic Arrian*: Greek historian (*c*.95–180), disciple and editor of the Roman Stoic philosopher Epictetus.

258 *hollands*: linen garments.

a haggard, inspired-looking man: generally accepted as a sketch of Edgar Allan Poe (1803–49). The most obvious model for his 'rhapsodical tract' is the metaphysical speculation he called *Eureka* (1848).

260 *bolus*: large pill.

262 *a confidential follower*: another caricature, of Henry David Thoreau (1817–62), the author of *Walden, or Life in the Woods* (1854). Fourteen years younger than Emerson, he lived in his household for parts of the 1840s, but was not subsequently as closely associated with him as is suggested here.

263 *meekly standing like a Raphael*: allusion to *Paradise Lost*, vii. 217.

old Memnon: an Egyptian colossus which gave out a musical sound each dawn.

264 *Seneca . . . Bacon . . . Swedenborg*: the Stoic philosoher allegedly misused his position as counsellor to Nero; Bacon, the Lord Chancellor under James I, was banished from the Court for accepting bribes; Emanuel Swedenborg, the

eighteenth-century Swedish mystic, was originally a scientist and engineer.

268 *my friend is above receiving alms*: mocking Thoreau's view of friendship, particularly in 'Wednesday' in *A Week on the Concord and Merrimack Rivers* (1849), where charity and friendship are treated as incompatible.

271 *a stranger is better than a brother*: Proverbs 18: 24 and 27: 10. Solomon, who also figures in the epitaph for China Aster in Chapter 40, was regarded as the author of Proverbs, Ecclesiastes, and the apocryphal Wisdom of Solomon. See *Moby-Dick*, Chapter 96.

his Essay on Friendship: in 'Friendship' Emerson assigns 'politics, and chat, and neighbourly conveniences' to 'cheaper companions', so that friendship is reserved for higher concerns.

274 *the first-born of Egypt*: Exodus 12: 29.

276 *CHINA ASTER*: china asters and orchids are both plants, one plain and one exotic; etymologically aster means 'star', orchis 'testicle'.

Marietta: Ohio town, at the junction of the Ohio and Muskingum rivers.

280 *poor old pauper Job*: the Old Testament patriarch who suffers many misfortunes.

287 *Death himself on the pale horse*: Revelation 6: 8.

Come-Outers: religious dissenters.

298 *All the world's a stage*: the opening of the 'seven ages of man' speech by the misanthrope Jacques in *As You Like It*, II. vii. 140–67.

299 *Souter John and Tam O'Shanter*: hero and his drinking companion in Burns's poem 'Tam O'Shanter'; Somnus and Morpheus were Roman personifications of sleep and dreams.

300 *the angels who, in man's form, came to Lot's house*: Genesis 19: 1–26.

the devils who, in man's form, haunted the tombs: Matthew 8: 28–34 (story of the Gadarene swine), Mark 5: 2–18 (story of Legion).

301 *Thersites*: in Homer's *Iliad*, Thersites is famous for railing against the Greek leaders, such as Agamemnon, in the Trojan War. In *Troilus and Cressida* he is a cynical observer of the war.

305 *the same sign that Timon traced*: the hero of *Timon of Athens* composes his own epitaph, which is found with his body in the cave: 'Timon is dead, who hath outstretched his span. / Some beast rear'd this; there does not live a man' (v. iii. 3–4).

307 *I am Philanthropos, and love mankind*: echo of Timon's words 'I am Misanthropos and hate mankind' (IV. iii. 53).

307 *the three kings of Cologne*: the Cathedral at Cologne possessed bones supposedly belonging to the three magi of the Nativity story, viewed by Melville in 1849.

An enemy speaketh sweetly with his lips: Ecclesiasticus 12: 16.

314 *I believed not his many words*: echo of Ecclesiasticus 13: 11.

317 *Hamlet . . . Don Quixote . . . Milton's Satan*: the three authors have different degrees of influence on Melville; traces of Don Quixote and Milton's Satan are present in Ahab in *Moby-Dick*, of Hamlet in *Pierre*, which contains further reflections on literary originality (Book XVIII, i).

318 *Drummond light*: lime light, an intense white light developed in the 1820s; used in lighthouses, and by P. T. Barnum in New York in the 1840s.

an effect . . . akin to that . . . in Genesis: illuminating the darkness and chaos like God at the Creation (Genesis 1: 2–5)—an obvious play on origin/genesis.

320 *solar lamp*: form of oil lamp.

a horned altar: the site of animal sacrifice throughout the Old Testament, e.g. in Exodus 27: 2–8, where God also instructs Moses to keep an eternal lamp burning in the court of the Tabernacle.

321 *Simeon*: in Luke 2: 25–35, a devout man who sees the infant Jesus at the Temple in Jerusalem, fulfilling a prophecy.

323 *with much communication he will tempt thee*: the following lines combine several verses from Ecclesiasticus 13: 4–13.

Wisdom of Jesus, the Son of Sirach: alternative title of the book of Ecclesiasticus.

324 *apocrypha . . . apocalypse*: the Greek sense of the first word is 'hidden things', of the second 'uncovering'.

Take heed of thy friends: Ecclesiasticus 6: 13.

326 *auto-da-fe*: Port. act of faith, the punishment of heretics by the Inquisition of the Catholic Church in Spain and Portugal, usually by burning; victims would wear robes depicting the torments they faced in hell.

Murillo's wild beggar boys: Bartolomé Esteban Murillo (1618–82), Spanish painter, usually of religious subjects; *Redburn*, Chapter 49, describes 'such a boy as Murillo often painted'.

329 *Counterfeit Detector*: one of several periodical publications listing counterfeit money in circulation, and identifying signs by which they could be detected.

look a lie and find the truth: proverb usually in the form 'tell a lie . . . ', etc.

331 *Vicksburgh Trust and Insurance Banking Company*: Franklin notes that all currency issued by Mississippi banks was unreliable in this period, as banking had not yet been regulated.

332 *a perfect goose*: plays on the sense of 'fool'.

324 *a Committee of Safety*: presumably the angels, but the Committees of Public Safety in the French Revolution were state agencies which organized the Terror.

Jehovah shall be thy confidence: Proverbs 3: 26.

335 *Life-preserver*: apparatus for saving the passenger from drowning.

a brown stool with a curved tin compartment: a commode.

336 *special providence*: usually, an intervention by God in human affairs.

The Oxford World's Classics Website

www.worldsclassics.co.uk

- Browse the full range of Oxford World's Classics online

- Sign up for our monthly e-alert to receive information on new titles

- Read extracts from the Introductions

- Listen to our editors and translators talk about the world's greatest literature with our Oxford World's Classics audio guides

- Join the conversation, follow us on Twitter at OWC_Oxford

- Teachers and lecturers can order inspection copies quickly and simply via our website

www.worldsclassics.co.uk

American Literature

British and Irish Literature

Children's Literature

Classics and Ancient Literature

Colonial Literature

Eastern Literature

European Literature

Gothic Literature

History

Medieval Literature

Oxford English Drama

Poetry

Philosophy

Politics

Religion

The Oxford Shakespeare

A complete list of Oxford World's Classics, including Authors in Context, Oxford English Drama, and the Oxford Shakespeare, is available in the UK from the Marketing Services Department, Oxford University Press, Great Clarendon Street, Oxford OX2 6DP, or visit the website at www.oup.com/uk/worldsclassics.

In the USA, visit www.oup.com/us/owc for a complete title list.

Oxford World's Classics are available from all good bookshops. In case of difficulty, customers in the UK should contact Oxford University Press Bookshop, 116 High Street, Oxford OX1 4BR.